Whether you need help with the bottom-line insights in the Results Bucket or need to add more fun to your workplace with the best practices in the *Hoopla!* Bucket, *Mastering the Management Buckets* can help you to become a more effective manager. Buy a bucketful of books and bless your hard-working team members!

FRANK LOFARO
President and CEO, Christian Management Association

John Pearson has written a wonderful book that is not only for those aspiring to leadership positions but also for those who have been in the management ranks for years. I enjoyed it and learned a few things to boot! Buy the book, grab a cup of coffee, put your feet up and take notes!

DIANE PASSNO
Senior Vice President, Focus on the Family

As World Vision helps transform the lives of the world's poorest children and families in nearly 100 countries, we strive to be leaders and managers who honor God every day. That's not easy! *Mastering the Management Buckets* is a fresh reminder of the complexity of the leadership challenge—yet it also delivers practical management insights for our leaders and our in-the-trenches people.

RICHARD E. STEARNS
President, World Vision U.S.

MASTERING THE
MANAGEMENT
BUCKETS

20 CRITICAL COMPETENCIES FOR LEADING YOUR BUSINESS OR NONPROFIT

JOHN PEARSON

Regal

From Gospel Light
Ventura, California, U.S.A.

Published by Regal
From Gospel Light
Ventura, California, U.S.A.
www.regalbooks.com
Printed in the U.S.A.

Library of Congress Cataloging-in-Publication Data
Pearson, John W., 1946-
  Mastering the management buckets / John Pearson.
     p. cm.
  Includes bibliographical references (p.   ) and index.
  ISBN 978-0-8307-4594-4 (hard cover)
  1. Church management. I. Title.

BV652.P43 2008
254—dc22

2007047144

1 2 3 4 5 6 7 8 9 10 / 15 14 13 12 11 10 09 08

Rights for publishing this book outside the U.S.A. or in non-English languages are administered
by Gospel Light Worldwide, an international not-for-profit ministry. For additional information, please visit www.glww.org, email info@glww.org, or write to Gospel Light Worldwide, 1957
Eastman Avenue, Ventura, CA 93003, U.S.A.

This book honors

Janet Beneditz,
Faithful Servant of the Crisis Bucket

Without Janet and her servant colleagues worldwide,
no leader or manager would make it through the day!

CONTENTS

The Cause

The Community

The Corporation

FOREWORD

By Bob Buford

John Pearson, a friend and colleague of almost 30 years, has been a life-long student and practitioner of management applied to the growth of Christian organizations. Under the umbrella of Christian Management Association and the Willow Creek Association, he has hosted and pro-vided a platform for the leading thinkers of our time.

The two of us share a loyalty to the thinking of Peter Drucker, often called "the Father of Modern Management," whose work has been both profound and useful to many Christian ministries. John traces his Drucker lineage back to Drucker's debut appearance 20 years ago at a 1986 Leadership Network Summit Conference of large church and para-church leaders in Estes Park. These vital organizations have not only ad-vanced God's kingdom, but have also been central to the stability and moral foundation of American culture, still the envy of the world.

Peter Drucker often emphasized that churches and parachurch organizations were spiritual and moral enterprises at the core, instru-ments for serving God's purposes on earth. Peter was quoted in *Forbes* magazine, whose cover story called him "Still the Youngest Mind," as saying, "The pastoral megachurches are surely the most important so-cial phenomenon in American society in the last thirty years."

A recipient of the Christian Management Award presented by Chris-tian Management Association in 1990, Peter told us that those think-ing of religious organizations needed to consider three factors:

1. **The eternal**—that is, things that never change. Three months before his death in what was probably his last media inter-view, Peter expressed his view of the eternal:

Tom Ashbrook: You've lived a long life and focused intensely on life and how it's lived. Now you're 95. What about an afterlife? What about God? How do you think about the moment of transition that you are inevitably approaching?

Peter Drucker: Well, I happen to be a very conventional, traditional Christian. Period! And I don't think about it. I am told! It's not my job to think about it. My job is to say, "Yes, Sir."

Tom Ashbrook: That must be very comforting.

Peter Drucker: It is and I say every morning and every evening, "Praise be to God for the beauty of His creation. Amen."[1]

2. **The culture**—always and forever changing. Culture is different from one continent to another and from one time period to another, which makes it critical for religious organizations to change forms while preserving the essence of their message and work.

3. **The tools**—almost always developed in secular culture, but they are then useful in Christian culture.

There would, of course, be no megachurches were there not freeways, air conditioning, sound systems, printing and a host of other innovations. But Peter once told me, "Religious organizations have a tendency to eternalize the tool." It is incredibly important for leaders never to confuse the eternal with the culture or the tools.

Peter always said, "The purpose of management is not to make the Church more businesslike, but more Church-like." The mission of God's Church is, of course, distinctive from that of an entrepreneurial business organization, but most of the tools are the same.

Drucker used French economist J. B. Say's definition of an entrepreneur as "one who takes resources from a state of lower to higher yield and performance." That feature of management is the same for Bill Hybels as it is for Bill Gates.

John's new book *Mastering the Management Buckets* gives Christian leaders—so in need of a 101-level course in management—a wise distillation from a sea of management material (Drucker alone produced 10,000 book pages) of the practical tools they need to help their organizations grow and serve God's purposes. John puts the cookies on the lowest shelf.

This is a very practical, supremely useful book. It deserves a wide audience. It is certainly one of the first books a Christian leader should read.

Bob Buford
Chairman of the Board, The Buford Foundation and Leadership Network
Author of *Halftime, Game Plan, Stuck in Halftime* and *Finishing Well*

ACKNOWLEDGMENTS

It takes a village to raise a manager. I'm most grateful for the long-suffering bosses and boards that gave me amazing leadership opportunities over the years. My years in association management enabled me to visit hundreds of companies, churches and ministries in North America and other countries to observe their best practices firsthand.

From 1979 to 1990, I was privileged to serve as CEO of Christian Camping International/USA, now known as Christian Camp and Conference Association (www.ccca.org). In 1990, Bill Hybels and Don Cousins at Willow Creek Community Church invited me to join the management team. From 1992 to 1994, I served as the first president of the Willow Creek Association (www.willowcreek.com), and then from 1994 to 2005, I was president/CEO of Christian Management Association (www.cmaonline.org). My Rolodex from those 25 years of association management is still treasured.

It also takes a village to raise a book. My friend Russ Robinson has always urged me to write more, so in 2006, Joanne and I launched our management consulting practice, John Pearson Associates, Inc. Finally, the manuscript for this book bounced out.

As every author says about his publishers—but I really mean—I'm very grateful to Bill Greig and Dr. Gary Greig at Regal Books for their enthusiasm for both the material and its potential impact in the marketplace and in churches and ministries.

Joanne gave me the gift of time to write the book. Her parents, Gordon and Ethel Anderson (now in heaven), influenced me profoundly. My son, Jason—one of the most creative entrepreneurs I know (www. pearpod.com)—designed the cover and the charts, but more importantly, has engaged enthusiastically in our non-stop leadership and management dialogue his entire life. He gets it. Plus, he and Melinda have blessed us with four grandchildren (triplets plus one!) . . . all future managers, I'm sure.

And finally, Suzy West, the incredibly competent and always cheerful Vice President of Administration/Finance at Christian Management Association, applied her amazing gift of proofreading to this manuscript. I'm grateful.

It took a village.

MASTERING THE
MANAGEMENT
BUCKETS

20 CRITICAL COMPETENCIES FOR LEADING YOUR BUSINESS OR NONPROFIT

BUCKETS 101

The workshop room was crowded with Christian camp directors. Oozing in passion and enthusiasm, these leaders had traveled from around the world to Christian Camping International's 1971 annual convention at Green Lake Conference Center.

The workshop topic was counselor training and I was writing notes as fast as I could (no laptops back then), when someone tapped my shoulder. I turned to see my wife, Joanne, motioning for me to exit the meeting. Expecting bad news, I followed her outside.

"I don't know what workshop you're attending, John," she began, "but it doesn't matter. Olan Hendrix is teaching an all-day seminar on Management 101, and he just described you to a *T*. You've been through college and seminary, but you've never read a management book, never taken a management course—and you could be the poster boy for everything managers and camp directors are doing badly. Just follow me back to Olan's session. Some day you'll thank me!"

That day-long crash course in Management 101 changed my life. I have thanked Joanne a zillion times—and Olan Hendrix[1] dozens of times.

The truth is, I was unprepared for leadership. I didn't know what I didn't know. But over the years, patient bosses, boards and mentors guided me in my life-long learning journey. I'm still learning.

Somewhere along the way, I created my 20 management buckets system. The 20 buckets are categorized into three arenas: *Cause, Community* and *Corporation*. Your *Cause* is all about your mission, your customer, your strategy, your programs, products and services—and your results. Your *Community* is about building, equipping and celebrating team members—for the sake of your Cause, but also because honoring people is the right thing to do. Your *Corporation* arena is about fiduciary responsibilities, hiring and firing employees, organizational charts and budgets—not as relational or inspiring as the others, but no less important to the health of your organization.

Each "bucket" represents a core competency that every effective organization must master. At the beginning of each chapter, you'll find a summary of the core competency—the "bucket"—that is fleshed out in the following pages. Within each bucket, there are two to six "balls," which represent the specific action steps needed to achieve that competency. Every "ball" is a verb—think *action, execution* and *implementation!* This system is not dry theory; it's in-the-trenches, real-life stuff.

When you use "buckets" and "balls" language with your team members, you help them see the big picture: how each person's work contributes to your organization's mission. No one person can master the core competencies in all 20 management buckets. No one leader or manager has the capacity or the giftedness to implement every ball in every bucket. Leaders of effective, high-impact organizations know that they must build teams of people with diverse experiences and strengths in order to master these critical core competencies.

The 20 management buckets work well for me, but you may want to use different labels for your "buckets" and "balls." The point is to perfect a leadership and management philosophy and system, and then—as Peter Drucker preached—practice, practice, practice the art of management.

In my camp director days, I'd marvel at the people skills of creative program directors but wince at their inability to energize their teams at weekly staff meetings. They had most of the core competencies in the Program Bucket but were unaware of the critical balls in the Meetings Bucket. Thus, their thoughtful programs, products and services were frequently derailed by uninspired and unmotivated staff. Good ideas. Poor execution.

Later in my career, I observed leaders and managers who excelled in the Customer Bucket, but didn't know what they didn't know in the People Bucket. Not all buckets are created equal, but to be effective, leaders must know the 20 buckets and the critical balls in each one.

This book is Buckets 101. It won't solve all your management challenges—no book will. Instead, it is a crash course in leadership and management. It's more pragmatic than comprehensive. It's part resource library, part filing system and part toolbox.

The Goal: Effective Management

When Jim Collins wrote *Good to Great and the Social Sectors*, his monograph for nonprofits that elaborates on his bestselling book *Good to Great*, he added this tagline: "Why business thinking is not the answer." I agree with him. When I read the *Wall Street Journal* each morning, I mentally chronicle the lapses of "good business" practices of many large corporations.

Nonprofits, in my opinion, often do it better with far fewer resources and far more obstacles. How many volunteers does IBM recruit every year? (By the way, if you're a marketplace manager today, God may some day lead you to the Church or the nonprofit side of management—or vice versa. Christians are in "full-time" ministry wherever they work. Some of us get paid by IBM or Starbucks, while some of us receive payroll checks from World Vision, YoungLife, First Community Church or The Salvation Army. Regardless, we're *all* in ministry.)

The test of management is not whether you are "business-like"; it's whether you are *effective*. There are leadership and management best practices found in both the for-profit and nonprofit sectors. Neither has a lock on success or failure, and the buckets introduced in this book can successfully be applied to either. While several buckets address specific nonprofit issues (donors, volunteers, boards, and so on), thoughtful business leaders won't skip those chapters because they know that communities are interdependent. We need each other.

Whether you are a business, church or nonprofit leader, there are four levels of management knowledge. You must mentor your team members so that they become life-long learners in all 20 buckets, moving from Level 1 to Level 4 when possible. No single person, of course, will master every competency, but your team members must *collectively* master the core competencies in order for your organization to reach its maximum potential. Here are the four levels:

Level 1: I don't know what I don't know.

Level 2: I know what I don't know.

Level 3: I have an action plan to address what I know I don't know.

Level 4: I am knowledgeable and effective in this core competency and can mentor others.

There are several different ways to use this book to increase your knowledge. After you've read it, create a buckets system for yourself. I'm partial to three-ring binders with 20 tabs, but you may prefer 20 file folders. When you find something helpful in the newspaper or at a workshop, drop the insight into the appropriate bucket filing system.

To move to Level 3 ("I have an action plan to address what I know I don't know"), consider these options:

- **Twenty Days.** Designate the next 20 working days and each day, for one hour, review one bucket (one chapter). Focus on one or two strategic next steps and add them to your To-Do List.

- **Twenty Months.** Set aside one full day per month over the next 20 months and learn all you can on that day and during that month to hone your core competencies within one bucket.

- **Twenty Years.** If you're under 45 and one of your top-five strengths is "learner" (see the Team Bucket), you might enjoy focusing on one bucket per year while cherry-picking insights from the other buckets along the way. If you invest 20 years in 20 buckets, you'll be a world-class management expert and some-one will name a bucket in your honor (see the Drucker Bucket).

Whatever your timeline, as you mentor your organization's team toward greater and greater knowledge and competency, remember to emphasize how each bucket works together. When team members see the big picture—it takes all 20 buckets to build a sustainable organiza-tion—they will be more cautious about moving ahead with incomplete information. But once they have a handle on the buckets (pun intended!), their confidence will grow exponentially. They'll learn how a ball in the Operations Bucket enhances the work in the Customer Bucket. Department rivalries will lessen and true teamwork, based on trust and interdependence, will result.

On Holy Ground

If you are a Christ-follower, you will appreciate the faith-based foundations of this book. I believe that the Bible is relevant to Wall Street, Madison Avenue and Silicon Valley. If you are somewhere in the process of your faith journey, you will learn how Christians attempt to connect the dots between the teachings of Jesus and the practical challenges of the contemporary workplace. There is no better venue for walking the talk than in the nine-to-five real-life laboratory.

There are 20 management buckets, and the "Jesus Bucket" is not on my list. Many years ago, I heard evangelist Leighton Ford say, "For many people, Christianity is an additive, not an alternative." For the fully devoted follower of Christ, however, life is a radical alternative to the unsatisfying, live-for-yourself rat race so common in the marketplace and even in some churches and nonprofit organizations. Faith is not merely an additive.

To master the core competencies of the management buckets, every breath and every bucket must emanate from a heart that seeks to glorify God. If you don't honor God in the Customer Bucket and the Culture Bucket, a quick dip into the Jesus Bucket every few Sundays won't cut it. Don't delude yourself. The apostle Paul mentored Timothy, "Concentrate on doing your best for God, work you won't be ashamed of, laying out the truth plain and simple. Stay clear of pious talk that is only talk. Words are not mere words, you know. If they're not backed by a godly life, they accumulate as poison in the soul" (2 Tim. 2:15-16). Leaders and managers must live out authentic walks with Christ in each bucket and with each ball.

The Christian leader knows that all of life is holy. There is no dichotomy between secular and sacred. There is no biblical category for "full-time Christian service." The calling of a Christ-follower is to follow Christ, full-time. Some of us get paychecks from churches and non-profit ministries, while some of us are paid from the marketplace. Regardless, the earth is the Lord's—wherever a believer walks, he or she walks on holy ground.

There's a popular myth that the devil is in the details. Wrong. God is in the details. As you read this book, visualize every bucket and the three arenas of Cause, Community and Corporation as being on holy ground. Proverb 16:3 says, "Put GOD in charge of your work, then what you've planned will take place." Honor God with every ball in every bucket.

At my two-day workshops, I share dozens of war stories from my reckless management years before I understood the 20 buckets. I wish I could go back and edit my life's video, but I can't. Hopefully, this book will save you some scars and scares, and also lighten your load on your God-honoring management journey.

John Pearson
www.managementbuckets.com
San Clemente, California

THE CAUSE

 **THE CAUSE**

The Cause is all about our mission, our customers, our strategy, our programs, our products and our services—and it's about the results we are targeting. The language of Cause is purpose-driven, energetic and many times laced with athletic and military imagery: "Okay, team . . . let's get out there and take that hill. Win one for the Gipper!"

THE RESULTS BUCKET

We focus on results. We are not activity-driven; we are results-driven. We measure what we value, so we celebrate both the writing and the achieving of team-blessed standards of performance for every staff member, board member and volunteer. We also abandon dead horses and sacred cows.

Strategic Balls in the Results Bucket

1. MANAGE for results.
2. FOCUS on outside results, not inside results.
3. PRIORITIZE results with S.M.A.R.T. standards of performance.
4. MEASURE your results.
5. SLOUGH OFF yesterday.

Whether you lead a for-profit company or you're the senior pastor of a church or you're a manager in a nonprofit organization, you must focus on results. If your water cooler conversations, board reports, donor letters, monthly updates and luncheon speech to the Rotary Club feature activities and anecdotes but not results, you're headed for disaster. If your sales people exceed their monthly goals for sales appointments but make no actual sales, that's not a sustainable business model. If your VP of development regularly golfs with the top donor prospects in town but never makes "the ask" and never brings back a check, what's the point? You must set performance goals that focus on results—not on activity.

In his 839-page book *Management: Tasks, Responsibilities, Practices*, Peter Drucker writes that the work of the manager involves five basic areas. Managers (1) set objectives, (2) organize, (3) motivate and communicate,

(4) measure results, and (5) develop people (including themselves).[1] These functions, when done well, equal stellar results.

Ball #1:
MANAGE for Results
Allocate resources to opportunities—not problems.

Peter Drucker saw the need for a simple yet rigorous tool that would help nonprofit and church leaders maximize their unique and important missions. So he created an assessment tool that is now titled *The Drucker Foundation Self-Assessment Tool.*[2]

They're known to many simply as the "Drucker questions." Used as levers to pry open and elevate your best thinking, the five questions will help you, your team members, your board and your boss find out where God is working—and how best to join up with Him.

When you can succinctly answer these critical questions, you'll have a ready-made 20-minute talk for any community group, new staff member orientation session, a volunteer briefing, or a one-on-one fundraising presentation. Most importantly, team-generated answers to these questions will enable your church, your business or your non-profit organization to stay focused on God's calling for you. You'll also enjoy your work more, confident that you're on the right track— God's track.

There are always key people in your organization that have not been brought up to speed: new team members, newly promoted managers, key volunteers and board members. You certainly have a short list of dependable vendors and conscientious consultants who could serve you more effectively if you brought them inside the circle. Schedule a day with your team or plan an off-site retreat and explore together these important questions that will help you manage for results.

The only way you can effectively manage for results is by answering the five Drucker questions. Question 4, "What are our results?" will force you to ask hard questions and to evaluate whether or not your work and activities are aligned with your mission (Question 1). Questions 2 and 3 focus on the customer (see the Customer Bucket in the following chapter).

When you truly know your customer, you'll see new vistas of opportunity as your customers increasingly trust you. But if you instead focus on your problems (the kind we'll try to solve in the Operations Bucket, for example), you may solve pesky problems that are *barriers* to results but not *carriers* to results.

> # The Five Most Important Questions Every Organization Must Ask
>
> 1. What is our mission?
> 2. Who is our customer?
> 3. What does the customer value?
> 4. What are our results?
> 5. What is our plan?

It takes a village of buckets and balls to lead and manage an enterprise. We're starting with the Results Bucket because it is absolutely foundational to the whole enchilada (that's a management term). But you must understand how the other 19 buckets and the dozens and dozens of other balls in those buckets complement and complete this critical focus.

For example, let's say that your team is committed to mastering the core competencies in the Results Bucket. You're passionate about results, so you take out Ball #1 (Manage for Results) and implement it with Ball #3 (Prioritize Results).

Yet one team member, Tripp, has endless questions, while another manager, Alison, was wounded by an abusive manager at her last job. She hates goal setting and writing standards of performance. In the past, doing so resulted in failure for her. How can you build up the core competencies in the Results Bucket when you are met with such resistance?

In order to forge ahead, both Tripp and you need to be competent with Balls #1 and #2 in the People Bucket. This means knowing the four social styles. Tripp's social style is "Analytical," so you can serve him with an abundance of information to affirm his style and to get his buy-in.

Alison's reluctance to set goals can likely be solved by Ball #2 (Mentor Your Team Members with Niche Books) in the Book Bucket.

Ask her to read chapter 3 in Bobb Biehl's paradigm-shattering book *Stop Setting Goals If You Would Rather Solve Problems*.[3] Because Alison is a *learner* (see the Team Bucket), she'll likely read the entire book in her thirst for knowledge and will then mentor others.

Ball #2:
Focus on Outside Results, Not Inside Results
Results and resources exist on the outside.

John Wood was Microsoft's director of business development for the Greater China region before he founded Room to Read in 2000.[4] The nonprofit organization's mission is to provide underprivileged children with an opportunity to gain the lifelong gift of education. Room to Read works in Cambodia, India, Laos, Nepal, South Africa, Sri Lanka and Vietnam.

In his book *Leaving Microsoft to Change the World: An Entrepreneur's Odyssey to Educate the World's Children*, Wood reflects on his quest to build the "Microsoft of Nonprofits." He writes about Steve Ballmer, Microsoft's CEO:

> Steve lives, eats, breathes, and sleeps results, results, results. Like a dog with a chew toy, he is manically focused and not willing to let anything distract him from performance. It was a lesson I kept top of mind as I began building Room to Read and sought to differentiate us from the thousands of other nonprofit organizations out there.[5]

Ballmer mentored John Wood well. Wood also lives, eats, breathes and *emails* results! Below his standard email signature (name, phone, and so on), Wood includes a jam-packed paragraph of results. It's a brilliant idea! My good friend Larry Entwistle forwarded an email to me that Wood had sent him in March 2007. The results speak for themselves:

We're all about results! We have opened 287 schools, established over 3,600 bi-lingual libraries and 110 new computer and language rooms. We've put more than 2.8 million books in the hands of eager young readers, and are funding long-term scholarships for 2,336 girls. Over 1,200,000 children now have access to enhanced educational infrastructure. Together, we are changing the world through the gift of education.[6]

Notice that John Wood's results blurb is not about fundraising or hiring more staff or recruiting volunteers. It's about results—*outside results*.

Where Are Your Priorities?

In 1986, Bob Buford and Fred Smith at Leadership Network[7] invited me to a week-long summit with Peter Drucker in Estes Park, Colorado. Drucker held court all day with about 30 Christian leaders. I'll never forget his insights on outside results versus inside results.

If a hospital, he said, focuses on keeping the nurses happy (inside results) but neglects the care of patients (outside results), the patients will all die and the hospital will go out of business. He acknowledged that it is good to keep the nurses happy. But when an organization focuses predominantly on inside results (administration, maintenance, policies and procedures) rather than on outside results (mission, customer, sales, donors, recipients), it is on the path to failure.

It's an easy trap. Of the three arenas—Cause, Community and Corporation—the Corporation side (budget, operations, systems, meetings) will take every ounce of emotional and physical energy you can muster. The Community side (people, team, *hoopla!*, donors, volunteers) will eventually whine and complain if it's not adequately fed. Rarely will external forces—your Cause—push you to invest time. It takes sheer discipline every single day to focus on outside results. But you can do it! Remember Drucker: "Results are obtained by exploiting opportunities, not by solving problems."[8]

Take the self-assessment below to see where your energy is focused.

WHERE ARE YOUR PRIORITIES? Where are you investing your time and resources?		
Five Signs You Might Be Focused More on Inside Results Than on Outside Results!		
What do you talk about and focus on in these activities?	**Inside Results**	**Outside Results**
1) Staff meetings		
2) Newsletters, donor letters, brochures and publications		
3) Elevator speech (What is your 60-second answer to "What does your organization do and how's it going?")		
4) Budget and financial reports		
5) Celebrations		

Figure 1.1

Ball #3:
PRIORITIZE Results with S.M.A.R.T. Standards of Performance
Create clear goals and a rigorous accountability system with celebration mileposts.

Imagine a world where your team members leave work on time every day. Imagine their day's work in sync with your organization's mission, with your Big Holy Audacious Goal, with your annual objectives. Imagine if in response to "How was work today, dear?" Annette beams to her husband and gushes, "Fantastic! We are 25 percent ahead of our team goals on Vision 2020! I'm a month ahead of my top-three standards of performance. Guess what? Paul suggested I take Friday off so I can join you at the surfing competition."

Well, maybe Annette doesn't actually *gush*, but paint this picture for your team: Passion, clarity and confidence *are* possible. When you help your team focus on results, with clear goals and a rigorous accountability system, you'll be amazed at what can be accomplished.

Activity-based work is subjective because the goals—if any—are fuzzy. Results-based work, on the other hand, is objective because the goals are well defined. Work becomes fulfilling. When a clear target is on the wall, it energizes your team.

As a leader and manager, you have two options:

> **Option #1.** Invest minimal time in goal-setting, live with fuzzy targets and use your superior motivational skills to pump up the sagging morale of your team. You'll actually save time this way because you'll never have to waste time celebrating success.

> **Option #2.** Invest time with your team in goal-setting. You've learned that every day invested up front on clear targets will eliminate days of expensive wrong turns, one-way streets and blind alleys—so your team is focused on clear goals that align with the mission. Your monthly celebrations

and your spontaneous affirmation moments (see the *Hoopla!* Bucket) keep your team's spirits high.

So what are S.M.A.R.T. standards of performance (SOPs) and how do you build in an accountability process? S.M.A.R.T. SOPs are *specific, measurable, achievable, realistic* and *time-related*. Remember this acronym:

Specific. The performance standard should clearly specify what results you want to achieve.

Measurable. It must describe, in quantifiable terms, the exact finish line (e.g., 300 widgets, 500 new donors, 25 trained volunteers).

Achievable. The performance standard must be attainable. No pie in the sky stuff here!

Realistic. It must also be rooted in reality and aligned with the resources you have allocated to the goal. Does the whole team agree that it's realistic?

Time-related. The SOP must have a specific date when the results will be achieved (e.g., December 31).

Every leader, every manager, every direct report—virtually every team member—must write 5 to 10 annual standards of performance. The SOPs must (1) meet the S.M.A.R.T. criteria, (2) be reviewed and approved by peers, direct reports and each person's boss or board, and (3) be part of a regular accountability/reporting process (usually monthly).

Many teams start with a two-day annual retreat and focus first on the mission, the Big Holy Audacious Goal, the G.N.O.M.E. Chart (more on these in the Strategy Bucket) and then—based on the coming budget year—discuss each team member's vital role in helping to accomplish the corporate goals for the year. Each person then submits 5 to 10 personal draft SOPs for group discussion.

Other teams use a consultant or a facilitator to keep the retreat process on track and to breathe new life into what could become a routine or stale annual exercise.

As SOPs are aligned with the emerging annual budget, your SOPs may go through several drafts. Ultimately, when every team member's SOPs are approved for the next fiscal year, it will be time to celebrate!

Ball #4:
MEASURE Your Results
Track your progress with leading indicators.

Faith-based SOPs

Proverb 16:9 says, "In his heart a man plans his course, but the Lord determines his steps" (*NIV*). If you are a Christ-follower, you know that the results of your work are up to God. But don't fall into the pseudo-faith trap that puts all the responsibility on the Lord. He expects us to think, pray, plan and work hard. The third verse of the same chapter says, "Commit to the Lord whatever you do, and your plans will succeed." Is your business, your church, your nonprofit about you or about Him? The Bible says that it's about Him—and we know that His plans will succeed.

Okay, you now know about three core competencies in the Results Bucket. Balls #1, #2 and #3 are critical to the Bucket, but if you don't know what you don't know about Ball #4, it's a bit like golfing 18 holes on a pristine California ocean-view course with new Callaway clubs . . . and no scorecard.

Most people want to be held accountable for their progress. They want to know how they are doing. Effective companies and organizations use a variety of accountability tools for tracking progress.

Start with a one-page Leading Indicators tracking form (see Fig. 1.2). This report—and a consistent monthly accountability team meeting—will revolutionize your work! (Some teams use other report names, such as Monthly Metrics, Dashboard Report or Goal Tracking, for example.) I encourage teams to review the Leading Indicators report once a month. It should be a regular report on the standard agenda for your monthly team meeting.

TOP 10 LEADING INDICATORS: MONTHLY UPDATE Approved by Management Team on October 15					
Leading Indicators	Point Person	ANNUAL GOAL (12 Months)	YTD Goal (6 Months)	YTD Actual (6 Months)	YTD Difference
1) Revenue	Bob	$925,000	$500,000	$517,000	+$17,000
2) New volunteers	Dale	250	175	195	+20
3) New donors ($500 or more)	Sue	175	75	125	+50
4) Partnerships	Fred	5	1	2	+1
5) Regional reps trained and certified	Rob	25	12	10	-2
6) Website product downloads	Rob	10,000	3,500	5,500	+2,000
7)					
8)					
9)					
10)					

Notes:
Melinda will compile and distribute this report by the fifth of each month and the Management Team will review it at our monthly meeting on the second Wednesday of every month.

Figure 1.2

Don't Obsess on Indicators

You measure what you value, but don't fall into the trap of obsessing about measurements. Invest adequate time toward tracking your weekly and monthly progress, but don't let the systems, the reports or the accountability meetings become your favorite activity. The results are not found inside the organization—they're outside (see Ball #2!).

If there were a management version of Mount Rushmore, who would you nominate to place alongside Peter Drucker and Ken Blanchard? Many managers would recommend Jim Collins, author of *Built to Last* and *Good to Great*. He offers savvy wisdom on this subject. Collins says that "all indicators are flawed." He writes, "It doesn't really matter whether you can quantify your results. What matters is that you rigorously assemble evidence—quantitative or qualitative—to track your progress."[9]

Collins understands that many organizations cannot readily quantify widgets sold per month. Many, such as the Cleveland Orchestra, operate much more on the soft side of results. In *Good to Great and the Social Sectors*, an easy-to-read 35-page monograph to accompany his bestselling book, Collins details how a nonprofit can rigorously assemble evidence to show that the organization is moving toward greatness.

As Christ-followers, we must remember that "greatness" is not the goal. Personally, our journey must be about becoming more like Christ, being apprentices to the Master. Organizationally, we must focus on results, not to be great but to be fruitful. Collins says that "the moment you think of yourself as great, your slide toward mediocrity will have already begun."[10] Proverb 16:8 says, "Pride goes before destruction, a haughty spirit before a fall" (*NIV*).

Ball #5:
SLOUGH OFF Yesterday
When the horse is dead, dismount!

Someday you may end up with 25 standards of performance and a 10-page Leading Indicators report. There is something in the North American business mystique that causes us to add projects and product lines quickly—but we are reluctant to dump programs and the good people that run them. That spells trouble.

Effective leaders know when to hold and know when to fold. Eventually, you must deep-six your typewriter catalog and start selling computers. Sunday night services are out; neighborhood small groups are in. Drop the records, eight-tracks and cassettes and replace them with MP3s and digital players.

How many dead horses are you still riding, attempting to resuscitate not just a losing program or product, but a dead loser? When the horse is dead, dismount! You may be focusing on results, even outside results, and measuring them religiously, but you may be missing the most important word in "focus on results": *focus!*

George Duff, my good friend and management mentor, led his vice presidents in a "Slough Off Yesterday" exercise each year. George served as president of the Greater Seattle Chamber of Commerce for 27 years (and had 27 different board chairs!), and once a year, he closed the doors to the conference room. Behind closed doors, he asked each VP to hypothetically trim their own budgets and their staff members by 20 percent. "What must we abandon and what must we strengthen in each department?"

> In your next interview, ask the job applicant about her top-three goals for the last 12 months and about her success at achieving them. If she is results-savvy, you'll have her up and running in half the time it normally takes. If you hire a person who is inexperienced in goal-setting, however, you will invest dozens of hours to coalesce that person into your results-oriented culture.

Then, one by one, his vice presidents reported on this emotionally painful but critically important exercise. It was just a drill—a confidential one—but it helped reveal the winners and the losers.

Sooner or later, you will have to make hard choices about abandoning a program, product or service. "We can do this the hard way or we can do this the easy way," says the knuckle-cracking tough guy in the movies, and it's the same at work. The hard way is to ignore reality, pretend that there are no program/product life cycles and then blame it on your boss or board when you're forced to drop a lagging program.

The easy way (actually, the *preferred* way—it is never easy) is to be intentional. Do the pruning drill and then plan for strategic abandonment—certainly not without thought and people care, but with God-honoring intentionality. Many times, this process also helps you gently eliminate sacred cows.

Jesus said in John 15:1-2, "I am the Real Vine and my Father is the Farmer. He cuts off every branch of me that doesn't bear grapes. And every branch that is grape-bearing he prunes back so it will bear even more." When you prune, it creates capacity to follow your dreams. When you add but never subtract, you cannot nimbly respond to new opportunities. When you find out what God is doing, you can't join Him if you're on overload.

Look at the "Strategic Program Development Criteria" list in the Program Bucket for a helpful tool on evaluating your current programs. Before you launch a new program, product or service, review these tough questions. The easiest kind of program to abandon is one you never launched!

The Results Bucket To-Do List

❏ *Order the participant guide and process guide for* The Drucker Foundation Self-Assessment Tool.

❏ *Read* The Most Effective Organization in the U.S.: Leadership Secrets of The Salvation Army by Commissioner Robert A. Watson.[11] Drucker said, "The Salvation Army is by far the most effective organization in the U.S. No one even comes close to it with respect to clarity of mission, ability to innovate, measurable results, dedication, and putting money to maximum use."[12]

❏ *Read "Ensuring Mission Impact: How to Move from Strategy to Results,"* by Matt Breitenberg and Art Caccese from the December 2003 issue of *Christian Management Report*, published by Christian Management Association.[13]

❏ *With your key leaders, formulate a Leading Indicators tracking form and* begin using it immediately to keep your team accountable.

❏ *Bless your team members by helping them write and achieve 5 to 10 annual standards of performance (SOPs).* Then they will have an answer to the daily question, "How was your day at work?"

❏ George Duff always concluded the "Slough Off Yesterday" exercise with a probing question to his vice presidents: "Which people on your team do you rely on so significantly that—if they were to leave—you would be in a jam? Do those people know how valued they are? *Be sure to tell them and affirm them in a special way this week.*" That's a profound reminder to all of us. The right people focusing on the right results will experience extraordinary accomplishments. You're the leader that can make this happen!

❑ *Introduce your church to the "Metrics Manual" in the appendix of William R. Hoyt's book, Effectiveness by the Numbers: Counting What Counts in the Church.*

TO DO OR TO DELEGATE?				
Priority A, B, C	Point Person	Task	Deadline Date	Done Date

THE CUSTOMER BUCKET

We know our primary and supporting customers. We segment our customers to more effectively meet their unique needs. We listen to our customers. We are zealots for researching and understanding our markets.

Strategic Balls in the Customer Bucket

1. FOCUS on your primary customer.
2. IDENTIFY your supporting customers.
3. LEARN how your customers will change.
4. MOVE customers from ignorance to purchase.
5. SEGMENT your customers prayerfully.
6. RESEARCH what your customer values.

The Father-Son Fishing Weekend was a blast for dads and their sons the first year my camp-director colleague hosted it in the Pacific Northwest, so he put more marketing dollars into the second annual fish fest. Bill mailed the four-color brochures multiple times to every father on his list. He segmented his database and paid special attention to his satisfied customers from the first annual weekend.

Oops! Eight weeks out, pre-registration for the second event was dismal. Bill was a marketing genius and knew that the brochure had all the right words, photos and pricing to appeal to fishing fathers and their sons. What was wrong?

Bill grew impatient waiting for the mail, so he cancelled all his appointments and assembled his team in the makeshift marketing "war room" at the well-managed Christian camp. They hit the phones with passion and determination.

"Joe! Hey . . . it was great having you and Bobby at the Father-Son Fishing Weekend last year. I remember you both caught your limit! But I just noticed you're not signed up yet for our weekend in May. Are you and Bobby joining us?"

Time after time, Bill and his team waited for an answer—and after a long pause, they got it.

"Just a second," the husband would say, "I need to ask my wife. Honey? Do you want Bobby and me to go to that fishing weekend again this year?"

Bill's war room research changed his strategy 180 degrees. He had his Five *P*s of Marketing lined up (Product, Price, Place, Promotion and People), but it was his telephone research that helped him hit a homerun. He learned that the "primary customer" for the Father-Son Fishing Weekend was the wife and mother, not the father or the son. After that, the annual fish fest brochure was always targeted to Joe's wife, the primary customer and decision-maker. Attendance grew and wives and mothers—and fathers and sons!—were happy . . . because Bill knew his customer.

In this chapter, we'll explore the dynamic tension between your mission and your customer, a tension that is equally valid in nonprofit and for-profit organizations. A software company with an eloquent mission statement and no customers will quickly slide into oblivion. A church that minimizes its prophetic message to attract customers may fill pews but won't change hearts.

Ball #1:
FOCUS on Your Primary Customer
You can't be all things to all people.

The five "Drucker questions" we explored in the last chapter should be asked and answered by every nonprofit and every business—every Fortune 500 company, the local dry cleaners, the women's shelter downtown *and* your neighborhood church. To recap, the questions are:

1. What is our mission?
2. Who is our customer?
3. What does the customer value?
4. What are our results?
5. What is our plan?[1]

Your "customer" may be a church member, a donor, a homeless person, a car buyer, a parent, a grocery shopper, a seeker, a college student, an orphan, a prisoner, a book reader, a radio listener, a pastor in the developing world, or someone else. But . . . stop right now, and underline this next sentence: *You can't be all things to all people.* Many business leaders and ministry leaders find it difficult to identify and focus on just one "primary customer," but you must if you want to be effective. Think of every other person you care about as a "supporting customer."

"Your primary customer," writes Peter Drucker, "is the person whose life is changed through your work."[2] It may seem obvious to you who your primary customer is, but beware: Many organizations do a 180 when they confront the brutal facts. Encourage thoughtful debate on the customer question. If you get this wrong, the unintended consequences are devastating. If you pray and hear from God and get it right, on the other hand, the rest of the management journey is exceedingly more joyful!

Heed this weathered sign from a dirt road in East Texas:

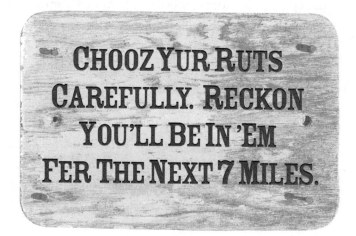

CHOOZ YUR RUTS CAREFULLY. RECKON YOU'LL BE IN 'EM FER THE NEXT 7 MILES.

Thousands of churches focus on reaching seekers. Their primary customer is a person who is somewhere in the process of understanding what it means to be a follower of Jesus Christ (see The Engel Scale in this chapter). Other churches invest serious money on the worship experience for their adult Christians. A few churches, by their missionary budget giving, demonstrate that non-Christians in the developing world are their primary customers. Some Christian radio and TV stations say that they raise most of their money for evangelism, but they focus most of their broadcasting to the already converted.

If you manage a hardware store, who is your primary customer? Are your newspaper ads, the parking lot layout, your exterior signage and your display racks designed for men or women? In what income bracket? (If you can answer the customer question, the other answers come easy.)

Maybe you're one of the real estate agents that flood my mailbox with those "Just Sold!" color postcards. I'm over 60. Are you sending the same card to my son and daughter-in-law, who are in their 30s? Who is your primary customer?

Whether you lead and manage a nonprofit or a for-profit organization, you must align your marketing, staffing and budget priorities with your primary customer. "The primary customer is never the only customer," writes Drucker, "and to satisfy one customer without satisfying the others means there is no performance. This makes it very tempting to say there is more than one primary customer, but effective organizations resist this temptation and keep to a focus—the primary customer."[3]

Your Organization's Calling

Does it feel like you're pushing JELL-O® uphill while your team's morale is sliding south? If you're focused on the wrong primary customer, the hill will only get steeper and your morale will nosedive deeper. You can juggle all the balls in the *Hoopla!* Bucket to fix morale, but if you haven't done the homework on your primary customer, you're doomed. Get this one right and the *Hoopla!* kicks in on its own.

Remember, you must move from "I don't know what I don't know" to "I know what I don't know." Don't be discouraged! (For fun, take a mini-break right now and visit jello.com to read the history behind the wiggle. After 100 years and more than 150 products, the JELL-O folks clearly know a thing or two about their customers. According to the website, their first ad ran in the *Ladies' Home Journal* in 1902 and targeted women with aprons.[4])

Just like JELL-O, ministries and churches must discern their unique calling. Who is the primary customer God wants you to reach and serve? It's also legal for Christians in the marketplace to ask God for customer insight. God has a purpose for your life and your work—nail down your primary customer ASAP.

This decision won't be easy. If you have not processed this critical issue in a disciplined, accountable way, schedule an off-site retreat and get the right people in the room. Engage an outside facilitator or consultant as your guide.

With everyone assembled, heed Peter Drucker's wisdom on encouraging constructive dissent: "All the first-rate decision makers I've observed," he writes, "had a very simple rule: If you have quick consensus on an important matter, don't make the decision. Acclamation means nobody has done the homework. The organization's decisions are important and risky, and they should be controversial. There is a very old saying—it goes back all the way to Aristotle and later became an axiom of the early Christian Church: In essentials unity, in action freedom, and in all things trust. Trust requires that dissent come out in the open."[5]

Ball #2:
IDENTIFY Your Supporting Customers
To be effective: focus, focus, focus.

Your supporting customers may include volunteers, vendors, donors, parents, members, employees, board members and other individuals and groups you serve. In order to achieve results (see the Results Bucket), you must also satisfy these important customers . . . but you must never lose your focus on your primary customer.

While many mega-churches offer a vast array of special programs for seemingly every people niche, most churches and ministries must prioritize. Companies must do the same. Once again, *you can't be all things to all people.* To be effective, you must focus, focus, focus—not on many, but the few.

To illustrate Ball #2 in the Customer Bucket, let's look at local churches in North America. They have a unique dilemma—and a stunning opportunity. For example, we can see from the Simplified Segmenting Chart (Fig. 2.1) that there are 12 broad "customer" groups that a church might attempt to serve. Few churches can serve the diverse needs of all 12 groups effectively. (These are broad categories, not niches. A niche, for example, would be a single mom in the 25 to 34 age category.)

If you're in church leadership, pray and ponder over these issues. Be honest: You can't serve every segment with world-class programs and services—and you don't want to. So prioritize the segments below and concentrate your passion, your people, your programs and your budgets on only three to five groups. And serve them well! Focus.

I know, I know . . . your church is already in a catch-22. You have programs from the cradle to the grave and your senior adults want their hymnals back (the red ones) and the fifth-grade boys want a skate park. Most churches do not have the leadership discipline to "downgrade" current programs and services of lower-priority groups in order to allocate re-

LOCAL CHURCH SIMPLIFIED SEGMENTING CHART Who is God calling you to reach and serve?			
SIMPLIFIED SEGMENTING Focus on 3 to 5 Groups	**CHILDREN**	**YOUTH**	**ADULTS**
CHRISTIANS who attend church	A	B	C
CHRISTIANS who *do not* attend church	D	E	F
NON-CHRISTIANS who attend church	G	H	I
NON-CHRISTIANS who *do not* attend church	J	K	L

Figure 2.1

sources to the highest-priority programs. But as you move forward, you can be prayerful, thoughtful and laser-like. Don't create expectations that you'll be world class in everything you do. God wants you to have a heart for people, yes—but He doesn't want you to be stupid about it!

Plan a day of prayer and then schedule a task force retreat to discern which groups in your church should be the highest priority. (Use the helpful resources from the Leader to Leader Institute.[6]) Remember, *you can't be all things to all people*. God doesn't expect you to do that. After a prayerful and thoughtful process over several months, determine your priorities:

Our Primary Customer is:

_____

Our Highest Priority Supporting Customers are:

Priority 1 _____

Priority 2 _____

Priority 3 _____

Priority 4 _____

Priority 5 _____

Stay on your knees until you hear from God. He has prepared and called your church to reach and serve specific segments.

When the Holy Spirit nudges you, follow Henry Blackaby's wisdom from his profound book, *Experiencing God*:

When God speaks,
it is important to write it down.[7]

When you identify your primary customer and your supporting customers, it will then be pruning time for your ministry. Admit that you can't be all things to all people and "dismount" from programs that need to be abandoned (see the Results Bucket).

Ball #3:
LEARN How Your Customers Will Change
You're serving a parade, not a crowd!

The president of the Greater Seattle Chamber of Commerce, George Duff, hung the insight pictured below on his office wall for the 27 years he led the Emerald City's chamber.

To reach and serve your primary and supporting customers, you must anticipate how your customers will change—and you must embrace those changes. The ethnicity of neighborhoods change. The Polish sausage shop has been replaced by an El Pollo Loco. The median age of your church (or your customer base) is getting older or younger. Busters have different values than their boomer parents. Those boomers may change their values and their thinking as they get older.

Your company, church or organization likely has team members who are experts at demographic, psychographic and lifestyle research and marketing. Invite them to help you understand the people you are reaching and serving—and how they will be changing in the years ahead.

Start with the obvious: age. If your website, brochures and newsletters are still one-

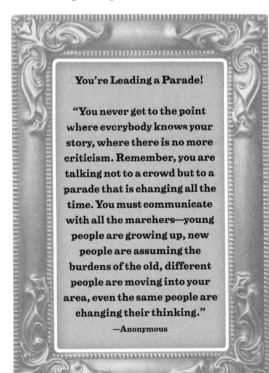

You're Leading a Parade!

"You never get to the point where everybody knows your story, where there is no more criticism. Remember, you are talking not to a crowd but to a parade that is changing all the time. You must communicate with all the marchers—young people are growing up, new people are assuming the burdens of the old, different people are moving into your area, even the same people are changing their thinking."

—Anonymous

size-fits-all, you're wasting time and money. Analyze the five major age groups and their unique differences (Fig. 2.2). Will one message, one ad, one email blast communicate effectively to all five generations? All of these generations may be in your parade. How are they changing?

THE FIVE GENERATIONS

LEADERSHIP ISSUE	SENIORS	BUILDERS	BOOMERS	BUSTERS	MILLENNIALS
1. Era they were born	1900-1928	1929-1945	1946-1964	1965-1983	1984-2002
2. Life paradigm	Manifest destiny	Be grateful you have a job	You owe me	Relate to me	Life is a cafeteria
3. Attitude to authority	Respect them	Endure them	Replace them	Ignore them	Choose them
4. Role of relationships	Long term	Significant	Limited: useful	Central: caring	Global
5. Value systems	Traditional	Conservative	Self-based	Media	Shop around
6. Role of career	Loyalty	Means for living	Central focus	Irritant	Place to serve
7. Schedules	Responsible	Mellow	Frantic	Aimless	Volatile
8. Technology	What's that?	Hope to outlive it	Master it	Enjoy it	Employ it
9. Market	Commodities	Goods	Services	Experiences	Transformations
10. View of future	Uncertain	Seek to stabilize	Create it!	Hopeless	Optimistic

Used by permission of Growing Leaders, Inc. (www.growingleaders.com)[8]   Figure 2.2

This is very hard work. Based on what you're learning about the changing needs of your customers, you will likely need to adjust your programs, products and services to meet those changing needs. Conduct focus groups, create an electronic suggestion box and poll your members. Retain consultants to help you. You need a diet of constant feedback. (Feedback is the breakfast of champions!)

Communicate Frequently!

If your customers are changing and your marketing and communication is ragged, it's a double whammy. Again, when you don't know what you don't know, the Law of Unintended Consequences (that is, "There shall be some unexpected result") will derail you. But when your radar is active and learning how your customers are changing, all the other balls in all the other buckets will be enhanced.

Let's dip into the Printing Bucket by way of example. Advertisers use the term "frequency of message" to remind themselves that a single brilliant full-page, four-color ad just won't do it. Some customers will miss the ad, others will forget it and others will not like it. It takes frequent repetitions to get your key message across. Effective communicators understand this principle. Great leaders practice it. Thoughtful managers create frequency systems so that customers hear the same message again and again and again.

If you announced a new program only in your quarterly newsletter, you might be shocked to learn how many people didn't read it, don't care or never understood it. If your *Vision 21st Century* initiative was launched last year with a notice in the bulletin and you're using the acronym *V21C* this year, guess what? Few people have a clue what you're talking about! Last month's important email to your members or customers has been deleted. Some of your customers who liked the program last year have changed their thinking about it this year.

Think about your long-term customers (donors, recipients, guests, members, and so on) at the front of the parade. What do they know that your newest customers at the back of the parade don't know? And what about the marchers in tomorrow's parade who have never heard of you? Do you know what they are thinking about? How are they changing?

People in your parade need new inspiration today, new stories today and new reasons to join your team today. It's hard work, but do the hard work and it will pay rich dividends—kingdom dividends. So know your customers. Some of them just changed their thinking today.

Ball #4:
MOVE Customers from Ignorance to Purchase
Use the right tools for the right people at the right time.

The trash can is the only place where one size fits all! One-size-fits-all is a very expensive and ineffective customer strategy. Successful companies target their messages to at least six levels of current and future customers. The goal is to move people from ignorance (Level 1) to purchase (Level 6):

Level 1: Ignorance
Level 2: Awareness
Level 3: Interest
Level 4: Trial or Consideration
Level 5: Preference
Level 6: Purchase

For example, consider the donor program (see the Donor Bucket) of a ministry that delivers wheelchairs to people worldwide.[9] In a single month, this ministry reaches out to new donors, thanks current donors and wonders why the list of former donors is growing so rapidly. And if they operate like many nonprofit organizations, they may send the same monthly donor letter to every segment: non-donors, small donors, major donors, lapsed donors and even angry "I'll never give again" donors. That spells trouble.

Instead, an experienced fundraiser creates a donor strategy for moving a person from "ignorance" to "purchase." She has a different marketing and communication plan for each of the six levels, because she knows that what works to move a Level 1 customer to Level 2 is not the same as what works to move a Level 5 to a Level 6. (If the word is out that you're a generous donor, you've likely been to more than your fair share of fundraising dinners. Many are ill-conceived because they're asking people at Level 1 to move to Level 6 in the space of two hours—or three, if the dinner drags on. Most of the time, it doesn't work.)

The key principle for the smart fundraiser: *Use the right tools for the right people at the right time.* Here's how this strategy works:

Level 1: *Ignorance.* A neighbor invites a new homeowner over for coffee and mentions their involvement in a wheelchair ministry.

Level 2: *Awareness.* The new neighbor reads a newspaper article about the ministry and remembers the neighbor's enthusiasm.

Level 3: *Interest.* The neighbor's teen daughter has a new friend that sponsors a wheelchair every Christmas. "Dad, check out their cool website!"

Level 4: *Trial or Consideration.* The family agrees to have a garage sale to raise money for wheelchairs. They give a one-time gift online.

Level 5: *Preference.* Within seven days, the ministry calls to thank the family for the gift. The call impresses the dad. "I like these folks!"

Level 6: *Purchase.* After attending a ministry fundraising event, the family makes a three-year major gift commitment and become volunteer zealots.

Use the Right Marketing Mix Tool

The next time you strategize about your customers (members, book buyers, radio listeners, donors, iPod users, or whatever they may be), fill your conference table with all of your brochures and marketing pieces. Then arrange them in six groups, from Level 1 to Level 6. Are you trying to communicate your story with the same brochure or website or newsletter to all six levels? *One size doesn't fit all.*

Begin now to create specific strategies for each group and then determine which tools are the right tools for the right people.[10] A grid like Figure 2.3 will help you think it through.

Whether you're the CEO, the marketing manager, the executive pastor or the receptionist, chances are that you have one or more brochures in the works. Stop the presses! Call your copywriter, graphic

THE RIGHT TOOLS FOR THE RIGHT PEOPLE! YOUR MARKETING MIX ▶	Marketing Mix Tool A **Brochures, etc.**	Marketing Mix Tool B **Websites**	Marketing Mix Tool C **Newsletters**
THE MARKETING MIX FOR MOVING PEOPLE FROM IGNORANCE TO PURCHASE			
1) IGNORANCE	CARD: Did You Ever Wonder?		
2) AWARENESS	BOOKMARK: 10 FAQS		
3) INTEREST	BROCHURE: All About Our Ministry		
4) TRIAL OR CONSIDERATION	ENVELOPE STUFFER: Thanks for Your Order!		
5) PREFERENCE	BOOKLET: You've Made a Great Decision!		
6) PURCHASE	PERSONAL LETTER (and CALL): Now That You're Part of the Family		

Figure 2.3

designer, webmaster and printer today! (Or call yourself if you do it all.) Before you go one step further on the brochure or website, determine which of the six levels you're communicating to. Then do some shoe leather research and ask your customers: *Does this communicate?*

Ball #5:
SEGMENT Your Customers Prayerfully
Are they a +5 or a -8 on
The Engel Scale?

When Jim Engel and Wil Norton wrote *What's Gone Wrong with the Harvest: A Communication Strategy for the Church and World Evangelism*[11] in 1975, they integrated Engel's marketing expertise with Norton's passion for evangelism and missions. Engel was a professor of marketing at Ohio State University and the University of Michigan and was founder and first chairman of the Association for Consumer Research. Norton was president of Trinity College and Evangelical Divinity School and also served as dean of the Wheaton College Graduate School of Theology. Their book helped ministry and church leaders to understand that it's not only okay to "segment the seeker," but that it also makes Kingdom sense. The book popularized The Engel Scale (Fig. 2.4), which

was suggested in 1973 by Viggo Sogaard, a student at Wheaton Graduate School. (I mention this to drive home the point that Kingdom work is a partnership: A marketing prof, a seminary president and a graduate student all contributed to this tool. Kingom advancement is an open process. Jump in!)

> Dear Friend,
>
> We know you've never sent even one dollar to our ministry. However, we've continued to send you our monthly donor letter for the last 10 years because we're lazy and incompetent and we've never segmented our mailing list.
>
> Sincerely yours,
>
> *Alec*
>
> Executive Director
>
> P.S. Please recycle.

The Engel Scale

On the following page, we have adapted the original diagram of The Engel Scale[12] by adding space for you to align your programs with the response segments.

I know, I know . . . we've said this before, but it will be on the test and you'll hear it again: *One size doesn't fit all.* The thoughtful preacher, teacher, evangelist, fundraiser and business person must always communicate the message in the right language to the right segment. It takes thoughtful prayer and hard work. (Did I mention the hard work?)

Look at The Engel Scale. Where are students at a YoungLife camp? Are they at a –8, –7 or a –4? Are the men who became Christians at last year's men's retreat still at –1, or have you helped them grow to +3, +4 or +5? Don't know? You must find out—and soon! Fifty-two weeks of Sunday sermons may be 52 weeks of miscommunication if the message is targeted to +3 Christ-followers when 50 percent of the congregation is still at –1. Yikes!

Engel and Norton call this miscommunication minefield "the peril of program orientation" (see the Program Bucket). If we had space, we'd reprint the entire second chapter of their book (but you'll have to find

ONE SIZE DOESN'T FIT ALL!
A Person's Response to the Gospel and the Alignment of Our Programs to That Reality

Position	Communicator's Role: Proclamation and Persuasion	Our Current (and Future) Programs to Communicate with This Segment
A Person's Response to the Gospel		
-8	Awareness of supreme being but no effective knowledge of the gospel	
-7	Initial awareness of the gospel	
-6	Awareness of fundamentals of the gospel	
-5	Grasp of the implications of the gospel	
-4	Positive attitude toward the gospel	
-3	Personal problem recognition	
-2	DECISION TO ACT	
-1	Repentance and faith in Christ	
A New Christian's Growth		
+1	Post-decision evaluation	
+2	Incorporation into the Body	
+3	Conceptual and behavioral growth	
+4	Communion with God	
+5	Stewardship	
•	Reproduction internally (gifts, character) and externally (witness, social action)	
↓	Etc.	
ETERNITY		

Adapted by John Pearson from The Engel Scale   Figure 2.4

your own copy of this out-of-print classic). To whet your appetite, here's a brief excerpt. It's a discussion about a fictitious pastor, Tom Bartlett, who has a gift for preaching, but "he really doesn't know his people."

Each week Tom must make decisions about sermon content. As Drucker points out, effective decisions start with an opinion as to what should be done but the correct decisions cannot be made until opinion is tested against reality.[13] In other words, Tom must be certain that his sermon content speaks to his people where they are and to their needs in terms they can understand.

When the opinion about what should be done is not tested against reality, the decision-maker is essentially an "armchair theorist" and is guilty of *program orientation*. The result can be a strategy that is a solution to a nonexistent problem. Program orientation is analogous to a business firm's designing a new product in a laboratory and then trying to coerce people to buy it through the exercise of advertising muscle. Although this may at times result in success, the more likely outcome is a sales disaster. A far better approach, the *adaptive orientation* is to begin with a study of the audience and the other elements of the environment to be faced and to adapt the organizational strategy to the realities of the situation to be faced.[14]

Prayerful Intentionality

Thoughtful ministry requires earnest prayer. You're serving people today. Where are they on The Engel Scale? What is God telling you? Do your programs align with the needs of your people? Are you moving believers along toward greater maturity in Christ? Does your methodology for reaching the unchurched sync up with their understanding of the gospel?

If you're in the marketplace, how does The Engel Scale impact your work? You've already realized that it's an excellent model for creating customer categories. Use it to your company's advantage.

And how does it impact you? As you find out where God is working among your colleagues, The Engel Scale could give you greater insight into the steps people are taking toward eternity. Pray.

Ball #6:
RESEARCH What Your Customer Values
Listen! Listen! Listen!

Dr. Robert D. Hisrich, the marketing savvy co-author of our book *Marketing Your Ministry: Ten Critical Principles*, preaches research, research, research. He writes, "If you have $10,000 to spend, invest $5,000 in researching and understanding the market."[15] Bob is a world-class guru in global entrepreneurship and has authored dozens of marketing texts, and he is rarely satisfied that companies, nonprofits and churches are ever serious enough about research.

"What does the customer value?" is the third of the "Drucker questions" that all organizations must ask and answer. So how do you find out what people value? *You ask*, says Hisrich. "Ask people what their real needs are, then shut up, and listen, listen, listen."[18]

Your customers will tell you what they value if you are strategic and intentional in asking them. Every Office Depot cash register receipt points customers to a feedback website and a chance to win $1,000. Restaurants and hotels use customer comment cards. Disneyland cast members, with clipboard in hand, smile and conduct quick guest surveys. Effective organizations are zealots for customer feedback.

> During the early years of Earth-Link, Inc., one of the nation's largest online service providers, CEO Garry Betty spent 30 minutes at the end of each day calling new customers.[16] And Lee Iacocca, the former chairman of Chrysler Corporation, said, "If you take care of your customers, everything else will fall into place."[17]

Below are several research ideas to help you determine what your customers value. At your next staff meeting, brainstorm additional ways to talk to your customers.

- **Online Survey for Pastors.** Email your congregation every Sunday afternoon for feedback on the weekly service and sermon. (Companies such as SurveyMonkey.com offer user-friendly and inexpensive research tools.)

- **Exit Interview After Events.** Conduct quick exit interviews after each event. Recruit a volunteer researcher who loves to gather and analyze data.

- **Monthly Phone Blitz.** Once a month, with pizza and soft drinks, give each staff member a list of 10 people to phone with two quick questions.

- **Annual Satisfaction Survey.** Once a year, ask a researcher or consultant to create a Customer Satisfaction Survey. Compare the results from year to year—and report the good news to your inside circle.

- **Workplace Survey.** Your supporting customers include your staff members. Participate in the annual Best Christian Places to Work[19] survey and learn what your employees value most.

The Customer Bucket To-Do List

❏ *Focus on Ball #1* (your primary customer), then pay attention to the other five balls in the bucket. If you're fuzzy about Ball #1, the other 19 buckets will be fuzzy. The Customer Bucket is all about Ball #1.

❏ *Know your customer.* When you mail the brochure or launch the website before you identify your customer and what your customer values, you've just made your first cash deposit into a bottomless pit.

❏ *What do you need to know about your customers that you don't know today?* Who is working on this? If the Customer Bucket is not one of your strengths (see the Team Bucket), ensure that someone on your team has it covered. (Did I mention that it's hard work?)

❏ *Read the startling survey that Willow Creek Community Church conducted in 2007* and what they learned about the spiritual growth patterns of their "customers" in their self-published report, *Reveal: Where Are You?* by Greg Hawkins and Cally Parkinson (visit www.re vealnow.com).

TO DO OR TO DELEGATE?				
Priority A, B, C	Point Person	Task	Deadline Date	Done Date

THE STRATEGY BUCKET

We plan, believing the results are up to God. We energize our people and customers with a Big Holy Audacious Goal (BHAG). We're systematic—never negligent—in our strategic planning. We know our mission statement by memory, and our programs, products and services are in alignment with the mission.

Strategic Balls in the Strategy Bucket

1. BUILD a team-crafted strategic vision statement.
2. MEMORIZE your mission statement.
3. BE STRATEGIC about strategic planning.
4. SUMMARIZE your plan with a G.N.O.M.E. chart.

Occasionally Pat Clements stops a team member in the hallway at Church Extension Plan (cepnet.com) and asks, "What are you working on today, Jennifer?"

As Clements told a gathering of CEOs in Palm Springs last year, these impromptu conversations between the president and a staffer are always upbeat until he asks the key question from the Strategy Bucket. Upon hearing Jennifer's answer, Pat is ready with his follow-up question: "How is that project connected to our Strategic Plan Poster?"

At Church Extension Plan, the creation of the 11×17-inch Strategic Plan Poster is an organization-wide process. When completed, the poster is presented to every team member and displayed—for reference and inspiration—in every office, on bulletin boards, on cubicle walls, in the staff lunch room and, of course, in the boardroom. The poster graphically describes CEP's mission, vision, core values, multi-year targets and strategic goals for the current calendar year.

Hopefully, Jennifer readily connects the dots between her current project and the organization's fine-tuned strategic plan. But if not, Clements has a warm, but straight-forward response: "Jennifer, I'd suggest you review your current project with your team leader today and ask her to drop this one and engage you in a project that has a direct tie-in to our mission, vision and current goals."

The Strategic Plan Poster is a brilliant antidote to the traditional eyes-glazed-over response to an organization's strategic planning process. "Our strategic plan? It's in a binder on a shelf somewhere." When the strategic plan is team-crafted and includes the compelling elements described in the four balls in this chapter, it becomes an awesome process for achieving results.

Without a plan, a blind leader is merely coaxing blind followers through endless meetings and meaningless activities. Picture junior high students learning archery skills with the finest bows and arrows— but no targets. Yikes!

Ball #1:
BUILD a Team-crafted Strategic Vision Statement
*Ignite the awesome power of a Big **Holy** Audacious Goal!*

Steve Holbrook, a consultant friend who is now consulting in heaven, counted the National Aeronautics and Space Administration (NASA) as one of his clients. According to NASA, "History changed on October 4, 1957, when the Soviet Union successfully launched Sputnik I. The world's first artificial satellite was about the size of a basketball, weighed only 183 pounds, and took about 98 minutes to orbit the Earth on its elliptical path."[1]

Almost four years later, on May 25, 1961, President John F. Kennedy made an exciting announcement: The United States would put a man on the moon by 1970! My friend Holbrook told me that the astronauts tweaked that monster goal with this addition: To put a man on the moon by 1970—and bring him safely back!

If you're old enough, you may remember that exciting day on July 20, 1969, when Neil Armstrong descended from Apollo 11 and walked on the moon. John Naisbitt says that "strategic planning is worthless—unless there is first a strategic vision."[2] NASA's strategic vision was to put a man on the moon by 1970. A strategic vision is far different than a mission statement; it's a short-term mega-target that is specific and has a clearly defined result and deadline. NASA's strategic vision, according to Naisbitt, "gave magnetic direction to the entire organization. Nobody had to be told or reminded where the organization was going."[3]

> "You can always amend a big plan, but you can never expand a little one. I don't believe in little plans. I believe in plans big enough to meet a situation which we can't possibly foresee now."
>
> —President Harry S Truman

Contrast NASA's compelling strategic vision statement—and its organizing focus—with its wimpy mission statement at the time: "We are going to be the world leader in space exploration." Mission statements are important of course, but strategic vision statements are powerful and inspiring. Team members will sign-up for the cause. Vendors will support it enthusiastically. In nonprofit organizations, donors and volunteers will be your greatest cheerleaders . . . *if* the target is audacious enough.

Jim Collins popularized the BHAG (Big Hairy Audacious Goal) in his book *Built to Last: Successful Habits of Visionary Companies.*[4] I suggest to my church and ministry clients that they define their BHAGs as Big *Holy* Audacious Goals.

What is your big plan? What is your target in the next three, four or five years? What is so audacious that it energizes every person in your organization? When you're recruiting a new team member, what will cause them to work for you versus another company? When your volunteers are planning the umpteenth event and making sacrifices to serve, what BHAG or strategic vision will fire them up yet again? When tight deadlines never end and personalities clash, what BHAG will unify your team one more time and be the cause for celebration?

Proverbs 16:3 says, "Put God in charge of your work, then what you've planned will take place." If you nail this one, the other balls and the other buckets will be in alignment. If you ignore this one and live with a fuzzy direction, I have a new logo idea for you: the deer in the headlights!

Ball #2:
MEMORIZE Your Mission Statement
If your team members cannot recite your mission statement from memory, take it off the wall and rewrite it.

A mission statement is a bit like an epitaph on a tombstone: "Here lies ABC Organization and this is what we want to be remembered for." Your mission statement is the central ball in the Strategy Bucket. Without a cogent mission statement, you'll have a fuzzy strategic plan and a fuzzier organization.

Your mission statement describes the primary reason you exist. It gives the primary result you want to achieve. An effective mission statement defines *why* you do what you do and leaves the *how* to the strategic plan and the annual plan. It focuses on opportunities. It describes the big picture, not the details.

And it fits on a T-shirt! When brevity wins over bureaucracy, your mission statement is more billboard than biography. It will sing, zing and zip.

Every team member must memorize your mission statement, so it must be short enough to be memorized and meaningful enough that it's not minimized. Whether you lead a nonprofit organization or a business, inspire your teams to stand and deliver when prompted for the mission statement.

If your current mission statement needs tweaking, roll that task into your annual strategic planning process. Identify the big ideas, and then find a wordsmith to fashion the phrases that will deliver a powerful punch. For more ideas on mission statements, read *101 Mission Statements from Top Companies: Plus Guidelines for Writing Your Own Mission Statement* by Jeffrey Abrahams.[5]

The slogan on your letterhead, your website and your brochures must align with your mission. Another phrase for slogan is "brand promise." If your mission statement runs a little long (and some do), your slogan/brand promise delivers the kicker—but the two must have synergy and alignment.

Your core values (see the Culture Bucket) must also be aligned with your mission and slogan. Yes, it's all hard work—but it's rewarding work. When you hear new team members articulating your mission, values and vision to your key customers, you might even get emotional! Teach it and preach it.

Ball #3:
BE STRATEGIC About Strategic Planning
"Insanity is doing the same thing over and over again and expecting different results."

It was Albert Einstein who said, "Insanity is doing the same thing over and over again and expecting different results." If your company or organization has gone three or more years without a written strategic planning process and you think that this year you'll finally get around to it, Einstein has one word for you: insanity!

You must be strategic about strategic planning. Here are six key steps:

1. *Retain a consultant.* There are very few leaders that have the discipline to do effective strategic planning internally. The biggest battle is time because the demands of daily life crowd out all but the necessities.

2. *Create a rolling three-year plan.* Strategic planning is not an event; it's a process. Begin with a three-year plan, but then update it like clockwork each year.

3. *Begin with the basics.* Buy a binder today with 15 tabs and a book on strategic planning—and *presto!* you're on your way.

Winston Churchill said, "There is in the act of preparing, the moment you start caring." Begin to assemble the obvious documents and resources.

4. *Assign a point person.* Who should lead your year-round planning process? Ask God to give you a champion who loves planning and is passionate about the Strategy Bucket.

5. *Work through the five "Drucker questions."* The Drucker Foundation Self-Assessment Tool is an invaluable resource for addressing the most important questions you must ask (see the Results Bucket).

6. *Pray for a breakthrough.* Many leaders have experienced the incredible joy of seeing God work through the planning process. Breakthrough strategies have evolved and erupted because God-honoring leaders and managers have taken the planning process seriously. Because of God's blessing on strategic plans—and because of prayers and audacious acts of faith—God has honored the work of Christ-followers. The result: Millions of people have been fed, clothed, blessed and saved.

Ball #4:
Summarize Your Plan with a G.N.O.M.E. Chart
This would have helped Christopher Columbus!

My consultant friend and partner in The Andringa Group, Dale Lefever, is a brilliant strategic planning facilitator. He shares this thought with his clients: "Columbus did not know where he was going when he left. When he got home, he did not know where he had been. And he did it all on borrowed money. There is hope for all of us!"

Columbus could have used my G.N.O.M.E. chart (Fig. 3.1). Use this simplified strategic plan chart to address the five basic parts of a plan:

THE G.N.O.M.E. CHART				
GOALS	NEEDS	OBJECTIVES	METHODS	EVALUATION
GOAL #1:		1.1		
		1.2		
		1.3		
GOAL #2:		2.1		
		2.2		
GOAL #3:		3.1		
		3.2		
GOAL #4:		4.1		
		4.2		

Figure 3.1

Goals. After sifting through all of your opportunities, agree on three or four key goals that are aligned with your mission and your BHAG, and that give direction to the next 12 to 36 months. A church, for example, would likely write one goal that addresses life transformation or spiritual formation.

Needs. Identify the needs of the people you're serving with each of your major goals.

Objectives. List one, two or three objectives (sub-goals) for each major goal. Some prefer to begin with objectives and label goals as their sub-objectives. (One problem: Your chart would be spelled ONGME, and who can pronounce that?)

Methods. Here's where you list the programs, products and services that are designed to accomplish your goals and objectives to meet the specific needs of your customers. For example, "life transformation" might be a major goal for a church, and "teaching" would be one of the objectives to accomplish that goal. That church might then have a Sunday morning worship and teaching service—not as a *goal*, but as a *method* to accomplish the goal. Yet where do most churches invest their time—clarifying the goals, needs and objectives, or having verbal fist fights over the Sunday morning methodology? Without thoughtful and prayerful work on the front end, the discussion about methods will be meaningless.

Evaluation. Finally, there must be an ongoing process of evaluation to determine if the goals, needs and objectives are being met by the methodology. For ideas on research and feedback (the breakfast of champions), review the ideas in the Customer Bucket and the Program Bucket.

The Strategy Bucket To-Do List

❏ *Take some time to discern where you are in the knowledge levels*—and where you want to be a year from now. The first three buckets of the Cause arena—the Results Bucket, the Customer Bucket and the Strategy Bucket—are foundational to *all* of the other buckets. These three are at the heart of building a sustainable business or organization.

❏ Einstein said, "Intellectual growth should commence at birth and cease only at death." *Help your team members create life-long learning strategies* and move quickly out of Level 1: "I don't know what I don't know." There is an abundance of books, resources, workshops and consultants available to help you go deeper into each bucket.

❏ *Choose one or two tools to use now, and get started.* The G.N.O.M.E. Chart and the Strategic Plan Poster (mentioned at the beginning of the chapter) are just two of the tools available to help your team build their competencies in the Strategy Bucket.

❏ *Recruit a point person.* When your strategic plan is created by planners, not decision-makers, it will sit on the shelf and have little, if any, impact on your organization. Effective strategic planning will always drive decision-making—every day, every week, every month, every quarter, every year.

TO DO OR TO DELEGATE?				
Priority A, B, C	Point Person	Task	Deadline Date	Done Date

THE DRUCKER BUCKET

We are privileged to be leaders and managers and we steward that privilege by being lifelong learners and practitioners in the art of management. We don't just give lip service to management—we are disciplined students of great leadership and management thinkers like Peter Drucker, Ken Blanchard, and others.

Strategic Balls in the Drucker Bucket

1. LEAD from your strengths.
2. PRACTICE the art of management.
3. READ or re-read one Drucker book each year.

Peter F. Drucker, the Father of Modern Management, was welcomed into his heavenly home on November 11, 2005, just a few days shy of his ninety-sixth birthday. According to Bob Buford, his last days were consumed with repeating the Lord's Prayer in German.[1]

Christian Management Association honored Drucker with its highest honor, the Christian Management Award, in 1990. CMA honored Bob Buford with the same award in 2005. I must mention Drucker and Buford in the same breath because it was Buford and his Leadership Network[2] that brought much of Drucker's wisdom and management insight to the leading Christian leaders and pastors of our day.

Certainly one of my top-10 life experiences was sitting at the feet of Peter Drucker for four days in Estes Park, Colorado, with 30 other Christian leaders in August 1986. Buford invited us. Drucker enthralled us. Several years later, I was privileged to be part of a reunion gathering with Drucker in Claremont, California. This remarkable management guru was a gift from God to both business and ministry leaders.

I've dedicated one of the 20 management buckets to Peter Drucker. There are just three balls in this bucket, but you'll discover Drucker-isms (his pithy management one-liners, such as, "Most of what we call management consists of making it difficult for people to get their work done"[3]) throughout each discipline of leadership and management. His seminal book *Management: Tasks, Responsibilities, Practices* runs 839 pages. (The phrase "prolific management writer" doesn't do him justice.) While I've positioned the Drucker Bucket in the Cause arena because he was all about mission and results, his insight impacts and integrates the Cause, the Community and the Corporation arenas.

So what are the balls in the Drucker Bucket? Think of the driving range at your golf course. Picture hundreds and hundreds of balls all over the range and buckets and buckets of balls lined up for both the pros and the hackers. Just like your community driving range, Drucker had something for all of us—the weekend duffer *and* Tiger Woods.

He was a category of one.

Ball #1:
LEAD from Your Strengths
Peter Drucker launched a movement to minimize weaknesses.

In my last few years at Christian Management Association, I passed along a Robert Mankoff cartoon from the *New Yorker* magazine to my board chair. In the drawing, a corporate board is meeting and the chairman tells the CEO, "Actually, we all think you're doing a pretty good job. We just feel it would be more fun to have a celebrity for C.E.O."

Drucker said, "Effective leadership is not about being liked; leadership is defined by results, not attributes."[4] It sounds simple, but it's radical. Lead from your strengths, not your weaknesses. Figure out who you are, what you enjoy doing, what you're good at, and then build a team around you to fill in the cracks. Focus on results and lead from your strengths.

Don't allow anyone else's leadership theory or strengths to be prescriptive for your unique style. Strong-willed but misinformed managers, board members and colleagues will force you into their mold. They'll tell you, "This is what a leader looks like. This is how leaders lead." Don't buy it. Lead from your own unique strengths. Don't take your own unique leadership eye off the ball.

Drucker's lead-from-your-strengths movement has many disciples. Bill Hybels, the senior pastor of Willow Creek Community Church and chairman of the Willow Creek Association, participated in that 1986 summit with Peter Drucker, and the impact it had on him was far-reaching. In 2002, he wrote *Courageous Leadership*, which described 10 different leadership styles.[6] The list includes motivational, visionary, directional, strategic, managing, shepherding, team-building, entre-preneurial, reengineering and bridge-building leaders. Hone your own style (Hybels lists 10—pick one) and lead from your strengths.

> "Follow effective action with quiet reflection. From the quiet reflection will come even more effective action."[5]
>
> —Peter Drucker

Ken Blanchard has written a full shelf of excellent leadership books (search "Ken Blanchard" at Amazon.com for the list). He has preached "lead from your strengths" tirelessly for years. Increasingly, Blanchard's message is faith-based, including a more recent book he co-authored with Phil Hodges called *Lead Like Jesus: Lessons from the Greatest Leadership Role Model of All Time.*[7]

The movement became a groundswell in this decade when the Gallup research on strengths was popularized in the book *Now, Discover Your Strengths*[8] and the latest update, *Strengths Finder 2.0*[9] (see the Team Bucket).

Max Lucado's *Cure for the Common Life: Living in Your Sweet Spot* challenges people to find their "S.T.O.R.Y." (Lucado's acronym for Strengths, Topic, Optimal conditions, Relationships and "Yes!" moments).[10] He popularizes the decades of research conducted by People Management International (PMI) with SIMA®, their proprietary discovery process that assesses the core strengths and natural motivation of individuals. (SIMA is the acronym for System for Identifying Motivated Abilities. For more information, visit their website at PeopleManagement.org.)

We can thank Drucker for his early insight. It has freed up millions to lead from their strengths.

Ball #2:
PRACTICE the Art of Management
Exercise your management muscles with a daily dose of Drucker.

Peter Drucker preached that you must practice, practice and practice the art of management. He said it was like any other discipline. World-class musicians hone their gifts up to eight hours a day. Athletes practice, practice and practice. Professional golfers finish 18 holes and head to the driving range. Tiger Woods has a coach.

What do hassled managers do? After the nine-to-five battle (more often 7:00 A.M. to 7:00 P.M.), they overeat, drink or distract their joyless days with mind-numbing entertainment. On the other hand, great managers stay at it—always digging for fresh insights and solutions. Drucker writes, "We now accept the fact that learning is a lifelong process of keeping abreast of change. And the most pressing task is to teach people how to learn."[11]

There are several suggested ways to master the management buckets in the introduction to this book. To practice and execute the art of management, you must commit time and thought. Create your own disciplined process for mastering the 20 management bucket competencies. Your plan might involve 20 days, 20 weeks, 20 months or 20 years. Make a plan. Just do it!

Read *The Daily Drucker* Daily
I know, I know . . . your office is piled high with good stuff to read (like this book). Stacks of the *Wall Street Journal* taunt you, "You management farce! How dare you pretend to mentor your team. You don't even take time to mentor yourself. Your sorry leadership façade is fueled only by the fumes of last year's trendy management gimmicks. Get real, you big fake!"

Guilt never inspires. Self-reproach and self-doubt are crippling. But there are hundreds of best practices for staying on top of the art of management. Your first step is to buy this book for every team member: *The Daily Drucker: 366 Days of Insight and Motivation for Getting the Right Things Done.*[12]

Similar to a one-year Bible in format, *The Daily Drucker* delivers a poignant and practical one-page management insight for every day of the year. Excerpted from the vast Drucker library of wisdom and pithy points, topics cover the Drucker waterfront: time management, results, innovation, and much more.

Here are five ways to leverage this book and bless your team members as they practice, practice, practice the art of management:

1. **Stand and read.** When your team gathers for their five-minute check-in meeting (see the Meetings Bucket), ask a team member to read the daily dose from Drucker.

2. **Boot and read.** Don't waste the two minutes watching your computer boot up. While emails from Nigerian hucksters fill up your inbox, read *The Daily Drucker*. Create a disciplined habit away from your desk, such as sitting in your guest chair while you read, reflect and pray. Ask the Lord to help you connect the day's management insight with a current management challenge or a perplexing people problem. I'm not suggesting, of course, that Peter Drucker replace Saint Peter, Saint Paul or Jesus. But I *am* suggesting that great managers are disciplined, lifelong learners. You probably agree, but unless you build the core value of lifelong learning into your calendar, you're a phony.

3. **Email and read.** Assign one team member per week to select a Drucker quote from the daily reading and email it to every team member. This "Daily Dose of Drucker" will at least benefit that week's researcher. Teachers learn more than students.

4. **Post and read.** Delegate this idea to the top Drucker zealot on your team. Ask her to post a weekly Drucker quotation on the bulletin board every week. I like this one:

> **QUOTE-OF-THE WEEK FROM PETER F. DRUCKER**
>
> *"People who <u>don't</u> take risks generally make about two big mistakes a year.*
>
> *People who <u>do</u> take risks generally make about two big mistakes a year."*
>
> Source: The Daily Drucker: 366 Days of Insight and Motivation for Getting the Right Things Done[13]

5. **Brown Bag and Read.** Once a month, invite your team to the "Drucker Deli" for lunch. Order deli sandwiches (or bring your own) and meet at a nearby scenic spot. (During my CMA years in San Clemente, California, our team sometimes enjoyed carry-out on the T Street bluff, watching dozens of surfers get axed in the Pacific.) The admission price for the "Drucker Deli" is cheap. Bring your underlined copy of *The Daily Drucker* and share your favorite insight from the last 30 days of readings. (Of course, it goes without saying that once a month you should also host a Bucket Breakfast or Bucket Brunch or Bucket Buffet or . . . okay, I'll stop . . . and have your team members share their favorite insights from *Mastering the Management Buckets*. For more ideas on team building, see the *Hoopla!* Bucket.)

Ball #3:
READ or Re-read One Drucker Book Each Year
The father of modern management knows best.

My good friend and mentor George Duff reads Peter Drucker's *The Effective Executive* once a year.[14] (To survive 27 years as president of the Greater Seattle Chamber of Commerce, you have to be an effective executive.) George is a Drucker zealot. If you have not yet read or listened to any of Drucker's books, *The Effective Executive* is an excellent beginning point. If you lead a church or nonprofit organization, be sure to read *Managing the Nonprofit Organization: Principles and Practices*.[15]

One of my treasured books, autographed for me by Peter Drucker, is a novel, *The Temptation to Do Good*, published in 1984. It's a great title and a quick read for busy leaders and managers who need a change of pace from the growing pile of must-read books. In this work of fiction, Drucker introduces us to Father Heinz Zimmerman, president of a Catholic university. He faces all the leadership challenges common to nonprofit CEOs: budgets, donors, staff conflicts, board members, ethical issues, and more. Throw in student and faculty expectations and you'll appreciate your current organization more—no matter how complex it is!

In just 152 pages, Drucker addresses the subtle "temptation to do good" syndrome that gets many religious leaders into trouble. You'll enjoy the story and Drucker's memorable insights.

This chapter would be woefully incomplete without listing the legacy that Peter Drucker left: his books. Check (✔) the titles that align with your current management challenges and commit to reading a minimum of one Drucker book per year.

Books by Peter F. Drucker—The Father of Modern Management

❏ *The End of Economic Man* (1939)
❏ *The Future of Industrial Man* (1942)
❏ *Concept of the Corporation* (1946)
❏ *The New Society* (1950)

❏ *The Practice of Management* (1954)

❏ *America's Next Twenty Years* (1957)

❏ *Landmarks of Tomorrow* (1957)

❏ *Managing for Results* (1964)

❏ *The Effective Executive* (1966)

❏ *The Age of Discontinuity* (1968)

❏ *Technology, Management and Society* (1970)

❏ *Men, Ideas and Politics* (1971)

❏ *Management: Tasks, Responsibilities, Practices* (1973)

❏ *The Unseen Revolution* (1976; reissued in 1996 under the title *The Pension Fund Revolution*)

❏ *People and Performance: The Best of Peter Drucker on Management* (1977)

❏ *An Introductory View of Management* (1977)

❏ *Adventures of a Bystander* (autobiography) (1978)

❏ *Song of the Brush: Japanese Painting from the Sanso Collection* (1979)

❏ *Managing in Turbulent Times* (1980)

❏ *Toward the Next Economics and Other Essays* (1981)

❏ *The Changing World of the Executive* (1982)

❏ *The Last of All Possible Worlds* (fiction) (1982)

❏ *The Temptation to Do Good* (fiction) (1984)

❏ *Innovation and Entrepreneurship* (1985)

❏ *Frontiers of Management* (1986)

❏ *The New Realities: In Government and Politics, in Economics and Business, in Society and World View* (1989)

❏ *Managing the Nonprofit Organization: Principles and Practices* (1990)

❏ *Managing for the Future* (1992)

❏ *The Ecological Vision* (1993)

❏ *Post-Capitalist Society* (1993)

❏ *Managing in a Time of Great Change* (1995)

❏ *Drucker on Asia: A Dialogue between Peter Drucker and Isao Nakauchi* (1997)

❏ *Peter Drucker on the Profession of Management* (1998)

❏ *Management Challenges for the 21st Century* (1999)

❏ *The Essential Drucker* (2001)

❏ *Managing in the Next Society* (2002)

❏ *A Functioning Society* (2002)

❏ *The Daily Drucker* (2004)
❏ *The Effective Executive in Action* (2006)[16]

The Drucker Bucket To-Do List

❏ *Focus on your strengths,* not your weaknesses. In *The Effective Executive,* Drucker says that "strong people always have strong weaknesses too. Where there are peaks, there are valleys. And no one is strong in many areas."[17] (More on this in the Team Bucket.)

❏ *Be a student of management.* To exercise your strengths, you must be a disciplined lifelong learner in the art of management. God has gifted you to lead. Steward that gift and practice, practice, practice.

❏ *Make time to read.* There is no relationship between the amount of time you spend watching TV golf and your competencies as a manager. There is a stunning relationship between reading books by Peter Drucker and your effectiveness as a manager. Your calendar reflects your convictions.

TO DO OR TO DELEGATE?				
Priority A, B, C	Point Person	Task	Deadline Date	Done Date

THE BOOK BUCKET

We believe leaders are readers! We create a culture that embraces a healthy appetite for leadership and management books, journals, articles and audio resources. We mentor team members with thoughtfully selected titles and chapters to help them leverage their strengths, grow in their faith and serve others with passion. We don't just talk about books—we actually read them!

Strategic Balls in the Book Bucket

1. AVOID management-by-bestseller syndrome.
2. MENTOR your team members with niche books.
3. MASTER the management buckets by reading.
4. CREATE your top-100 books list.

President Harry Truman said, "The only thing new in the world is the history you don't know." Leaders and managers are in the knowledge-management business. Mastering the management buckets requires a sane assessment of where you are in each of the 20 buckets—and of how you plan to move to the next level.

Level 1: I don't know what I don't know.
Level 2: I know what I don't know.
Level 3: I have an action plan to address what I know I don't know.
Level 4: I am knowledgeable and effective in this core competency and can mentor others.

The apostle Paul wrote to Timothy, "And the [instructions] which you have heard from me along with many witnesses, transmit and entrust [as a deposit] to reliable and faithful men who will be competent and qualified to teach others also" (2 Tim. 2:2, *AMP*). Core competencies must be passed along to build a sustainable ministry or company. When team members are confident at Level 4 and have mastered a management bucket, create opportunities for them to mentor others.

While overwhelming amounts of information are at our fingertips thanks to the Internet, wisdom is in short supply. More information is not the answer. The quality of information has been dramatically dumbed down. Any self-proclaimed expert can post information on Wikipedia, but what we really need is a Wisdompedia.

Passionate journalist-wannabes foist their typo-rich blogs onto our information highways and our email inboxes. Writing at 90 miles per hour, these lightning-fast postings reflect speed, but rarely substance. (Suggestion to bloggers: Write draft one, then take a long reflective walk or visit Starbucks. Return from walk, edit, then post.)

Andy Stanley nailed the problem—and the solution—with his insightful book *The Best Question Ever*. He writes:

> Every professional athlete knows that he or she will never reach, nor maintain, peak performance apart from outside input. Granted, the superstar pitcher may be the one with the skill, youth, money and fame. But none of that is enough to keep him performing at his peak. He needs a coach. He needs another set of eyes and another source of insight to help him judge his performance realistically.
>
> Not coincidentally, men and women who consistently make the right moves relationally, professionally, and financially are those who seek input from others. Again, they know what they don't know and aren't afraid to go to those who do know. And this private habit results in very public success.
>
> You will never be all you're capable of being unless you tap the wisdom of the wise people around you.[1]

(I don't want to spoil the discovery process for you—buy Andy Stanley's book yourself and discover the answer to "the best question ever.")

Leaders Are Readers

Here's the point of this chapter: Thoughtfully selected books can be powerful tools in your mentoring ministry with your team members, your colleagues and your family and friends. Everything you need to know has been written in a book somewhere.

Brian Ogne, one of the most enthusiastic camp and conference center directors I've ever met, once asked his grandfather if he'd like a special book for Christmas. He replied, "Why would I need another book? I already have one!" Don't be like Brian's grandpa!

Mastering the management buckets includes serious attention to books. Leaders are readers. I'm grateful to authors who disciplined their lives to share their leadership lessons in print. I've relied heavily on the wisdom from books in my leadership—and you'll see dozens of book recommendations throughout this one.

A timely book, well chosen and recommended by a friend, is a treasure. Dick Towner, the champion for the Good $ense Stewardship Movement at Willow Creek Association, urged me to read Andy Stanley's book—and I'm grateful.

When I was the CEO of Christian Camping International/USA (now known as Christian Camp and Conference Association), I received a letter from Jim Pancoast, a valued member in Texas. He wrote, "John, the most important benefit that I received from my CCI membership this year was your recommendation to read Ken Blanchard's book, *The One Minute Manager*.[2] It has dramatically changed the way we lead and manage here at Sky Ranch."

Books pack a punch!

Ball #1:
Avoid Management-by-Bestseller Syndrome
Management gimmick-of-the-month whiplash can be fatal!

When the author of Ecclesiastes wrote, "There's no end to the publishing of books" (12:12), he was more prophetic than his contemporaries ever realized! According to the bibliographic information management company R. R. Bowker, there were 291,920 new titles published in the U.S. in 2006, an increase of more than 3 percent over 2005.[3]

Hundreds, if not thousands, of those titles promised the latest, greatest leadership and management truths, trends, tactics and tales for revolutionizing your business, career, work relationships and income. *Caution!* The management gimmick-of-the-month approach will give your team whiplash. Thoughtful leaders build on the brilliant themes from last year and enhance and reinforce those learnings with complementary books and resources this year.

> Before you distribute the next required-reading title to your team, create the context: "Last quarter, we added another weapon to our arsenal when we read XYZ. This quarter's book builds on that methodology and zeroes in on one of the critical balls in the Customer Bucket. Please note that there's a $10 gift card for Starbucks in your book. Get out of the office for a few hours and enjoy some reading with your favorite beverage."

There are far more management methods and too many leadership theories to master. It's overwhelming! You must pick and choose. Should you master the Blue Ocean Strategy approach or retain a consultant to focus on Emotional Intelligence? What about the balanced scorecard or benchmarking? Is management by objectives still valid? What happened to management by wandering around (or was it *wondering* around)? What is values-based management? Should you go with Six Sigma or TQM, or do you need a SWOT analysis? Should you change your mission statement (even though the bronze wall plaque set you back $3,000)? Is your money on Drucker, Blanchard, Collins, Lencioni, Engstrom, Bakke, Deming, Laurie Beth Jones, Hybels, Warren or Maxwell?

Help!

While you must be well read, you can't possibly read everything. That's why I have zeroed in on Peter Drucker's work. His books build on one another and won't trigger management theory whiplash. You might want to create a Ken Blanchard bucket. (If you do, let him know. He'll love it!)

I first heard the phrase "management-by-bestseller" over coffee at Starbucks with Scott Vandeventer, chief operating officer at Evangelical

Christian Credit Union. He commented, "Too many leaders frolic from fad to fad, taking otherwise good ideas and making programs out of them for as long as their attention spans can handle it, without ever getting to their core values and their own unique business model or value proposition." Scott nailed it.

He added, "The issue isn't that the concepts are lightweight—they're often quite good—but when the leader is ever-searching, they never get to the root issues behind their search. We wouldn't describe *Good to Great* by Jim Collins as 'lite.' It has great ideas, but leaders jump into the ideas as if every single one applies to their case. That's a major error. They need to ask what they can take from the book into their world. Some organizations get dangerously close to Management-by-Bestseller Syndrome due to a kind of corporate attention deficit disorder, probably systemic to its leadership."

Ball #2:
MENTOR Your Team Members with Niche Books
Leverage their strengths with thoughtfully selected chapters.

"By working faithfully eight hours a day, you may eventually get to be a boss and work 12 hours a day," wrote Robert Frost. But really, it doesn't have to be that way. When your team is thriving at work, you too can leave on time and thrive at home. Many bosses teach, mentor, equip, encourage and motivate their team members with the simplest tools: books!

Avoid Management-by-Bestseller Syndrome that requires everyone to read this month's trendy book. Instead, build a management library in your office and recommend specific titles to specific people for specific problems or opportunities. How do you teach the priority of affirmation to a rookie manager? Help her understand "one minute praisings" from the classic *The One Minute Manager* by Ken Blanchard and Spencer Johnson.

Does a team member have a faulty sequential view of priorities (God first, family second, church third, career fourth)? Encourage him to read *Balancing Life's Demands: A New Perspective on Priorities.*

Author J. Grant Howard writes that a list of sequential priorities makes absolutely no sense. "It can't be intelligently explained. It can't be easily understood. It can't be logically lived out." He adds, "I am convinced that the existing sequential model is not only impractical it is unbiblical."[4]

You don't have to read every chapter of every book. Perhaps one of your managers has a heart to build more trust with a team member, but she's short on ideas. Ask her to read chapter 10 in *The Carrot Principle: How the Best Managers Use Recognition to Engage Their People, Retain Talent, and Accelerate Performance*. In just 20 pages, there's a goldmine of 125 recognition ideas in five categories: goal setting, communication, recognition, trust and accountability. Here's an example:

> Idea #104. What would it take to convince an employee that you are on his side? That you are part of a team? How about doing his least favorite job for a day? (Actually, it's not a bad idea to use at home either.)[5]

You get the idea. Build a massive management library and create a purposeful book culture. At your next staff meeting, ask team members to answer these two questions:

1. What's the most helpful management book you've ever read and why?

2. What are two or three of your "Reading 101 Principles" for getting the most out of a book?

Ball #3:
MASTER the Management Buckets by Reading
Put down the duckie!

If you grew up in the first *Sesame Street* era or are blessed with children or grandchildren, you may remember the hilarious upbeat tune, "Put Down the Duckie," that featured more than a dozen celebrities and musicians, including Paul Simon, John Candy and Danny Devito. Jazzman Hoots the Owl is teaching Ernie to play the saxophone, but Ernie won't put down his rubber yellow duckie.

Hoots sings, "You gotta put down the duckie. Put down the duckie. Put down the duckie, if you wanna play the saxophone!"[6] That's the message in the Book Bucket. If you're passionate about your mission and your BHAG, you must practice, practice and practice the art of management. In essence, you must "lay aside every weight and the sin which so easily ensnares us" (Heb. 12:1, *NIV*) if you want to lead and manage with excellence.

What duckie are you willing to put down today so that you can pick up a book and be a leader of excellence? Mastering the 20 management buckets may seem overwhelming to your team members—maybe even to you. But how do you eat an elephant? One bite at a time.

Start with three buckets and three books. Don't procrastinate. Start today. Identify the three buckets you'd like to master first and get one book recommendation for each bucket (from my list or from a peer or mentor). Read those three titles in the next 90 days. (To read my top-100 recommended books list, visit www.managementbuckets.com. You can also subscribe to the free eNewsletter, "Your Weekly Staff Meeting," which features a book review and a bucket insight each week.)

**Check the Three Buckets You'll Master
(and Three Books You'll Read) First**

OUR CAUSE

- ❏ The Results Bucket: *The Three Signs of a Miserable Job: A Fable for Managers (and Their Employees)* by Patrick Lencioni
- ❏ The Customer Bucket: *The Drucker Foundation Self-Assessment Tool* (Participant Workbook) published by Leader to Leader
- ❏ The Strategy Bucket: *Good to Great and the Social Sectors: Why Business Thinking Is Not the Answer* by Jim Collins
- ❏ The Drucker Bucket: *The Daily Drucker: 366 Days of Insight and Motivation for Getting the Right Things Done* by Peter F. Drucker with Joseph A. Maciariello

❑ The Book Bucket: *The Best Question Ever: A Revolutionary Approach to Decision Making* by Andy Stanley

❑ The Program Bucket: *Marketing Your Ministry: Ten Critical Principles* by John W. Pearson and Robert D. Hisrich

OUR COMMUNITY

❑ The People Bucket: *How to Deal with Annoying People: What to Do When You Can't Avoid Them* by Bob Phillips

❑ The Culture Bucket: *Winning: The Answers—Confronting 74 of the Toughest Questions in Business* by Jack and Suzy Welch

❑ The Team Bucket: *StrengthsFinder 2.0* by Tom Rath

❑ The *Hoopla!* Bucket: *Joy at Work: A Revolutionary Approach to Fun on the Job* by Dennis Bakke

❑ The Donor Bucket: *Revolution in Generosity: Transforming Stewards to Be Rich Toward God* by Wesley K. Willmer, general editor

❑ The Volunteer Bucket: *Simply Strategic Volunteers: Empowering People for Ministry* by Tony Morgan and Tim Stevens

❑ The Crisis Bucket: *The Effective Executive* by Peter F. Drucker

OUR CORPORATION

❑ The Board Bucket: *Good Governance for Nonprofits: Developing Principles and Policies for an Effective Board* by Fredric L. Laughlin and Robert C. Andringa

❑ The Budget Bucket: *2008 Church and Nonprofit Tax & Financial Guide: For 2007 Returns* by Dan Busby

❑ The Delegation Bucket: *The One Minute Manager Meets the Monkey* by Ken Blanchard, William Oncken and Hal Burrows

❑ The Operations Bucket: *The Minister's MBA: Essential Business Tools for Maximum Ministry Success* by George S. Babbes and Michael Zigarelli

❑ The Systems Bucket: *The E-Myth: Why Most Small Businesses Don't Work and What to Do About It* by Michael E. Gerber

❑ The Printing Bucket: *Associated Press (AP) Stylebook and Briefing on Media Law* published by the Associated Press

❏ The Meetings Bucket: *Death by Meeting: A Leadership Fable . . . About Solving the Most Painful Problem in Business* by Patrick M. Lencioni

Ball #4:
CREATE Your Top-100 Books List
Pick your top-3, top-10 and top-100 books.

This is for extra credit. In a journal or on your computer, begin to assemble your top-100 books list. One rule: You may only list books you have actually read, not read about. I recommend that you list them under the 20 management buckets, though you may have another system that works for you.

I created my top-100 list last year and it was a fascinating and joy-filled journey. Once again, I was with old friends. My heart beat fast as I savored the early morning hours I invested in *Experiencing God: Knowing and Doing the Will of God*, authored by Henry Blackaby and Claude King. I was reminded again of the savvy organizational chart system from *The E-Myth: Why Most Small Businesses Don't Work and What to Do About It* by Michael E. Gerber. (I immediately recommended the book to a client.)

TrueFaced: Trust God and Others with Who You Really Are, by the team at Leadership Catalyst,[7] Bill Thrall, Bruce McNicol and John Lynch, continues to have an extraordinary ministry in my life and the lives of others. To the right is one of their profound insights.

> "Performance-obsessed cultures can never promote healing. Rather, they create more wounding." [8]

When I added Bob Phillip's book *The Delicate Art of Dancing with Porcupines: Learning to Appreciate the Finer Points of Others* to my top-100 list, I reminisced about the week I learned that I was a "Driver" and that my wife, Joanne, was an "Analytical." That explained everything! (We've been married 38 years,

> You're in a meeting and a coworker recommends a hot new book, clearly impressing the boss. Ironically, that was the book you had just loaned your colleague last month. That's okay. President Harry Truman said, "It is amazing what you can accomplish if you do not care who gets the credit."

thanks to that course!) Phillips writes about the four social styles, and his easy-to-remember system has been hard-wired into my leadership and management thinking for 25 years.

Begin with your top-3 and your top-10. You'll enjoy the journey as you build your top-100 list. Remember that you'll change over the years and so will your needs and priorities. Don't hesitate to change your list, but don't ever eliminate the Management 101 books from your library. Your next hire may not ever have read Peter Drucker's *The Effective Executive* or Ken Blanchard's *The One Minute Manager* or *Strengths Finder 2.0* by Tom Rath.

The Book Bucket To-Do List

❑ *Take good notes.* When a great quote or an innovative idea jumps out at you in your reading, write it down and tuck it into your 20-buckets binder under the corresponding bucket. Remember to write down the book title, author and page number so that you can find it again! This will also help you recommend focused, appropriate resources to your team.

❑ Whether you mentor your team members with books or audio resources, *do it with laser-like accuracy.* Don't waste their time. Whet their appetite for life-long learning with thoughtfully selected books across the 20 disciplines of the management buckets.

❑ *Delegate your reading.* When someone recommends a great book, buy it—even if you don't have time to read it. Delegate some of your reading to the management zealots on your team.

❑ *Start your top-3 list now,* and then move on to your top-10. Set a strategic timeline for completing the list of your top-100.

TO DO OR TO DELEGATE?

Priority A, B, C	Point Person	Task	Deadline Date	Done Date

THE PROGRAM BUCKET

We are zealots for program effectiveness and so we research and understand our customer before launching new programs, products or services. We measure program results. We feed our primary programs and drop the losers—all in the spirit of discerning where God is at work.

Strategic Balls in the Program Bucket

1. GIVE program choices.
2. BUILD program capacity and sustainability first.
3. FEED your strongest programs and benchmark the others.
4. DON'T BE the eighth lemonade stand in a row of nine!

The flagship programs, products or services are the public face of your organization. Customers purchase surfboards, convertibles, iPods, bananas, dry cleaning, a week at a Christian camp, a venti Orange Crème Frappuccino® and baseball tickets because they satisfy a need or want—not because a nonprofit or a corporation has an excellent crisis plan in place (see the Crisis Bucket). It's the music, the teaching, the youth group or a divorce recovery program that attracts new attenders to your church—new people don't join because of the back office efficiencies (the Operations Bucket) or the board governance systems (the Board Bucket). Programs, products and services are the magnets for customers.

Programs are cause-driven. An apprentice program helps homeless people learn job-related skills, enabling an urban ministry to achieve its objectives. A university's "Semester in Africa" program aligns with its mission to prepare young men and women to be global Christians. An organization's prison ministry connects volunteers with its Big Holy

Audacious Goal (BHAG): "to place 500 ex-offenders in full-time employment over the next three years."

But! No bucket is an island. When the other 19 buckets fail to align with the Program Bucket, the program and your entire operation can quickly spiral out of control. For example:

- The quarterly concert sells out, but the event loses money. (The program folks need more training in the Budget Bucket.)

- The megachurch's six services are jam-packed, but the parking inefficiencies and rude volunteers squelch the spiritual impact within 12 minutes of the closing praise song. (They need help from the Systems Bucket and the Volunteer Bucket.)

- During the new CEO's honeymoon phase at the rescue mission, major donors gave generously. One hundred days later, they want her to document the measurable results that their gifts will generate. (There's a ball in the Results Bucket that can help her.)

In this chapter, we'll explore the four balls in the Program Bucket and how you can help your team integrate them with the other 19 buckets.

Ball #1:
Give Program Choices
When the only two answers are yes or no,
you're not satisfying customer needs.

When my son, Jason, was about four, I taught him an important marketing principle I learned from Bob Hisrich, co-author of our book *Marketing Your Ministry: Ten Critical Principles.*

Late one afternoon, Jason asked his mom for a cookie. "No," Joanne said. "It's too close to dinner time."

I took Jason aside and gave him my fatherly advice on effective marketing. "Here's how to get your cookie, Jason," I began. "Tomorrow, go into the kitchen and ask Mom this simple question: "Can I have one cookie or two?"

My street-smart kid learned fast. The next day, he joined his mom in the kitchen and asked nonchalantly, "Mom? Can I have one cookie or two cookies?"

The answer was immediate: "Just one!"

Jason enjoyed his chocolate chip cookie that afternoon because he gave his mom the opportunity to say no and still say yes. He gave her choices. It's a simple marketing rule of thumb, but it's easy to overlook in the Program Bucket: Give people the choice to say no to a few options—yet still say yes.[1] For example . . .

Event Registration Forms Options: Always include at least two options on registration forms: the "early bird" rate and the regular rate. Add another option and ask for $15 more for the advanced purchase of a CD, book or T-shirt (again, more choices).

Donor Options: Before you mail 10,000 donor letters, test several options with 100 donors:

- ❑ 1 camp scholarship = $147
- ❑ 2 camp scholarships = $294
- ❑ 10 camp scholarships = $1,470
- ❑ 1/2 camp scholarship = $73

Your test with a few donors will give you the data you need to determine which options will work best for 10,000. Always give options.

Volunteer Service Options: "Jennifer, our team members have prayed and we'd like you to be the junior high coordinator. Would you prefer a 12-month or an 18-month term?"

Coffee Options: Go to your favorite Starbucks or other coffee shop and look at the amazing array of options: cup sizes, flavorful coffees from multiple continents and tempting extra ingredients. After you've made those choices, the well-trained Starbucks partner (their word for employee) continues presenting options: "We have seven bagel selections for you this morning, John. Would you like the sesame seed with crème cheese? Shall I bag half a dozen bagels for the hard-working team at your office?"

Budget Options: "I'm recommending that the director of programs receive a salary increase of either 5 percent or 10 percent. I'd like your feedback." (Remember, if you ask for just one cookie [5 percent], the answer might be no. Give options for which both options are yes.)

Compare the vast array of options that can be provided to customers and team members with lackluster choices that quickly disengage people:

- The service is Sunday at 11:00 A.M. You comin' or not?

- T-shirts go on sale Wednesday. We have one color: black.

- All tickets are $19. First-come, first served.

- The whole church will be studying 40 days of budgeting. Join a small group on May 1. We offer this course just once a year.

- Whether you're a new employee or you have your 25-year pin, everyone must attend Friday's six-hour workshop on improving employee morale. Bring your own sack lunch. Don't be late.

Give people options and they'll say yes to something! Execute this critical ball in the Program Bucket and you'll be amazed at the response.

Ball #2:
BUILD Program Capacity and Sustainability First
You never have a second chance to make a first impression.

It was an answer to their prayers: A young ministry with a bold vision caught the attention of the editor of *Focus on the Family* magazine. Their resources for parents made the magazine's cover story. Thousands of people swamped the organization with phone calls and letters.

Eric Buehrer, president of Gateways to Better Education[2] told me, "The second we hung up the phone, it would ring again. That went on all day. It was exciting. Then the mail started pouring in on top of that! It was a blessing, but we were unprepared for such an avalanche of responses." Gateways quickly outsourced their customer response operations to an experienced company. The ministry had high competence in program content, but very limited experience in customer service and back office operations.

We all know this scenario. The CEO or senior pastor comes down off the mountain and announces, "God told me to start the Dorcas Dream Ministry for hurting people. We can do it. You guys work out the details and I'll announce it next week." It reminds me of the Dilbert cartoon where the boss has gathered the team for yet one more meaningless meeting and announces, "Sales are dropping like a rock. Our plan is to invent some sort of doohickey that everyone wants to buy." After this pronouncement, Dilbert's boss sits down and proudly concludes, "The visionary leadership work is done. How long will your part take?"

It's tough on visionaries to be held back by the realists: "What do you mean, build capacity first? God told me to do this!"

Whoa, Silver! Effective CEOs, senior pastors, senior leaders, managers, board members and key volunteers have core values in place that affirm the importance of teamwork, collaboration and the integration of spiritual gifts and strengths. The launching of a new program should never be a Lone Ranger event, because new programs require multitalented teams to factor in capacity and sustainability from the get-go.

Did you ever watch *The Lone Ranger* TV series? "Return with us now to those thrilling days of yesteryear. The Lone Ranger rides again!" Here's the problem: In real life, your Lone Ranger leader can't mount his fiery white horse with the speed of light, a cloud of dust and a hearty, "Hi-yo, Silver . . . away!" Your masked man leads a team—a team with discernment and analytical gifts and intuitive street-smart common sense.

So when your lone leader shouts the made-for-TV mantra, "Hi-yo, Silver, away!" the team won't buy it—and that's good. There's a better way.

Here are the top-10 questions effective leaders should ask about program capacity and sustainability before they launch a new program:

Top-10 Questions to Ask About Program Capacity and Sustainability

Check the three most important for your organization.

❏ 1. Does this program align with our mission statement?

❏ 2. Does this program align with our Big Holy Audacious Goal (BHAG)?

❏ 3. Does this program have written goals that meet the S.M.A.R.T. test (Specific, Measurable, Achievable, Realistic, Time-related)?

❏ 4. Do we have the people capacity to both launch the program and maintain it (a staff champion, support staff, volunteers, and so on)?

❏ 5. Have we answered the five Drucker questions?

❏ 6. Have we invested adequate time and money in researching *Who is the customer?* and *What does the customer value?*

❏ 7. Does this program align with our culture and our core values?

❏ 8. Have we conducted due diligence to assess the program's sustainability (including revenue and expense) over the next three to five years?

❏ 9. Under what conditions do we agree that we will "pull the plug" on this program if the goals are not achieved by the target dates?

❏ 10. Have we been diligent in asking our inside circle for constructive criticism or have we spiritually hyped it so much that naysayers have been silenced?

SUSTAINABILITY!
Count the Cost

"Is there anyone here who, planning to build a new house, doesn't first sit down and figure the cost so you'll know if you can complete it? If you only get the foundation laid and then run out of money, you're going to look pretty foolish. Everyone passing by will poke fun at you: 'He started something he couldn't finish.'"

Luke 14:28-30

Build Sustainability

There are many excellent resources available to help you build sustainability. Google the word or query all the sustainability books at Amazon.com. Any good Sustainability 101 course will alert you to one financial fallacy that nonprofit organizations (and many businesses) often miss: *We lose money on every sale, but we make it up in volume.* Ministries and churches sometimes assume that faith or God's blessing will overrule business principles—but the last time I checked, people of faith are still governed by the laws of gravity. Likewise, people of faith must be governed by sound business practices.

Here's an example of what happens when sustainability issues are ignored or not understood ("I don't know what I don't know"):

Your ministry just launched an academy that teaches high school seniors a Christian worldview. A week's tuition is $500, but you provide a $250 scholarship for each student.

In the program's first year, you'll serve 100 students, so you'll need $25,000 in extra contributions. That's doable because it's just 10 percent of your organization's $250,000 annual fundraising target. You have several zealot donors who give larger gifts. It appears that God is blessing.

But fast forward ahead three years. The program mushrooms in success and it is now serving 1,000 kids. Yikes! You must now raise $250,000 in annual gifts to subsidize each student's fees. In three years, you've doubled your fundraising target. Few organizations can do that.

The program now has a waiting list, a stunning faculty and Christian leaders from three other countries begging you to start programs there. You've doubled your support team, signed a five-year lease on larger offices, expanded the board of directors—but you're sinking in red ink. Your donor base can't sustain the program's success.

That's called *subsidy creep*. A great idea with a modest budget has turned into a nightmare.

The next phase is not pretty. You begin the cutbacks. Staff members are laid off and programs are sliced. Quality dips. Morale plummets. Visionaries withdraw. Prayer meetings are scheduled. Blamers pontificate. Whiners turn up the volume. Board members start talking out of school.

News Flash! Cancel the prayer meeting; it's not a spiritual problem. It's not a leadership problem. It's not even a problem in the Budget Bucket. It's a *sustainability* problem. The business model doesn't work. Sometimes you can figure this out in advance with wise counselors and consultants and sometimes you can't. But if "sustainability" is not yet in your program vocabulary, write the word on your whiteboard right now along with Luke 14:28-30.

Ball #3:
FEED Your Strongest Programs and Benchmark the Others
All programs are not created equal.

Every program, sacred cows included, needs a disciplined strategic plan that includes an evaluation process (see the Results, the Customer and the Strategy Buckets). All programs are not created equal, and you must determine which programs you'll feed and which ones must survive without substantial corporate nourishment.

Many companies and organizations have a benchmarking process (Google that word, too) that regularly analyzes each program, product and service under the effectiveness microscope. Some programs are cash cows; some are losers. Some need more time. Others should have been abandoned last year.

Where should you invest your time, people and money? As Henry Blackaby recommends in *Experiencing God*, you must find out where God is working and then join Him. Once that has been established, it's time for some research, especially if the capacity and sustainability concepts are new to your program team. Check out articles and books on program effectiveness, the sigmoid curve and other topics related to program and product lifecycles. Ask a research zealot or volunteer to help you on this.

Many organizations segment their programs into two basic groups: *primary* and *secondary*. Primary programs are the life blood of the organization. Secondary programs are the ones often dropped when time or money is in short supply.

Feed your primary programs. Make them stronger. Be sure that your entire team (staff, board, volunteers, key donors, key customers) agree on which programs are primary. Don't allow the 80/20 rule to kick in, when you spend 80 percent of your time managing the problems and hassles created by your secondary programs (the 20 percent).

Adapt the following tool (Fig. 6.1) as a template to create your own standards and evaluation process for determining how to segment your programs into primary and secondary categories.

Ball #4:
DON'T BE the Eighth Lemonade Stand in a Row of Nine!
It's risky to be the first program—it's high risk to be the last.

There are 10 fundamental marketing principles that impact program design, capacity and sustainability. My co-author of *Marketing Your Ministry: Ten Critical Principles*, Dr. Robert Hisrich, created these principles

STRATEGIC PROGRAM DEVELOPMENT STANDARD Annual Evaluation of Current and Future Programs Primary Programs and Secondary Programs					
Rate each program on a scale of 1 to 5 for each standard. 5 = Currently meets or exceeds standard. 4 = Has met or exceeded standard at least 2 out of the last 3 years. 3 = Has not met the standard, but we agree it will likely meet it in the next year. 2 = No reason to believe it will meet the standard. 1 = Based on this standard, it is time to drop this program.	Program A	Program B	Program C	Program D	Program E
A) Program serves a minimum of ___% of our customers (members, donors, etc.).					
B) Program generates a net income of $_____.					
C) The measurable results of this program are improving each year.					
D) Customer research and feedback indicate this program has strong appeal and/or potential.					
Add Additional Standards Here:					
E)					
F)					
G)					
H)					
I)					
J)					
TOTAL SCORES					

Determine score ranges for primary programs and secondary programs.
(Example: Primary programs must score at least 37 out of 50 points.)

Figure 6.1

over dozens of years in his worldwide academic and consulting work. As you design programs, remember that when you don't know what you don't know, you're in the danger zone.

You must understand these 10 critical principles and align them with your current program design plans. Space prohibits an extensive discussion of each principle, but here are the Cliffs Notes.

Critical Principle #1
If you have $10,000 to spend, invest $5,000 in researching and understanding your audience.

As we learned in the Customer Bucket, research is fundamental to marketing. Look at our definition of marketing and you'll understand how critical research is to the marketing process:

> Marketing is the analysis, planning, staffing, implementation and control of programs composed of various controllable activities to bring about exchanges with target markets in order to satisfy these target markets and accomplish the objectives of the ministry.[3]

When your Moses-type leader comes down from the mountain with the next latest, greatest new program idea, recommend that you launch the research project immediately to determine if the customers agree.

Critical Principle #2
You can't be all things to all people.

Look at the mind-numbing array of toothpaste options at your drugstore. Wikipedia (the free online encyclopedia) has 35 pages describing "brands of toothpaste"—and that's just for the U.S.![4] Colgate Total is "clinically proven to protect against cavities, plaque, tartar, gum problems and bad breath for 12 hours."[5] (Which customer cares about all these things?) Crest Barbie® BURSTIN' Bubblegum Toothpaste asks, "Got a Barbie girl? Your kid will love the sparkling gel that has a kid-tested bubblegum flavor . . . Plus the superior cavity protection you expect from Crest."[6] (Retired NASA engineers are unlikely to buy this product.) While researching this chapter, I ran across an Aquafresh® promotion pitch to teenyboppers: "Amp Up the Clean" and get up to 30 free music downloads with the purchase of participating Aquafresh toothpaste and toothbrushes.[7] They know their customer.

You can't be all things to all people. Toothpaste hucksters understand this principle, so they research, research and research even more to target their marketing programs to a carefully defined and responsive niche audience. Their research focuses on four major areas: demographic, geographic, psychological and product-related.

Demographics: age, education level, family size, income, nationality, occupation, race, religion, residence, sex and social class.

Geographic factors: city size, climate, county size, market density, region of country and terrain.

Psychological elements: lifestyle, motives (emotional or economic) and personal attributes like extrovert/introvert, dependent/independent, leader/follower.

Finally, product-related segments: benefits desired (durability, enhancement of esteem, status from ownership, and the like), brand loyalty, controllable marketing elements, end use and volume of consumption.

Your program must be targeted to a narrow niche—a select and well-defined market. You must know your customer.

Critical Principle #3

Ask people what their real needs are, then shut up and listen, listen, listen.

Many nifty programs have bitten the dust even though the four-color brochure was spiffy and the website won awards. The problem: The actual program didn't meet customer needs. You must invest money on the market survey before you develop the product or service you want to offer. Do mothers still care about cavities? Do teenagers want toothpaste that promises fresh breath and free music downloads? Your market survey will tell you what people need and where to spend your advertising dollar.

How many organizational newsletters go from the mailbox to the round file because they don't meet the needs of the recipients? How many programs are propped up with hype and email overkill because the content doesn't address the real needs of people?

How many Sunday sermon series have been preached on topics of interest to the pastor but fail to meet the needs of church members? And while I'm preaching here, can someone explain to me how—in our sophisticated culture of specialization—one 30-minute Sunday morning sermon can meet the needs of everyone at that service: seekers, new Christians and long-time fully devoted followers of Christ? Colleges don't do that; they have courses at 101, 201, 301 and 401 levels. And what about the wide age segments in the pews?

We're deluding ourselves to think that Sunday mornings at 11 are effectively meeting needs. They may be meeting the needs of the preachers, but not the customers. *I'm* not the expert at this—the customers are the experts. Are we asking them?

How do you determine what people need? Research. Ask them with mail surveys, telephone surveys, online surveys, focus groups, one-on-one personal interviews, exit interviews after an event, "phone us today" campaigns, "write to us" months, suggestion boxes . . . the list could go on.

And then listen, listen, listen.

If I were a pastor, I would email every church member every Sunday afternoon with a two-minute survey about the service.[8] I would constantly ask about their needs and how the church could help meet their needs. I would expect the research to dramatically impact the content and preparation for future Sunday services. I would share that data with the staff and the elders. I would likely be on my knees more often.

Critical Principle #4

If you don't know where you're going, any road will get you there.

Leaders must be ruthless in rejecting bad ideas for new programs, products or services. Reject all programs that do not align with your mission statement and your BHAG, and be relentless about using the "Top-10 Questions to Ask About Program Capacity and Sustainability." In the absence of a clear direction, almost any program can be added to your menu of programs and services. Often, the mark of a disciplined organization is the number of program ideas you reject each year.

Critical Principle #5

Know your strengths, roll out from them, and then make sure others know them, too.

If your donor letters or Sunday morning offering appeals are the thirty-second verse of that old hymn, "Help Us Make It Through the Fiscal Year," you won't excite anyone. But if you focus on your strengths—your flagship programs, products and services, and how they are changing lives for the better—you'll create momentum, loyalty and engaged donors, members and customers.

To roll out from your strengths, you need programs, products and services that you are well known for. Invest think time in identifying those programs that qualify for your strengths list, then create a thoughtful strategy to talk them up in your newsletters, on your website, at board meetings and presentations, and in your elevator speech. When someone asks, "How's it going?" that's your cue to talk about your strengths.

Critical Principle #6

Don't be the eighth lemonade stand in a row of nine.

Avoid being the Johnny-come-lately to a product, service or program. Being the first guy on the block with a new model or an innovative program is always risky. You never know if it will fly.

Then if it flies, the copycats will come out with a better, cheaper model. Suddenly the first guy begins to lose out to the competition—unless he had enough time to establish himself as the leader.

Does your church, nonprofit organization or company have a long history of being the eighth lemonade stand in a row of nine? Should your new logo be a pitcher of lemonade?

Critical Principle #7

Don't over-engineer. Your audience won't pay extra for something they cannot appreciate.

In the book *Marketing Your Ministry*, we describe a fictitious ministry that marketed teaching tapes to new believers.[9] The plan was to create high-quality audio messages with musical introductions packaged in vinyl binders with attractive graphics. The novice marketing team segmented their potential customers into seven niches and produced seven different audio series. The products didn't just fizzle—they never got lit.

When a consultant named Skip asked Brooks, the nonprofit CEO, what went wrong, Brooks didn't have a clue. He whined, "We figured if kids will pay 10 bucks for a hard-rock tape, they would be willing to pay 10 bucks for a teaching tape—especially a quality one. I mean, what does it say about Christianity when our products are cheaper than the world's?"

Skip pointed out that the sin of over-engineering is common in many organizations and companies. Researchers, scientists, program directors and technicians often develop more bells and whistles on products, programs and services than the consumer wants to pay for. Many times the consumer is not even aware that a product has such advanced features. To pay for the technology, the manufacturer must charge a premium price. Customers are often eager to pay for quality, but they don't want to pay for extra features they don't use.

Once again (in this example), an organization spent thousands of dollars on product development, graphics, advertising and staff time, but zero dollars on researching and understanding the market. In this case, a one-day consultation with a marketing consultant would have saved the ministry thousands of dollars.

Don't over-engineer—consumers won't pay for it.

Critical Principle #8
Caution! People are creatures of habit.

Your church changes its Sunday morning service from 11:00 A.M. to 10:30 A.M. You've sent product information to your retailers on the first of every month, but you now send it bi-monthly to save money. You used to include return envelopes with your donor receipts, but you don't anymore—and now church attendance, product sales and donations have dropped off.

People are creatures of habit. What do you do in the first 10 minutes when you return home at night? Fold your arms across your chest—is your right hand on top of your left arm or under it? Look at the route you drive to work. You're a creature of habit.

Customers, donors, members, volunteers and your staff members are also creatures of habit. An "expressive," one of the four social styles (see the People Bucket), embraces change and is bored with routine. An "analytical," on the other hand, accepts change slowly. So when you make drastic changes in your program, you'll get push back (if you're listening). If your program people love making changes for change's sake, they may be insensitive to the pain and discomfort that even minor changes cause some customers.

Critical Principle #9

Give people the choice to say no to a few options—but still say yes.

My son, Jason, enjoyed his chocolate chip cookie because he learned quickly the importance of giving people—like his mom, who controlled the cookie inventory—options. Review your registration forms, order forms and website sign-up options and assess whether or not you are giving your customer plenty of chances to say yes.

Critical Principle #10

One clever direct mail piece does not a marketing plan make. People buy a total package.

Read our marketing definition again: "Marketing is the analysis, planning, staffing, implementation and control of programs composed of various controllable activities to bring about exchanges with target markets in order to satisfy these target markets and accomplish the objectives of the ministry." It takes an A to Z, comprehensive program management mindset and an integrated marketing plan to effectively satisfy the customer and accomplish the objectives of a business or nonprofit.

A cutting edge website and great advertising copy will never cover the challenges of a weak program, product or service. Savvy program people understand that they must create a total program experience, because people buy a total package. The experience begins with the first point of contact (phone call, website, brochure, word of mouth) and continues as long as possible—months or even years after the event or the sale.

The glossy sales brochure of the new Volkswagen Beetle will have little impact if the gum-snapping receptionist or the aggressive sales person irritates the customer. Or let's say your neighbor down the street receives a series of innovative postcards from your church, beginning four weeks before Easter. She calls the church on Sunday morning for information regarding childcare, yet on the busiest day of the church week, the office is closed. "If this is an emergency, please press 17."

I organized a junior high retreat in Seattle during my college days that made a spiritual impact on many students, but the high quickly became a low when the bus load of students returned to the church. One rambunctious junior higher (is there any other kind?), tired of waiting for his ride home, tested the fire extinguisher in the church basement. The janitor spewed out such foul and angry expletives at this young man that I'm sure the seventh-grader never returned to the youth group.

Program begins when the first person arrives and ends when the last person leaves—and everything that happens in between contributes to the overall quality of the experience. One clever marketing piece is the least of your worries!

Peter Drucker said that "the purpose of business is to create and keep a customer."[10] The Program Bucket, for churches and nonprofit ministries, builds on that wisdom and leverages program opportunities for Kingdom advantage. Program effectiveness is not just a theoretical nine-to-five exercise. God calls us to be His people (in ministry *and* in the marketplace) as we steward the programs, products and services that usher in life transformation. We are standing on holy ground.

The Program Bucket To-Do List

❏ *Step back and envision how God could maximize your programs, products and services*—and how much He desires that your customers receive spiritual value from your programs.

❏ *Research!* You get what you pay for. You also get what you research. Launching a new program without researching and understanding your customer, donor or member increases the likelihood for a spectacular program disaster.

❏ *Evaluate your existing programs* using the strategic tool (Fig. 6.1) and be ruthless in rejecting new programs that do not align with your mission and goals.

TO DO OR TO DELEGATE?				
Priority A, B, C	Point Person	Task	Deadline Date	Done Date

THE COMMUNITY

 **THE COMMUNITY**

The buckets in the Community arena are no less important than those of the Cause, but the vocabulary is softer. Here, we hone our core competencies in people skills and seek to create a God-honoring culture with three to five core values. In Community, we build and equip team members and celebrate results using tools from the *Hoopla!* Bucket. We invest time in affirmation . . . not because it increases revenue, but because it honors people. Leaders of nonprofit organizations and churches who work with donors and volunteers must balance Cause rhetoric with the warm language of Community—"We are extraordinarily blessed by our volunteers"—and business managers must do the same for their employees, their vendors and their customers.

THE PEOPLE BUCKET

We celebrate the God-designed uniqueness of our team members, our customers, our donors, and our volunteers. We are diligent about understanding the four social styles—Analyticals, Drivers, Amiables and Expressives—and helping our people find their comfort zones as they grow in their interpersonal versatility skills.

Strategic Balls in the People Bucket

1 KNOW your own social style.

2 COMMUNICATE creatively with the four social styles.

Don German saved my life! Twenty-five years ago at a Christian camp and conference center directors institute, he presented a two-day workshop on the four social styles. What I learned was life-changing and marriage-saving.

The institute was designed by Bob Kobielush, who is now president of the Christian Camp and Conference Association.[1] The institute was God-breathed from the beginning. When Bob invited Don German to join the faculty, Don was in awe of the divine appointment: Just 24 hours before Bob's phone call, Don and his wife had prayed for a significant opportunity to engage in more Kingdom projects! Don is based in Houston, Texas, and has been coaching and consulting with company presidents, senior executives and managers for many years. He lives his faith deeply whether he's facilitating a training module at a Fortune 500 company or helping local church and nonprofit ministry leaders apply social styles to Kingdom work. The impact of that prayer, their call and the institute is remarkable—Don's faithfulness launched a holy ripple effect that continues to this day.[2]

The People Bucket is the key to all 20 buckets. This is a bold statement, but it's true. When you understand the four social styles (Analyticals, Drivers, Amiables and Expressives) it impacts the other 19 buckets in extraordinary ways. Without knowing your own comfort zone—and of those you work with—you will struggle and wound people needlessly.

I love the People Bucket, but I must also model some competencies in the Delegation Bucket. It was prudent (and less work!) to "delegate" this chapter to my friends Don German and Bob Kobielush. Both of them are social-styles zealots and far more gifted in communicating these critical balls in the People Bucket. Don wrote Ball #1 and Bob collaborated with me on Ball #2. Thanks, Don and Bob![3]

Ball #1:
KNOW Your Own Social Style
Find your comfort zone and help others feel comfortable.

Alex Thomas (not his real name), a division manager of a growing Christian camp and conference center in the Midwest, had a plan.

The camp was operating beyond its capacity. Every year, there was a waiting list for both campers and guests that wanted to use the facility. Alex had become convinced that this represented a great opportunity to extend the ministry. In order to accomplish his plan, he knew that he would have to persuade his boss, the executive director of the camp, to become the "champion" for the expansion idea.

Alex was a very meticulous, detail-oriented person, and he prepared his proposal accordingly. He did extensive research and studied the financial history of the camp. He studied property values in the area, tax rates and many other details required to help his boss make a positive decision. He did lengthy contingency analyses.

He put all of this together in a written presentation that ran about 60 pages, with an extensive appendix that was full of charts and tables to illustrate the plan. Alex was ready!

He decided to meet privately with his boss, Dan Wilson (also not his real name), in Dan's office. Alex had always had a very good relationship with him. Before coming to the camp, Dan had been a successful commercial real estate entrepreneur. Colleagues knew him as a hard-charging, dominant individual who, when committed to something, was known to be extraordinarily single-minded and determined.

Even at board meetings, Dan was always the person in charge and, while courteous and polite to the chairperson and others, he would interrupt when he became impatient. It was clear that the board placed great stock in what Dan had to say on any subject. Alex knew that if Dan believed in this plan, the board would go along.

In addition to the extensive written plan, with all of its documentation and appendices, Alex prepared a fairly sophisticated PowerPoint presentation that summarized the content of the plan. When Alex asked Dan for an appointment, Dan readily agreed.

During the meeting, Alex tried to get right down to business. However, Dan was interrupted five times with "urgent" phone calls and two other employees who brought him documents to sign. Almost an hour of the allotted two hours for the meeting had elapsed by the time Alex began the "meat" of his presentation. Alex knew that he would have to hurry through the presentation in order to finish "on time."

Without much preamble, Alex launched into his pitch. Dan did not seem to be paying much attention while he thumbed through the very extensive proposal book. Dan hardly looked at the PowerPoint images on the screen.

At first, Dan maintained some eye contact with Alex and was about to ask a question. Instead, Alex asked him to save his questions for the end of the presentation. As Alex went on, Dan glanced at his watch and began to fidget and give other signs of distraction.

At the end of the spiel, Dan told Alex that his initial impression was that this plan was premature and would involve going into debt. He said he would not commit to any plan that involved significant debt, having lived through an era in which the camp was deeply in the red and had a debt load that almost sunk the organization.

Dan then told Alex that he was really out of time and had to go on to another appointment. Dan didn't even suggest that they discuss it further. Alex left very disappointed and discouraged. In spite of his work, he felt as if he had failed completely.

Understanding the Differences in Social Styles

Why did Alex fail to achieve his objectives? You certainly couldn't fault him for a lack of preparation.

Alex was doing what came naturally. Dan was doing what came naturally to him. They were both behaving in somewhat predictable patterns consistent with their "social styles."

Everyone has a preferred social style. Your social style is a summary of what you say and do when interacting with others. It is comprised of two fundamental dimensions of your behavior: *assertiveness* and *responsiveness*.[4]

Assertiveness is a measure of how others, such as your boss or board chair, perceive the degree to which you make an effort to influence the actions and thinking of others. This dimension is illustrated below:

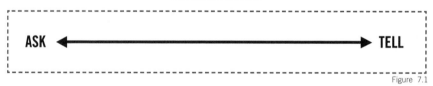

Figure 7.1

Some people engage more in telling behavior. They readily tell others what is on their minds and appear to be making an effort to influence the thoughts and actions of others. Other people engage more in asking behavior. They are more reticent and tend to ask more questions than telling people what they think. Alex's boss, Dan, showed strongly assertive behavior in numerous ways, while Alex demonstrated more asking behavior.

More assertive people tend to speak rapidly, move their bodies abruptly and may give the impression that they think quickly. They also tend to make swift decisions.

Conversely, less assertive people tend to speak slowly, move their bodies deliberately and may give the impression that they think slowly. Their decision-making process tends to be more cautious and calculated.

Responsiveness is a measure of how others perceive the degree to which you make an effort to control your expression of feelings and emotions. This dimension is illustrated below:

RESPONSIVENESS

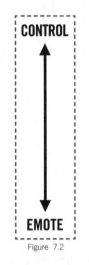

Figure 7.2

More responsive people (perhaps you, your boss or both of you) tend to readily express their feelings and emotions and appear to make little effort to control their expression of how they feel about things.

Less responsive people tend to be a bit more secretive about how they feel and tend to work to express their thoughts as if they are facts. Thus, those people tend to appear to behave in a more fact-oriented fashion, compared to the emotive types who tend to appear to be more feeling-oriented. The less emotive people tend to come across as more task-oriented than the more emotive people, who tend to be seen as more feeling-oriented. In the case of Alex and Dan, they were both of the more non-responsive type, but they were quite different in their assertiveness.

When you combine these two key dimensions of behavior and place the vectors at right angles to one another, you form a model of four basic social styles:

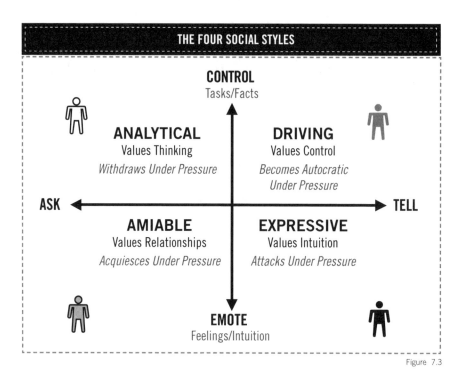

Figure 7.3

The style that is a combination of assertive and non-responsive be-havior is called "Driving." People in the Driving social style tend to make a strong effort to control the environment around them, to con-trol themselves and, to some degree, to control the behavior of others. You could label them "control specialists." When frustrated or defen-sive, this type often attempts to force the result they want and falls into their "backup style." The Driver's backup style is *autocratic*, an exaggeration of their natural style. Captain Kirk of the Star Ship Enterprise was depicted as a Driver.

The style that is a combination of more non-assertive and non-responsive behaviors is called "Analytical." People in the Analytical style tend to make a strong effort to make sure they have all of the facts before they take action, to be accurate and precise. They come across as "thinking specialists." They can appear somewhat impersonal as they try to manage interpersonal relationships through logic and facts. When under pressure or defensive, they tend to withdraw from the situation and simply avoid the problem. The Star Trek character Mr. Spock was depicted as an extreme Analytical.

The person that tends to habitually behave in an assertive and emotive fashion fits into a social style called "Expressive." Expressives tend to want to influence others through persuasion and by reaching them emotionally. They will readily "play a hunch." They have a low need for structure and often charge off into unknown waters. When frustrated or defensive, they tend to take out their frustrations on others, exhibiting a backup style of *attack*. The Star Trek character Bones came across as an Expressive.

> When the four social styles have their backs against the wall, Analyticals withdraw, Drivers dominate, Amiables give in and Expressives attack.

The style that is seen to combine high responsiveness and non-assertiveness is called "Amiable." These are people who seek to build and maintain relationships with others. The number and quality of relationships are important to them. When under pressure or defensive, their backup style is to appear to acquiesce to the needs of others, even when they may strongly disagree with a given course of action. The Star Trek character Scotty exhibited behavior common to this style.

The Key to Communication: Interpersonal Versatility

So what happened with our division manager and his boss? We observed a person with an Analytical social style preparing a detailed presentation for a Driver. If Alex had understood Dan's social style, he would have prepared a very different type of presentation.

Instead of a voluminous presentation book and a lengthy Power-Point presentation, Alex should have prepared a five-page executive summary, presented his case in a brief overview and invited lots of input from Dan. Instead, Alex probably lost his boss in the first 10 minutes of the presentation. He never found out what Dan's goals were for the camp—or what his concerns might be toward any expansion, for that matter.

Alex might have had a successful presentation if he had adapted his own style to meet the needs of the other person, the situation and then his own needs. Had he done that, he would have been practicing *interpersonal versatility.*

Interpersonal versatility is the third dimension to this system. This dimension is a measure of how others view your ability to adapt to different people and situations. A key principle of understanding social styles is this: There is no good or bad style!

There are effective bosses, division managers, CFOs, board members and board chairs in all four social styles. There is no correlation between success and a given social style. There is, however, a high correlation with people who are successful in interpersonal relationships and their interpersonal versatility! It is very unlikely that we could change our basic social style; however, we can change our versatility.

Let's look at the contrasts in high and low Versatility behavior, as illustrated below:

INTERPERSONAL VERSATILITY	
LOW VERSATILITY	**HIGH VERSATILITY**
Concerned for self	Concerned for others
Reduces tension for self	Reduces tension for others
Narrow interests	Broad interests
Rigidity	Flexibility
Unwilling to adapt	Adapts
Resistant to feedback	Open to feedback

Figure 7.4

Versatility does not come easily for most of us. It takes practice. But until you're a "versatility warrior," moving easily from one social style to another, you must understand what to do—and what *not* to do—to effectively relate to people outside of your preferred style. The chart on the next page can be a valuable tool in improving your versatility and interpersonal skills.

Knowing your own social style and the styles of your boss, co-workers, board members, donors, family members and others is critical for long-term success. There is no "best" style. Be versatile and adapt your approach to meet the needs of others—especially your boss. Investing time in charting yourself and the other members of your organization can be of great assistance in building a team.

Do's and Don'ts for the Four Styles 🚫			
Driving 🧍	**Expressive** 🧍	**Analytical** 🧍	**Amiable** 🧍
DO	**DO**	**DO**	**DO**
• Speak in terms of concrete results • Focus on the present, the short-term • Stick to the point • Do your homework • Stress how the Driver will "win" with your proposition	• Seek ideas, input • Focus on the future • Illustrate concepts with stories • Focus on the big picture • Stimulate their creative impulse • Stress how the Expressive will stand out from the others	• Be logical and well organized • Focus on past, present and future • Give facts, evidence, and lots of data • Focus on detail • Allow time to ponder • Stress how the Analytical can be assured of being right	• Be personal and personable • Focus on tradition • Emphasize a team approach • Be flexible • Allow time to "feel good" • Stress how the Amiable can be "safe"
DON'T	**DON'T**	**DON'T**	**DON'T**
• Be ambiguous • Focus on the long-term • Back down if you're convinced you're right • Give too much detail • Get into a control contest	• Put down the Expressive's enthusiasm and excitement • Be cool and impersonal • Be impatient with side trips and creativity • Be too serious • Give too much detail • Nit-pick	• Rush things • Be intolerant of details • Overlook the past • Be too personal • Be too emotional • Press for immediate action • Appear to not be serious	• Press hard to change things • Push for too much detail • Push for immediate commitment • Be cool and impersonal • Attack • Be dictatorial or autocratic

Figure 7.5

Ball #2:
COMMUNICATE Creatively with the Four Social Styles
Just one communication style will fail miserably!

As I mentioned, I've "delegated" this chapter to my friends Don German and Bob Kobielush. For a change of pace, listen in as Bob and I discuss how to effectively communicate to all four social styles. Bob is brilliant at this and gives us several important rules of thumb.

JOHN: Bob, I like your first rule of thumb: *Everyone tends to stereotype people anyway—so use a "stereotyping" system that is designed by God and science-backed.*

EVERYONE TENDS TO STEREOTYPE PEOPLE ANYWAY —SO USE A "STEREOTYPING" SYSTEM THAT IS DESIGNED BY GOD AND SCIENCE-BACKED.

BOB: Exactly. Let's say you're meeting with Frank, a donor prospect, for the first time. In about 15 seconds, you'll have a "first impression" about Frank based on his handshake, his dress, his speech and his body language. You've immediately stereotyped him. If you understand social styles—the whole package—you'll be able to make Frank more comfortable and also communicate in his preferred style.

But without training or a system like social styles you'll often make incorrect assumptions about people. It's only natural, but most people think that everyone else thinks like them—or they stereotype men one way and women another way.

The truth is that our social styles are designed by God and thoughtful scientific research has given us tools for understanding these four important distinctions among people.

WHEN PASTORS PREACH, TEACHERS TEACH, OR MANAGERS LEAD DEPARTMENT MEETINGS, THE AUDIENCE WILL INCLUDE ALL FOUR SOCIAL STYLES— AND JUST ONE COMMUNICATION STYLE WILL FAIL MISERABLY!

JOHN: Let's say Frank is an Analytical. How should you communicate with him about donor opportunities?

BOB: Analyticals need lots of information. For them, *no* decision is better than the *wrong* decision—so you must be factual, accurate and, most important, you can't blow smoke. I have another rule of thumb that explains this: *When pastors preach, teachers teach or managers lead department meetings, the audience will include all four social styles—and just one communication style will fail miserably!*

JOHN: Yikes! We've all done that! I prepare talks that I would like to hear myself—but I'm not as thoughtful about speaking to the other three social styles.

BOB: You're right, John. You're a Driver. You like to be direct, speak in bullet points and do a wrap-up with at least three commandments that should be accomplished in the next 24 hours! Drivers are very action-oriented.

But that's not comfortable for an Amiable, it's probably not enough information for an Analytical, and it's likely boring for an expressive because you left out the fun and the stories. The "Just Do It Now" approach only works for Drivers.

JOHN: Yikes, again! So how should I communicate so that the message is crystal clear to all four social styles? Is it even possible?

BOB: The experts encourage business people, pastors, teachers, trainers and anyone leading a meeting to literally chart their talks. Create four columns, one column for each social style, and write down how you want to communicate to each of the four groups—describe what you want them to know, to feel and to do when you're done. (To remind yourself of what each style values, refer to Fig. 7.6.)

JOHN: That sounds like something an Analytical speaker would do!

UNTIL YOU'RE A "VERSATILITY WARRIOR," MOVING EASILY FROM ONE SOCIAL STYLE TO ANOTHER, YOU MUST UNDERSTAND WHAT TO DO—AND WHAT NOT TO DO—TO EFFECTIVELY RELATE TO PEOPLE OUTSIDE YOUR PREFERRED STYLE.

BOB: Actually, all great speakers understand the most important component of social styles: versatility. Interpersonal versatility does not come easily for most of us. It takes practice and can be improved with education and experience, so there's hope for all of us. Here's Don German's rule of thumb on this: *Until you're a "versatility warrior," moving easily from one social style to another, you must understand what to do—and what not to do—to effectively relate to people outside your preferred style.*

JOHN: Having a high degree of interpersonal versatility, though, is not the same as being "wishy-washy," right?

BOB: Right. Let's say you're a Driver (like you, John) and you have four direct reports: an Analytical, an Amiable (like me), a Driver and an Expressive.

Most managers want to manage from their preferred style—in this case, like a Driver. But it's a turn-off for the other three styles. An effective manager will pray, think and plan, and then take social styles into consideration before and during each important meeting with a team member. He or she will be versatile enough to engage each employee according to his or her preferred style.

JOHN: So even though you're an Amiable, if you're meeting with a Driver you'll get to the bottom line first—and then if there's still time in the meeting, end up with the more relational stuff?

BOB: Close enough, John. Only a Driver would call it "rela-
            tional stuff"!

GENERAL OVERVIEW OF THE FOUR SOCIAL STYLES				
	ANALYTICALS	DRIVERS	AMIABLES	EXPRESSIVES
Reaction	Slow	Swift	Unhurried	Rapid
Orientation	Thinking and fact	Action and goal	Relationship and peace	Involvement and intuition
Likes	Organization	To be in charge	Close relationships	Much interaction
Dislikes	Involvement	Inaction	Conflict	To be alone
Maximum effort	To organize	To control	To relate	To involve
Minimum concern	For relationships	For caution in relationships	For affecting change	For routine
Behavior directed toward achievement	PRIMARY EFFORT: Works carefully and alone	PRIMARY EFFORT: Works quickly and alone	SECONDARY EFFORT: Works slowly and with others	SECONDARY EFFORT: Works quickly and with team
Behavior directed toward acceptance	SECONDARY EFFORT: Impress others with precision and knowledge	SECONDARY EFFORT: Impress others with individual effort	PRIMARY EFFORT: Gets along as integral member of group	PRIMARY EFFORT: Gets along as exciting member of group
Actions	Cautious	Decisive	Slow	Impulsive
Skills	Good problem-solving skills	Good administrative skills	Good counseling skills	Good persuasive skills
Decision-making	Avoids risks, based on facts	Takes risks, based on intuition	Avoids risks, based on opinion	Takes risks, based on hunches
Time frame	Historical	Present	Present	Future
Use of time	Slow, deliberate, disciplined	Swift, efficient, impatient	Slow, calm, undisciplined	Rapid, quick, undisciplined

Figure 7.6[5]

The People Bucket To-Do List

❑ *Work on your versatility!* The sooner you learn that you cannot relate
to everyone in the same way, the better you'll sleep at night. God
made everyone unique. Psalm 139:14 celebrates God's breathtaking
design: "I am marvelously made!"

❑ *Order a resource book on social styles today and schedule a staff development
day.* You'll bless your team members, your friends and your family
as you discover your own social style and learn to embrace the
unique and delightful differences all around you.

❏ *Identify the social styles of the 10 most important people in your life* (boss, direct reports, board chair, key donors, family, and so on).

TO DO OR TO DELEGATE?				
Priority A, B, C	Point Person	Task	Deadline Date	Done Date

THE CULTURE BUCKET

We strive to create a corporate culture with core values that are crystal clear. We yearn for a God-honoring workplace where grace and trust are alive and well. Because we are human we will always have relational conflicts, so we are zealots about resolving conflict early. We invite those who won't live out our values to exit. We experience true joy at work.

Strategic Balls in the Culture Bucket

 INVOLVE your team members in defining your culture.

2 PREACH and live your values.

3 CUT the cord.

The way some theorists and management authors describe corporate culture, it sounds like a mystical, unattainable la-la land. After reading their books and articles, you still can't get your arms around their blue-sky vision of a workplace heaven-on-earth. But really, understanding corporate culture is not that complicated. Creating a God-honoring corporate culture, however, is very demanding.

John Wooden, the esteemed UCLA basketball coach, has an easy-to-remember formula for success, which was part of the corporate culture he created on the practice court, in the locker room and on Bruin game days. Wooden's dad gave him "two sets of threes" when young John was in grade school:[1]

John Wooden's 2 Sets of 3
Don't lie.
Don't cheat.
Don't steal.

Don't whine.
Don't complain.
Don't make excuses.

We have all experienced corporate cultures that could use a hefty dose of Wooden's two sets of threes. While some companies and organizations might re-phrase their core value statements on the positive side (truthfulness, integrity, accountability, and so on), the coach's six "do not" statements are memorable and crystal clear.

Ball #1:
INVOLVE Your Team Members in Defining Your Culture
When your culture and values are crystal clear, your new people will embrace them with confidence.

What happens when team members who don't walk the talk line their walls with your plaques and awards? What do reserved parking spaces communicate to your employees, customers and visitors?

THIS PARKING SPACE RESERVED FOR HIS HIGHNESS, OUR CEO.

Is your leadership group named the "Management Council," the "Management Team" or the "Leadership Cabinet"? Does it matter?

Why do people leave your organization? Do you ask them? Are they honest? When you announce the next great idea, are naysayers valued or quieted? Is there a trash can underneath the bottomless suggestion box?

All of these—and more—create the stew that is your corporate culture.

In *The Minister's MBA*, George S. Babbes and Michael Zigarelli discuss the McKinsey 7-S framework for organizational design (Structure, Systems, Style, Staff, Skills, Strategy and Shared values at the core). They write, "You might find it helpful to think of your ministry's culture as a canary in a coal mine. Like the canary that dies when an invisible toxin is in the air, your culture's health will also indicate dangerous dysfunctions. It will tell you if one or more of the other Ss are underdeveloped or otherwise out of alignment."[2]

Mentor your entire team to keep an eye on the canary in your company, church or nonprofit ministry. Every team member, board member and volunteer—if you cast a vision for an enriching corporate culture—will help you build and enhance it. They will sound the alarm when your culture is being violated. Give them permission to call a timeout even if the canary sings off-tune. Something might be amiss.

Likewise, don't come down off the mountain and announce the planks of your new corporate culture platform. Instead, involve your team, over a series of months, in defining the unique corporate culture that aligns with your unique mission, BHAG and talented team members. Don't let a book or a consultant give you the prescription—*you* need to own this one and work through the process.

Bill Hybels at Willow Creek Community Church (near Chicago) has led his team in creating a distinct corporate culture and a set of values that truly honor God. Yet the culture at Saddleback Community Church (in Southern California), which is also God-honoring, is about 180 degrees different from Willow Creek. Rick Warren is a gregarious hugger in a Hawaiian shirt. Hybels is not. The Saddleback culture works in Orange County, but not in South Barrington, Illinois.

Survey Your Team Members

If your corporate culture is not crystal clear to new employees (or new volunteers), appoint a small task force to assess the culture and write a brief document that defines the cultural reality. Here are two ways to conduct the research:

Narratives. When you're interviewing your next potential employee, ask several team members to describe the culture at your company for the job prospect. You might be surprised at their answers, but write them down and add the narratives to your research.

Written Surveys. Distribute a survey (online or paper) to your staff, board members and volunteers. In addition to the rating scale (1 to 5), leave space for open-ended responses. Here is a sample format with some agree/disagree statements:

OUR CORPORATE CULTURE
Your Confidential Assessment

How strongly do you agree or disagree with the following statements?	1 Strongly Disagree	2 Disagree	3 No Opinion	4 Agree	5 Strongly Agree
1. The majority of our people are very professional in their work.					
2. Most of the time, we are inappropriately casual at work, and we need to be more professional.					
3. Every team member—no matter his or her title or longevity— is highly valued here.					
4. Having fun at work is a core value for our leaders and managers.					
5. Too often it appears that our programs, products and/or services are more important to us than the people we are serving.					
6. We squander too much time in unnecessary meetings.					
7. Leaders here receive most of the perks and recognition while others "in the trenches" get very little affirmation.					
8. We are diligent about focusing on results and being accountable for results.					
9. Our leaders and managers strive to be God-honoring in their work and in their personal lives.					
10. Based on past experience, when someone has to deliver bad news to a manager, they experience a lot of anxiety about how it will be received.					
11. There seems to be an unhealthy legalism on some issues here, yet other behaviors (gossip and materialism, for example) get a free pass.					

12. If you could add, drop or change just one thing about our corporate culture or core values, what would it be?

Figure 8.1

When your corporate culture is crystal clear, your new team members will work with blazing confidence from the get-go. Why?

Every new employee brings their delightful dysfunctions with them from their previous place of employment. The old reality is their only reality. If they got yelled at over at Acme Fireworks, they will assume the same yell level exists at your shop: *Do they really want my feedback or do they just want my blessing? Does this faith-based organization serve wine at dinners? Is there a strict nine-to-five mentality, even though I did three hours of email last night at home? Do we stop to pray in meetings when we hear God nudge us or is prayer just for mealtimes? And speaking of meals, is this a doughnut and caffeine culture or an obsession-with-weight club? Will accounting gossip about my expense reports? Will someone mentor me when I violate a value? Help! There are too many things about this new culture.* "*I don't know what I don't know!*"

If the differences between your corporate culture and Acme's are obvious and clearly communicated, new employees and volunteers will experience far less anxiety and far more confidence.

Ball #2:
PREACH and Live Your Values
Ten core values will never be remembered—much less lived.
Focus on three or four and make them hum!

Trust me—I'm not suggesting a re-write here of Holy Scripture, but put this book down right now and write out the Ten Commandments. You get extra credit if you can list them in order.

Done? How did you do? How would your team members do? Compare that memory exercise with how well you remember the two big ideas of the Great Commandment in Mark 12:29-31:

Jesus said, "The first in importance is, 'Listen, Israel: The Lord your God is one; so love the Lord God with all your passion and prayer and intelligence and energy.' And here is the second: 'Love others as well as you love yourself.' There is no other commandment that ranks with these."

As you begin to flesh out what's important to you in the Culture Bucket, you will be tempted to write too much. Think of your personnel policies or staff handbook (if you must have one) as your Ten Commandments and your core values as the Great Commandment. Less is more for the latter; *less will be lived out more.*

Consider the U.S. Navy, which preaches three core values: honor, courage and commitment. When Dennis Bakke co-founded The AES Corporation, he preached four shared values: to act with integrity, to be fair, to have fun and to be socially responsible. Brad Smith, president of Bakke Graduation University of Ministry preaches five values: passion, celebration, respect, integrity and community.

Most team members can remember three or four—maybe five. Once you've organized a thoughtful process for crafting team-owned core values, don't just nail them to the wall and go back to business as usual. Honor people who live out the values. Catch them doing something right, as Ken Blanchard would say, and make a big deal out of it. (See the *Hoopla!* Bucket for more ideas on the power of recognizing people who live your values.)

Is trust one of your core values? If it is, here's how you live it out: When you trust your people, you say yes 100 percent of the time to their vacation requests. Your team members know the corporate calendar and they know the priority of their personal calendars. They thoughtfully balance their work and personal lives with wisdom and good judgment. You hired them—trust them!

A Critical Core Value: Resolving Conflict

In 1990, I joined the management team at Willow Creek Community Church. Within 12 months, we were planning the launch of Willow Creek Association, and Bill Hybels asked me to serve as WCA's first president. During those years, I sensed something about the place that intrigued me: the smell! There was something different in the air and in the day-to-day fabric of relationships.

Willow Creek team members certainly had their fair share of disagreements and conflict. I expected that, because we all bring our dysfunctions to work. But there was an amazing scent of grace on the campus. Conflicts didn't fester—they got resolved. That was unbeliev-able! I don't think the Willow Creek team understood how unusual this was—they just thought that resolving conflict was biblical, and that other ministries and churches functioned biblically. (Yeah, right!)

When Bill Hybels held the standard high—that we would resolve conflicts readily—it actually happened. If a team member passed me in the hallway and didn't say hello, I didn't worry that Wendy was upset with me. If I offended Doug in a staff meeting, I knew Doug would have the guts and the integrity to talk to me.

Here's how it worked: "John, when it's convenient for you, I really need to go into the tunnel of chaos with you. We need to talk."

Gulp. That always got my attention. When Doug graciously gave the code words "tunnel of chaos," I knew something was up—this was impor-tant to Doug, and I needed to make time for a one-on-one meeting.

In his book *Honest to God?*, Bill Hybels writes that the tunnel of chaos is "where hurts are unburied, hostilities revealed, and tough ques-tions asked." He adds, "no matter how unpleasant the tunnel of chaos is, there's no other route to authentic relationships."[3]

According to the Peacemaker Ministries' "Slippery Slope of Conflict," there are three escape responses practiced by people who don't want to resolve a conflict: denial, flight or suicide.[4] None of those options, of course, are acceptable for the Christian.

At Willow Creek, we tried to resolve our conflicts quickly. If neces-sary, we added a third party according to Matthew 18 principles. That one core value, lived out, created an amazing working environment of in-tegrity and grace. It wasn't easy—but it was God-honoring and fruitful.

Contrast Willow Creek's experience with the all-too-typical busi-ness or ministry pseudo-community:

- "We can't put Andy and Dick on the same task force, because three years ago they almost came to blows."
- "Remember not to seat Mrs. Romano and Mr. Wong at the same table. They had a major issue following last year's day of prayer."
- "I know I should talk to Amanda about it, but she's not open to any dialogue. She thinks I created the problem."

When you preach and live out your values, the results are powerful. Team members are enthusiastically engaged, turnover is less and joy at work is a reality.

Ball #3:
CUT the Cord
Have the guts to terminate people who don't live your values.

In their book *Winning: The Answers—Confronting 74 of the Toughest Questions in Business Today*, Jack and Suzy Welch comment on "The Ultimate Values Test." They warn not to get rid of value offenders with surreptitious excuses such as, "Charles left for personal reasons to spend more time with his family." Instead, they say, inform your team publicly and "announce that Charles was asked to leave because he didn't adhere to specific company values."

Jack Welch, chairman of GE for 20 years, says that managers should be evaluated on two key areas: their performance and how well they live out the corporate values. This means that, at the end of the day, there are four kinds of managers.

Managers in Group 1 deliver great results and adhere to good values. "They should be praised and rewarded at every opportunity," says Welch. Managers in Group 2 deliver poor results but adhere to the values. They "deserve another chance, maybe in another position within the organization." Group 3 managers deliver great results but have lousy values. This kind, says Welch, "deliver the numbers, but usually on the backs of their people. Companies very often keep these jerks around for way too long, destroying morale and trust as they do." Managers in Group 4 have poor performance and poor values. This one's easy to deal with, says Welch. "When you finally get the guts to cut the cord, you'll wonder why you didn't do it sooner."[5]

Here's how I diagram Welch's insights. Discuss these four groups at your next staff meeting—*if* your corporate culture and core values are crystal clear.

THE ULTIMATE VALUES TEST — Where are your team members today?	LIVES OUR VALUES	DOES NOT LIVE OUR VALUES
GREAT PERFORMANCE	Group 1: Praise and reward!	Group 3: Warning! Start walking the talk or you're outta here!
UNSATISFACTORY PERFORMANCE	Group 2: Give them another chance.	Group 4: Cut the cord!

Figure 8.2

"In The Room of Grace," write the co-authors of *TrueFaced*, "one of the greatest gifts we can offer another person is a safe place to fail."[6] As you define and refine your core values in the Culture Bucket, pray for a discerning spirit to know when you must show grace and when you must show someone the door.

The Culture Bucket To-Do List

❑ *Create an ongoing feedback system* so that both new and long-term team members will continue to help you monitor and improve your culture. What's the fun of hitting your targets in the Results Bucket if you have unresolved relational conflict between your team members?

❑ *Hire for attitude, not aptitude.* Max DePree said, "The corporation can never be something we are not."[7] When you recruit outstanding people for your team—with God-honoring hearts—they will bring the right core values with them.

❑ *Read The Peacemaker: A Biblical Guide to Resolving Personal Conflict.*[8] Ken Sande summarizes the Christian peacemaking process with the Four Gs: Glorify God (1 Cor. 10:31), Get the log out of your own eye (Matt. 7:5), Gently restore (Gal. 6:1), and Go and be reconciled

(Matt. 5:24). "A Peacemaker's Checklist" in the appendix is worth the price of the book.

TO DO OR TO DELEGATE?				
Priority A, B, C	Point Person	Task	Deadline Date	Done Date

THE TEAM BUCKET

We believe that a balanced life honors God, each other, our families and our friends, so we leverage the unique set of talents and strengths given to each person by God. Thus we serve with more fulfillment and joy. We also leave work on time, physically and mentally.

Strategic Balls in the Team Bucket

 1 CREATE a time-block culture for your team.

2 LAMINATE your strengths!

Joanne's question at dinner was routine that evening: "How was your day today?"

"I cannot get caught up at the office," I whined. "It's like stabbing a shovel into a mountain. You wouldn't believe what I'm wrestling with. The deadlines are killing me." I continued to eat, mumble and complain until I sensed a quiet on her side of the table.

Apparently my prolonged groan and rolling eyes were even more discouraging to her than normal. "What would it take," Joanne began, "for you to get caught up at work?" Her question was caring, but serious. She had never asked me that before.

"Are you serious?" I probed back. "What would it take for me to get caught up at work? Are you kidding?" I half-laughed.

But Joanne was absolutely sincere. She was open to hearing my solutions. I figured I had just moments to leverage this incredible opportunity, but not show my cards.

"I don't know," I responded matter-of-factly, stalling for time while my brain whizzed through a dozen options. "I suppose if I worked maybe three weeks straight, seven days a week, say from 7:00 A.M. to 11:00 P.M., I could make a heap of headway and get caught up. Of course, that would never work with you. But . . . that's probably what it would take."

Her response stunned me. "So why don't you do that?"

That's all she said.

Then I got scared. *She really means this. She's giving me permission to get my work done with those extreme hours and she said yes so easily.*

Her offer—21 straight days of blissful catching up at work—quickly clouded my discernment. I mentally salivated at the work-a-thon ahead. (In retrospect, she had just given an alcoholic the treasured keys to the liquor cabinet. Booze was not my problem, thanks to good Baptist roots, but workaholism was my drug of choice. It's the "addiction that America applauds," according to one self-help book that I had scanned.)

After about six different questions, asked six different ways, I was confident that the proposed Catch Up at Work Campaign was approved. We agreed Day 1 would begin in the morning and my 7:00 A.M. to 11:00 P.M., hit-the-trenches, macho marathon would begin in earnest.

But Joanne wasn't finished. "John, you might as well be at work all the time," she added. "Because when you're here, you're not here. You would rather be at work anyway—so just go to work where you're happier. I don't want to get in the way of your work."

For once in my life, I didn't defend myself or blame her or others. We had always talked through everything. She was wise. But this evening, she had given up . . . thrown in the towel. Had I won or lost?

Joanne understood—long before I did—that my problem was not being buried by my work. Work breathed life into me. It gave me a creative outlet for my strengths and my social style that nothing else did.

My problem was that I had only ever experienced adrenaline rushes, appreciation from others and a sense of significance through my accomplishments at work. That was my "normal." I could justify the high expenditures of time, energy and emotion toward work because I had created a work environment dependent on me.

I became a gifted rescuer through a dysfunctional Catch-22 formula. The process went like this:

Creativity → new programs →
more pressure for the team →
John to the rescue → Herculean workload→
mission accomplished!

I was the hero at both ends, but no one questioned what it was costing my family.

On the Road Again

That first morning, with Willie Nelson's "On the Road Again" blasting from my car stereo, I stuffed the previous evening's feelings as far down as I could and raced to the office. The beauty of a 7:00 A.M. start time was that I had at least an hour of quiet before others arrived. I made my "21 Days to Victory List" and then made lists of my lists. The adrenaline returned and I was in The Zone.

That evening I called Joanne before going to McDonald's for dinner. She was still okay with my 21-day marathon and I promised I'd be home by 11:00 P.M.

I was on a roll that whole first week and interruptions didn't bug me as much as usual. After all, I had a secret weapon: the quiet sanctuary of my office all day Saturday and Sunday! *Finally,* I thought, *the CEO of Christian Camping International/USA will be on top of his game. No more excuses. No more missed deadlines. No more piles of paper or pressing projects. This place will be humming!* The fantasy was delicious.

I was 40 during this 21-day breakthrough, so I had energy to burn. Today, I have far less energy and a lot more wisdom.

In addition to completing tons of important tasks, I confess that I yielded to temptation and started several new projects in Week Two. (All good ones, of course.) These new initiatives would help camping leaders, our faithful in-the-trenches members. We must activate, motivate, mobilize, reach new heights, envision our future, inspire the team and trust God for great things! Ready! Fire! Aim!

I think it was about Day 10 that I called Joanne about 6 P.M. to check in. She was amazingly okay with all of this. She, too, realized, I thought, that if I could just catch up once and for all, then the rest of life would be a breeze. (Did I mention I was an idiot back then?)

"Hi! I have some good news," I began. "I'm making such great progress, I think I will come home early this evening rather than working until 11."

Joanne asked simply, "Are you all caught up with your work?"

"No," I responded, not catching on. "But—this is amazing—I'm plowing through the projects and have been incredibly productive. I still have a lot to do, but I thought you might appreciate my coming home early tonight." (*And*, I told myself, *I'm getting a tad tired.*)

Joanne's response was probably the all-time wisest response in the history of spousedom. She held her ground and said calmly, "Well, if you're not all caught up with your work, don't come home until 11."

My spirit sagged, but I got the message.

I worked until 11 P.M. that night—ditto for the next few nights, even into the second weekend. But I knew that my days were numbered. I terminated the craziness near the beginning of the third week. Yes, it took me *that* long to realize that I would never, ever, ever get caught up.

I returned home. There was no welcome home party, nor should there have been. Joanne's patience prevailed. I am eternally grateful.

And guess what? When I finally let go and blessed my team members with more authority and responsibility, we had a banner year. But even if it had been a down year, I moved in the right direction: honoring God with my work.

Some years later, buoyed by the supportive community of Willow Creek Community Church and Willow Creek Association, I enjoyed a life-changing series of counseling sessions over many months. I learned what had fueled my extreme workaholism.

Carl Bard said, "Though no one can go back and make a brand-new start, anyone can start from now and make a brand-new ending." I share all this not as a prescription for every leader and manager, but because when Joanne and I talk about it in workshops and informal settings, the story and the outcomes strike a chord and touch deep hurts, often in spouses. Be assured, I am a work in process. Actually, I'm a workaholic in process. It's a daily discipline.

Ball #1:
CREATE a Time-Block Culture for Your Team
Your work will never be done—so go home!

Ted Engstrom, a wonderful friend and mentor, was welcomed into heaven in 2006 at age 90. He wrote more than 50 books, and we're blessed that the wisdom of World Vision's president lives on. In countless CEO Dialogues,[1] Ted admonished busy CEOs to schedule their week using 21 time blocks.

Here's how it works: Divide your time into 7 morning blocks (7 A.M. to noon), 7 afternoon blocks (noon to 5 P.M.) and 7 evening blocks (5 P.M. to 10 P.M.). Adjust the duration of the blocks according to your lifestyle, but end up with 21 blocks of time per day.

Then agree with your team and your spouse (if you're married) how many time blocks you'll work each week. Most people work 5 morning blocks and 5 afternoon blocks for a total of 10 blocks. Some people add 1 or 2 evenings and perhaps a Saturday morning. If your job requires weekend speaking or travel (2 to 3 blocks), you may need to take time off during the week (skip work on 2 afternoons, for example).

Sometimes CEOs and division leaders must leave the office at 5:00 P.M. to give others permission to leave at 5:00 P.M. "Speed of the leader, speed of the team" is a common mantra at CEO gatherings. Maybe we need a new one: "When the leader goes home, he blesses his team members and their families."

The main point: Work hard when you're working, but don't dabble at work when you're not working. ("I just need to check my email, then I'll take the kids to the park.") Strive for a balanced life. And most important, get agreement from your board or your boss—and your spouse—on the proper balance of work time versus off time.

I know an executive assistant who monitors her boss's schedule. When the time blocks hit the maximum number for a week, she schedules the remaining blocks on his calendar for golf or family. He works hard, but he's not a workaholic.

Distribute the form on the next page to your team members and discuss the concept at your next meeting. (Before you do so, review the four social styles in the People Bucket. Remember that each style will respond to this concept in a different way.)

THE 21 TIME BLOCKS — TOWARD A GOD-HONORING BALANCED LIFE!

	SUN	MON	TUES	WED	THUR	FRI	SAT
MORNING							
AFTERNOON							
EVENING							

MY AFFIRMATION:
- My boss/spouse/family and I agree that on average, 7 out of 8 weeks,
  I will work a maximum of _____ time blocks per week.
- I will have two consecutive days off (6 time blocks) at least every ___ week(s).
- I will take compensatory time religiously.
- I will take holiday and vacation time religiously.

Signed_____ Date_____

Figure 9.1

(Note: I've deposited the time-block ball in the Team Bucket, but you might drop it into the Operations Bucket. It's also a core competency in the Volunteer Bucket . . . how many time blocks do you expect from volunteers at your church, for example?)

Ball #2:
LAMINATE Your Strengths!
No one has the whole package, so leverage your top-five strengths.

"I will praise thee," David wrote, "for I am fearfully and wonderfully made" (Ps. 139:14, *KJV*). While Scripture celebrates our amazing uniqueness, preachers, parents and bosses often do the opposite.

A parent admonishes his son over a low grade in science, but ignores the straight *A*s in every other course. "Why can't you be more like your sister?"

A pastor hassles a small-group leader about Scripture memorization, but ignores her 10 years of faithful hospital visitations.

A team member exceeds her quarterly sales goals, but is dressed down for rarely reading a business book. "Look at Dick—he's learning, learning, learning all the time."

Few leaders and managers practice the art of leveraging the unique strengths of each person on their team, even though the "strengths revolution" has become a cottage industry for authors, consultants and trainers. According to Tom Rath, a Gallup study of more than 10 million people revealed that the "vast majority of people don't have the opportunity to focus on what they do best." The author of *Strengths Finder 2.0* estimated that more than 70 percent of the workforce do not leverage their unique strengths at work.[2] That's a crime!

The research and resources from Gallup are noteworthy. Beginning in 2001 with the bestselling *Now, Discover Your Strengths*, authors Marcus Buckingham and Donald O. Clifton ("the father of strengths psychology") created a new vocabulary that has emboldened employees and managers to play to their strengths, not to their weaknesses.[3] When you multiply talent times investment, it equals strength.

> How effectively and consistently do your team members play to their unique strengths? Does Zuzana work all day on tasks that bore her? Did you notice how Emelia blossoms when she's up front presenting? Look at the high-fives Anderson receives when he fixes network software problems!

Rath's 2007 Gallup Press book, *Strengths Finder 2.0*, builds on that foundation. Gallup has identified 34 talent themes, such as Achiever, Arranger, Connectedness, Developer, Harmony, Relator and Woo (winning others over), to name just a few. The book and website provide an array of resources. Each book includes a unique access code so that you can take the Strengths Finder 2.0 online assessment at StrengthsFinder.com. Once you've completed the assessment, you receive an email with your top-five talents, in priority order, along with a narrative summary.

Here's the amazing part: According to Buckingham and Clifton, "Very few people share your signature themes (in fact, there are over thirty-three million possible combinations of the top-five, so the chances of your meeting your perfect match are infinitesimal.)"[4] You are fearfully and wonderfully made!

Ask your team members to complete the Strengths Finder 2.0 assessment and then distribute a chart to your team with each person's top-five strengths. Help team members become students of their own strengths and the strengths of their colleagues. It will launch a revolution in your workplace!

MANAGEMENT TEAM TOP-5 STRENGTHS					
TOP 5 STRENGTHS	DeWAYNE	DICK	JOHN	MARSHA	SUZY
Strength 1					
Strength 2					
Strength 3					
Strength 4					
Strength 5					

Figure 9.2

When you focus on strengths instead of weaknesses, you learn what uniquely motivates each person. Is it Harmony or Learning? Is it Significance or Responsibility, or both? No one has the whole package. No one scores high in all 34 talent themes. Yet each person has talents that they can hone into strengths for the good of your Cause, Community and Corporation!

Laminate!

Bob Shank, founder of The Master's Program,[5] encourages each person to laminate their top-five strengths and carry them in their wallet or purse. That way, when you're tapped for an assignment, you can whip out your strengths card and check the request against your strengths. "Nope!" you will often respond. "Not my strength!" That gets you off the hook and saves your energy for Kingdom assignments that align perfectly with the talents and strengths God has given you.

This is the wallet-size card I carry:

JOHN PEARSON'S TOP-5 STRENGTHS

1. **FOCUS.** You can take a direction, follow through, and make the corrections necessary to stay on track. You prioritize, then act.

2. **RESPONSIBILITY.** You take psychological ownership of what you say you will do. You are committed to stable values such as honesty and loyalty.

3. **SIGNIFICANCE.** You want to be very important in the eyes of others. You are independent and want to be recognized.

4. **BELIEF.** You have certain core values that are unchanging. Out of these values emerges a defined purpose for your life.

5. **MAXIMIZER.** You focus on strengths as a way to stimulate personal and group excellence. You seek to transform something strong into something superb.

If you ignore the two balls in the Team Bucket, there's really no point of honing your competencies in the other buckets. Success at work but not at home is not success, and there will be no lasting success at work if you don't leverage the unique strengths of each team member. Do it!

The Team Bucket To-Do List

❏ *List the top-five strengths of yourself and your boss* on the "Weekly Update to My Supervisor" template (see the Meetings Bucket). Imagine how this will revolutionize your weekly one-on-one meetings when both of you are leveraging your strengths instead of your weaknesses. Wow!

❏ *Recognize how intricately life balance and team member strengths are connected.* When your people identify their top-five talents and you all invest time in honing those into strengths, you'll have a more joyful and more fulfilling workplace. You can then delegate more because you're delegating to the strengths side.

❏ *Make sure you reward those on your team who are getting it right.* Who receives the accolades and the recognition on your team—the workaholics or those with God-honoring balanced lives? Gallup studies indicate that "people who do have the opportunity to focus on their strengths every day are six times as likely to be engaged in their jobs and more than three times as likely to report having an excellent quality of life in general."[6]

❏ *Give your team members Andy Stanley's book,* Choosing to Cheat: Who Wins When Family and Work Collide.

TO DO OR TO DELEGATE?				
Priority A, B, C	Point Person	Task	Deadline Date	Done Date

THE *HOOPLA!* BUCKET

We harness the power of hoopla! for celebration, recreation, intentional food and fellowship gatherings, and just plain fun. We thrive on knock-your-socks-off spontaneity. We believe *hoopla!* honors God. We budget funds for *hoopla!* to mitigate workplace stress and, most importantly, to show our team members how much they are loved and appreciated!

Strategic Balls in the *Hoopla!* Bucket

1. CELEBRATE the appointment of your new international executive vice president of *hoopla!*
2. LAUNCH your *hoopla!* program with a knock-their-socks-off surprise event!
3. AFFIRM your team with a F.A.X. (Flipchart Affirmation eXercise)!
4. RECOGNIZE your team's contributions with spontaneous *hoopla!*

You won't find "*Hoopla!* 101" listed in any business school curricula, nor a chapter devoted to the subject in the standard management textbooks. So what's all the fuss about *hoopla!* and why are more and more companies, nonprofit ministries and churches taking fun so seriously?

In his book *Joy at Work: A Revolutionary Approach to Fun on the Job*, Dennis Bakke writes, "We have made the workplace a frustrating and joyless place where people do what they're told and have few ways to participate in decisions or fully use their talents."[1] Bakke is waging a war on CEOs, senior pastors and managers who keep all the fun (that is, decision-making) to themselves. His Top-10 *Water Cooler Wisdom* rules summarize his radical—but distinctively Christian—beliefs about the transformational changes needed between the hours of nine and five.

I've known Dennis since the eighth grade, and when he reads the Parable of the Talents in Matthew 25:14-30, he actually believes there's a message for us. "Enter into the master's joy" (Matt. 25:23, *KJV*) means just that: God expects there to be joy at work. Bakke's aspirations for the workplace come through loud and clear in Rule #3 of his Water Cooler Wisdom Top-10:

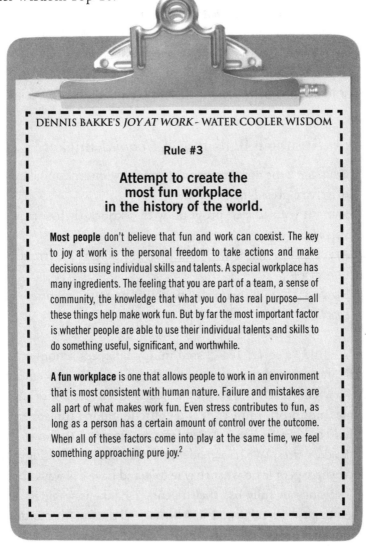

DENNIS BAKKE'S *JOY AT WORK* - WATER COOLER WISDOM

Rule #3

Attempt to create the most fun workplace in the history of the world.

Most people don't believe that fun and work can coexist. The key to joy at work is the personal freedom to take actions and make decisions using individual skills and talents. A special workplace has many ingredients. The feeling that you are part of a team, a sense of community, the knowledge that what you do has real purpose—all these things help make work fun. But by far the most important factor is whether people are able to use their individual talents and skills to do something useful, significant, and worthwhile.

A fun workplace is one that allows people to work in an environment that is most consistent with human nature. Failure and mistakes are all part of what makes work fun. Even stress contributes to fun, as long as a person has a certain amount of control over the outcome. When all of these factors come into play at the same time, we feel something approaching pure joy.[2]

Hoopla! Defined

First of all, let's agree that *hoopla!* should always be in italics (for emphasis) and always spelled with an exclamation point (for fun!) . . . but what does it mean?

Google the word and you get a mixed bag. *Hoopla!* turns up related ideas, such as hullabaloo, excitement, commotion and ballyhoo. Here's our working definition: Every email, event, effort and energy expended to enhance fun, affirmation and recognition in the workplace is *hoopla!*

And the more *hoopla!*, the better!

When Bakke was co-founder, president and CEO of The AES Corporation in Arlington, Virginia, the company employed 40,000 people worldwide. "Fun" was one of their four shared values (see the Culture Bucket). The idea, Bakke said, came from his biblical understanding of work and how leaders must affirm and value their people.

> Marketplace managers often have larger *hoopla!* budgets, while pastors and nonprofit organization leaders are often reluctant to spend donor dollars on "fun." No matter where you're serving and ministering today, don't think of *hoopla!* as a luxury or a perk. It's basic. It's people care. It's Management 101. It's imperative. It's a core competency. It's God-honoring.

For the Christian leader and manager, *hoopla!* is holy, whether your ministry is in the marketplace or at a church or nonprofit. *Hoopla!* zealots demonstrate a heart for people, and a fun workplace backs up the talk with the walk. Creating a *hoopla!* culture is a powerful tool, but the reverse of that is almost lethal. Imagine your team members praying, "Lord, use my life to serve the people around me—the poor, the widows, the orphans and the forgotten. Amen. . . . P.S. Please forgive me for hating my job so much. As You know, Lord, I'm not appreciated much here."

You've probably seen the motivational poster of the barrel-chested pirate cracking a nasty whip over the heads of the hapless sailors in the hold of the ship. The slogan reads, "Floggings will continue until morale improves." Scott Adams, the insightful creator of the *Dilbert* cartoon strip, tells about a company that eliminated annual raises, but promised year-end bonuses if the company achieved at least five of their seven annual corporate goals. Unfortunately, only four of the seven goals were met that year, so there were zilch bonuses. One of the goals they missed, according to Adams, was "employee morale."[3]

A recent Gallup poll reported that "65 percent of Americans received no praise or recognition in the workplace in the past year."[4] That's both shocking and sad. *Hoopla!* never came naturally to me in my 30 years as a CEO. I always had too much to do and too little time. "The tyranny of the urgent" could well have been the slogan on my letterhead! *Okay, we'll celebrate yet one more birthday (if there's decent cake), but let's keep the interruption under 12 minutes. The FedEx guy will be here at 4:00 P.M., and those graphs aren't done yet.*

Then one year at my professional association meeting, the American Society of Association Executives (you got it—there's an association for people who lead associations!), I attended a workshop: "How to Put Fun Into the Workplace." In one hour, I got a $10,000 idea. It's the perfect event for launching *hoopla!* in your organization (see Ball #2). When the fun is poured out of the *Hoopla!* Bucket, generously drenching your people, they'll know for sure that they are appreciated and recognized as important members of the team.

But first things first. You need a *hoopla!* coordinator.

Ball #1:
CELEBRATE the Appointment of Your New International Executive Vice President of *Hoopla!*
From this moment forth, hoopla! *is a core value.*

Okay, let's be clear here: You're not really going to give someone a big promotion, hefty salary increase and a corner cubicle. But you are going to make a big deal out of this "promotion."

Your assignment is to identify the best person on your team for the new honorary position, International Executive Vice President of *Hoopla!* Recruit your perfect candidate, brief the person on what you're looking for—*and why it is important*—and then encourage her or him to volunteer. Sure, it's more work (not less), but the right *hoopla!* zealot will jump at the chance to be your party planner. Here are the bullet points:

Honor team members with a year-round *hoopla!* culture.

Organize *hoopla!* events, parties and celebrations.

Overwhelm the team with spontaneous fun.

Pay the *hoopla!* bills from your *hoopla!* budget.

Laugh a lot—and inspire others to have fun.

Affirm and appreciate the team with regular doses of *hoopla!*

Many times, but not every time, the best EVP of *hoopla!* is an Expressive (see the four social styles in the People Bucket). Expressives plan a party at the drop of a hat . . . they turn any hat into a party hat! If you want to tone down the *hoopla!* a tad (if your office culture requires some decorum), appoint an Analytical. A Driver will get the *hoopla!* train moving on time and on budget. *Hoopla!* events organized by Amiables will focus on relationship building. (You get the point—be intentional with this recruitment task, based on the outcomes you want.)

Once you've inspired your *hoopla!* coordinator with the big idea and briefed your new champion on the details, then celebrate (of course) this historic appointment with appropriate *hoopla!* You want to signal your team that from this moment forth, *hoopla!* is a core value.

Here are three ideas to get your *hoopla!* juices flowing to give your EVP announcement some traction:

Idea #1: *Morning Email Blast:* "Hey! Take a break and meet me in the conference room for Krispy Kreme Doughnuts! I have an important staff announcement to make. The first three people to arrive will each receive a $15 iTunes Gift Card."

Idea #2: *Bulletin Board Memo:* Post a news flash on your staff bulletin board announcing the new position!

Idea #3: *Business Cards:* Print business cards with your new EVP's honorary title and distribute them when you announce your next *hoopla!* event. Ask team members to submit honorary titles for themselves (VP of Water Cooler Wisdom, Manager of First Impressions, for example). Ask your new EVP to order these whimsical business cards for everyone who submits a title. When the cards arrive, host an awards luncheon for "Best New Title," "Funniest Title," "Title Least Likely to Succeed," and so on.[5]

Ball #2:
LAUNCH Your *Hoopla!* Program with a Knock-Their-Socks-Off Surprise Event![6]
Make emotional deposits in relationship bank accounts.

You have now recruited a new International Executive Vice President of *hoopla!* You've handed off the *hoopla!* baton and ordered another copy of this book (my publisher insisted I mention this) for your new *hoopla!*

champion. Congratulations! But now your first big *hoopla!* event must rock and knock their socks off! Let the fun begin . . .

Have a Ball at the Mall

During my first month as CEO of Christian Management Association, we announced that I would provide lunch for our team of 11 in the conference room the next day. Everyone eagerly arrived on time, but instead of deli sandwiches in their brown bags, they found the lunch sacks bulging with Halloween candy.

"Oops," I bluffed, "the deli made an error. Well . . . let's go out for lunch." So I took them to a great restaurant where I had already made reservations. We ordered from the menu and had a relaxing meal.

But that was just the start.

After dessert, each team member received a sealed envelope and I read the rules for this *hoopla!* adventure.

> ## Have a Ball at the Mall!
>
> Congratulations! You now hold in your hot little hands an envelope with cash that must be spent in the next 60 minutes at the mall next door. <u>You may spend the money only on yourself.</u>
>
> Buy whatever you'd like, except a gift card. Leftover cash must be returned to me. We'll meet at exactly 2:30 p.m. by the fountain for "Show and Tell."
>
> If you're late, you owe me 50 bucks! **Ready. Set. Go!**

Staff members leaped out of their chairs and dashed into the mall like there was no tomorrow! Each envelope contained $50, and not one person returned one red cent an hour later. And—get this—before I left the restaurant, several customers asked if we had any openings at our organization!

That day is still a vivid memory for every team member, and the good-will it created lasted a long time. It was the right *hoopla!* event at the right time for the right team. They felt appreciated because they *were* appreciated.

According to *The Carrot Principle*, "one-third of the people you give a cash award to will use that money to pay bills. Another one in five won't have any clue in a few months where they spent the money or even how much they received."[7] Think about it: A $50 bonus check makes almost no impression, but a $50 shopping spree with your co-workers is magic.

When you create a fun and affirming culture, you're making emotional deposits in relationship bank accounts. It's a fun thing to do. It's the right thing to do. And it's a God-honoring thing to do. Post this on your bulletin board: "A cheerful disposition is good for your health; gloom and doom leave you bone-tired" (Prov. 17:22).

Your *hoopla!* champion may have other innovative team-building ideas to suggest. "A Ball at the Mall" is just one. (Caution: A CEO friend tried this idea but asked his people to draw names out of a hat. Each person had to buy a $50 gift for their "secret pal." The idea fizzled.)

Ball #3:
AFFIRM Your Team with a F.A.X.
(Flipchart Affirmation eXercise)!
Write a word or a short phrase of affirmation for each person.

Not all *hoopla!* must be fun and games. Remember that the focus of this core competency is "most importantly, to show our team members how much they are loved and appreciated!"

When we launched the Willow Creek Association in 1992, my sterling team that first year included just six or seven people. The ministry opportunities were stunning, and we were behind in our work from Day 1. The team worked hard, but times for celebration and affirmation were often postponed as we grasped at the next deadline.

Preparing one day for our weekly staff meeting, the Lord gave me the perfect idea. Dispensing with the routine of our standard agenda,

I listed each staff member's name on a flipchart both horizontally and vertically. I asked everyone to write a word or a short phrase of affirmation for each person. One at a time, while the others enjoyed coffee and healthy snacks (a core value at Willow Creek), a team member added to the colorful appreciation mosaic.

I've changed the names to protect the innocent, but it looked something like this:

Flipchart Affirmation eXercise (F.A.X.)

WRITE YOUR AFFIRMATIONS HORIZONTALLY BUT DON'T AFFIRM YOURSELF!	AFFIRMATIONS FOR **DICK**	AFFIRMATIONS FOR **GEORGE**	AFFIRMATIONS FOR **LUIS**	AFFIRMATIONS FOR **MERI**	AFFIRMATIONS FOR **PAUL**	AFFIRMATIONS FOR **TONI**
DICK		Deadline-focused	Cheerful servant!	Super Encourager	Incredible Thinker	Prayer Warrior
GEORGE	Loves Us		Gentle Admonisher	WOW!	Detailed Analyst	Listens to God
LUIS	Thinks the best of us	Organized		Brightens the room!	Busy, but patient	Random acts of innovation!
MERI	Positive	Lifelong learner	Restorer		Really Smart Decision-maker	Faithful and Fruitful
PAUL	WOO-ER	Balanced discipline	High view of our customers!	Connects our dots with color		Wordsmith
TONI	Heart for God	Goodness	Low ego	Joy, Joy, Joy, joy, down in her heart!	Faith!!!	

Figure 10.1

For example, Dick chose a purple marker and filled in the first horizontal line with his affirmation of George, Luis, Meri, Paul and Toni. George then took a red marker and the second line, and affirmed each person with a word or phrase.

"No rules," I said. "Just pray and write from your heart to bless your colleagues."

Each person filled their horizontal line with affirmations of the others, and then we gathered at the conference table. We focused on one person at a time, and each of us shared our affirmation. We affirmed Luis first. Dick began and added his color commentary to the word or phrase he had chosen for Luis.

Comments often began with, "Luis, I'm sorry I've never taken the time to tell you this, but you are one of the most cheerful servants I have ever known. You are amazing—and you are an incredible gift to our team." Wow! After we had all blessed Luis, we focused on another person.

Participating in the F.A.X. was powerful! You could have bottled the goodwill and warm fuzzies that this simple exercise created. Our team had been moving so fast, we realized that morning, that we'd scarcely realized how we were blessed beyond measure by the gifts, strengths and hearts of our co-workers.

We wrapped it up while a few Amiables and Expressives dried their tears. Then, being the focused Driver that God made me to be, I assumed that the exercise was over and done.

Not!

Wendy Guthrie Seidman (her real name) was the first salaried employee of Willow Creek Association. She was an incredible gift to us and had keen people skills. As we exited the room, she quietly removed the flipchart sheet and disappeared into her office. With scissors and God-honoring flair, she prepared the most significant element of the F.A.X. (What did I know about this affirmation stuff?)

Later that day, with her contagious warmth oozing, Wendy presented each of us with our own mounted sheet of affirmations. Whoa! For at least a year, those hand-written columns of kudos decorated our personal bulletin boards. Every day, in the midst of the chaos and the craziness of a start-up, we looked up and were profoundly blessed by the thoughtfulness of our co-workers.

Hoopla! is powerful.

Ball #4:
RECOGNIZE Your Team's Contributions with Spontaneous *Hoopla!*
Keep your nose to the ground and ask, observe and experiment.

Many leaders and managers seemingly have built-in *hoopla!* barometers in their brains (and their hearts), so they know when more fun, affirmation or recognition is needed. If you don't have that sixth sense, keep your nose to the ground and ask, observe and experiment. Peter Drucker said you must practice, practice, practice the art of management[8] (see the Drucker Bucket).

Some occasions are obvious. Your whole team is working late on a deadline project, so you order a team dinner. Three of your key people spend more time at airports than at home, so your *hoopla!* EVP has pizza delivered to their families. Your executive assistant just sent his zillionth email for you this quarter, so you chase him out of the office with afternoon matinee movie tickets.

> Don't let *hoopla!* get out of hand. See the Results Bucket for maintaining that careful balance between inside results and outside results. A hilarious *hoopla!* culture will be a lot of fun, but if you're not hitting your numbers, achieving results and accomplishing your mission, *hoopla!* is a sorry substitute for success.

Scheduled *hoopla!* is also appreciated, especially by the Analyticals who are comforted by their calendars. "This Thursday is the first anniversary of the Main Street Partnership. To celebrate, wear your boat shoes and meet at the pier for lunch and a two-hour boat ride. Here are the new company polo shirts. Please take two each—or three if you spill a lot!"

Need more *hoopla!* ideas? Try these and check the ones that fit your culture and your needs:

❏ **Starbucks Gift Cards.** Buy $5 gift cards 20 at a time from Starbucks so that they're always available for including with hand-written thank-you notes and your public "Job well done!" affirmations.

❏ **31 Smiles.** The minute your team gathers for your weekly staff meeting, cancel it and take them to your local Baskin-Robbins. BR is the largest chain of ice cream stores in the world. The original idea of 31 flavors (one for each day of the month) has grown to more than 1,000 flavors. Between spoonfuls of Maui Brownie Madness®, discuss the tasty ingredients of vision and growth (see the Strategy Bucket).

❏ **Stress Reduction.** Once at a Willow Creek Association staff meeting, I gave everyone a $5 bill. "Buy a stress reduction device for your office or cubicle," I announced. "So when we drop by, you've got something whimsical or fun to distract us for a moment."

The creativity was mind-boggling! One guy installed a Nerf basketball hoop. I brought in some garage sale golf putters and a mini-putting green. Others featured twirly gizmos on their desks and dart boards on their walls. Someone else had a Slinky®. (When was the last time you chased a Slinky down the stairs?)

The *hoopla!* prize went to Jim Mellado, now president of Willow Creek Association. Feigning disinterest and procrastination, he waited for two weeks and then at the end of a staff meeting, asked people to remain for one more agenda item.

"I completed my assignment," he smiled, and then sprayed every surprised team member in the room with his bright orange Super Soaker® squirt gun!

❏ **Elevator Meeting.** Need to make a quick decision? Schedule the meeting in the elevator. "Okay, team . . . enjoy the ride, but we're not leaving until we have a decision on the Nelson Project." No elevator? Take a team walk and don't turn back until you've made the big decision! Once made, celebrate the decision—immediately!—with iTunes gift cards for everyone.

❏ **Time Magazine Person of the Year!** It's official. I was named the 2006 Person of the Year by *Time* Magazine . . . and so were you! The Person of the Year was "You." Mention this to your graphic design team and see what they come up with for your next *hoopla!* recognition event.[9]

❏ **Ban Boring Birthdays.** One word of caution about birthdays: Don't peak too soon! You may celebrate birthdays one at a time or once a month, but whatever you do, don't let it become routine. Likewise, if you pull out all stops for Mary and then Harry's 15 minutes of fame is stilted and ill-prepared, that ain't good. Some organizations give employees the day off on their birthday with some birthday bucks. Many prefer the day off to the boring cake, candles and "Oh, what a surprise!" fakery from the not-surprised recipients.

❏ **Sleuth for Success.** *The Carrot Principle* features 125 recognition ideas. Here's Number 34: "Each day, spend ten minutes looking for someone doing something that furthers your company's goals. When you find it, recognize the person on the spot."[10]

❏ **Need More Ideas?** If your *hoopla!* coordinator is excellent on execution but short on ideas, get acquainted with the resources from Barbara Glanz Communications, Inc. Barbara is one of those amazing motivators with a heart for God who believes that every team member should be a zealot for workplace appreciation. She brilliantly explains why and how *hoopla!* and customer care must go hand in hand (see the Customer Bucket).[11] Check out the invaluable resources at her website, www.barbaraglanz.com.

The *Hoopla!* Bucket To-Do List

❏ *Choose three of the ideas above* to harness the power of *hoopla!* and show your team members how much they are loved and appreciated.

❏ *Promote your EVP of Hoopla!* as soon as you find the right candidate, and give them everything they need to make a hullabaloo.

❏ *Take fun seriously.* The morale, spirit and passion of your team are directly proportional to the amount of time and resources you invest in the *Hoopla!* Bucket.

TO DO OR TO DELEGATE?				
Priority A, B, C	Point Person	Task	Deadline Date	Done Date

THE DONOR BUCKET

We believe that extravagant generosity is the biblical norm, not the exception. We challenge donors to give liberally to Kingdom causes. We urge prayerful giving to God's work, not for tax benefits nor for budget needs. We scrutinize our methodologies not against what works, but against God-honoring principles.

Strategic Balls in the Donor Bucket

1. UNDERSTAND that fundraising is hard, but transformation is harder.
2. CREATE a God-honoring development plan.

"Tell those rich in this world's wealth to quit being so full of themselves and so obsessed with money, which is here today and gone tomorrow. Tell them to go after God, who piles on all the riches we could ever manage—to do good, to be rich in helping others, to be extravagantly generous. If they do that, they'll build a treasury that will last, gaining life that is truly life" (1 Tim. 6:17-19). The Bible is crystal clear: Pastors, ministry leaders, business leaders—*all* Christians—are to encourage other Christ-followers to be extravagantly generous when giving to God's work.

While many nonprofit ministry leaders excel at communicating this biblical value, it seems that local church leaders often sprint the other way. The neglect and under-emphasis of teaching true biblical giving has harmed the cause of Christ and all nonprofit organizations. Few pastors and leaders would dispute the importance of preaching and teaching the foundational doctrines and essentials of the gospel, yet God's Holy Word teaches that believers must be extravagant givers—and somehow far too many pastors, church elders and board members just don't believe or practice it.

What can be done?

Horace Bushnell wrote, "One more revival—only one more—is needed, the revival of Christian stewardship, the consecration of the money power to God. When the revival comes, the Kingdom of God will come in a day."[1] Fundraising gets a lot of bad press and, unfortunately, many pastors and Christian leaders still consider this side of their ministry work to be distasteful. Their donor letters are apologetic. "I wish we didn't have to ask you for money this month." Others create unbiblical dichotomies between "ministry" and "fundraising." God never intended that.

Whether you're a pastor, a church leader or a manager in a for-profit company, don't skip this bucket. If you're active in your community or church, you've already given to numerous causes and you're on dozens of fundraising lists. You may serve on the board of your church, a parachurch organization or a local nonprofit agency. Your company likely gives to important causes. You may assume you're well versed (no pun intended) in the principles of biblical fundraising.

Yet this chapter is not about "fundraising" or "the cause"; it's about *the giver*. That's you.

Ball #1:
UNDERSTAND that Fundraising Is Hard, but Transformation Is Harder
Where your treasure is, there your heart will be also.

Martin Luther said that "people go through three conversions: The conversion of their head, their heart and their pocketbook. Unfortunately, not all at the same time."[2] We read in Matthew 6:21 that Jesus said, "Where your treasure is, there your heart will be also" (*NIV*). Jesus was basically saying, "Show Me the money! Let Me look at your checkbook, your portfolio, your possessions and your tax returns, and we'll all know where your heart is."

Willow Creek Community Church has a seven-step strategy for turning irreligious people into fully devoted followers of Christ. The seventh step is all about stewardship, and the symbol for that step is a heart—not a dollar sign. True biblical giving, extravagant generosity, will never happen until there is a transformational change of heart.

Generous giving doesn't pop out the moment a person becomes a Christian. It takes time. That's why Willow Creek's leadership teaches that only a heart change (becoming a fully devoted follower of Christ) causes people to loosen the tight grip they have on their checkbooks. Once they understand that God—not them—owns it all, transformation begins.

And there's the rub.

Fundraising is hard enough. Waiting around for true transformation to kick in is even harder. I understand the dilemma—I led nonprofit ministries for more than 30 years.

Fundraising goals are increased every year. We're passionate about the cause, but extravagant donors (the biblical kind) are in short supply. So often, we decide that we need gimmicks to pry those tightly held dollars out of the hands of those Christians who are "still in the maturing process." (And, hey, we're not fussy . . . we'll take dollars from non-Christians, too.)

If Christians won't play by God's rules, why should we? If the secular charity on the other side of town clears $50,000 on an auction, we'll pray, ask for God's blessing and clear $75,000. *Give to God and He gives you a luxury resort weekend!*

If Christians won't give generously for the homeless or the hungry or the families of prisoners, maybe they'll come to our golf tournament. Yeah, that's the deal. Make it fun! *Come to our 36-hole golf-a-thon, win some prizes, get a tax receipt and enjoy God's smile. It's a win/win/win.*

> Randy Alcorn's Treasure Principle Key #1 is "God owns everything. I'm His money manager."[3] If that's the baseline for a Christ-follower, then all the best practices in the Donor Bucket must emanate from this foundational biblical principle.

Book the big-name speaker and the glitzy ballroom and follow your consultant's instructions to the last detail, and you too can raise big bucks at the annual benefit dinner. (Or do the non-dinner: *Dear Donor: You don't have to come to our dinner this year. Spend the evening with family and friends, but send us a lot of money in appreciation for our thoughtfulness in* *allowing you to stay home for one evening. P.S. We recommend the $100 per month option, which earns you this super-sized commuter coffee mug with your favorite Bible verses.)*

In his ground-breaking book *The Seven Deadly Sins of Christian Fundraising*, R. Scott Rodin warns us about the extreme danger of living in two kingdoms—God and mammon. He writes, "The Christian development office and the local church too often help accommodate this false two-kingdom view. We do it by allowing people to live in this two-kingdom world and never challenging it as unbiblical and soul-destroying. Even worse, we too often develop stewardship programs that operate on these same two-kingdom principles, which means we are not only passively accommodating this distorted view but we are actually supporting it."[4] The Bible doesn't teach the golf, glitter and gimmicks approach to funding Kingdom projects. Paul simply tells Timothy to teach people to be "extravagantly generous" (1 Tim. 6:18).

At the historic convocation described in 1 Chronicles 28 and 29, King David gave a fundraising pitch to the nation of Israel as he presented the temple blueprints (the To-Do List) to Solomon. Look how he begins his spiel:

> And you, Solomon my son, get to know well your father's God; serve him with a whole heart and eager mind, for God examines every heart and sees through every motive. If you seek him, he'll make sure you find him, but if you abandon him, he'll leave you for good. Look sharp now! God has chosen you to build his holy house. Be brave, determined! And do it (28:9-10)!

It's as if David is saying, "Solomon, if your motive is your own glory or your own fun, or a charitable deduction for playing golf or bidding on that luxury vacation . . . don't be deluded. God will not be mocked!" God sees through every motive. CEO David had created an extraordinary plan, clearly given to him by God (note that!), and had coalesced people and resources so that Solomon could launch this building program. Read David's encouraging words later in that same chapter:

Take charge! Take heart! Don't be anxious or get discouraged. God, my God, is with you in this; he won't walk off and leave you in the lurch. He's at your side until every last detail is completed for conducting the worship of God. You have all the priests and Levites standing ready to pitch in, and skillful craftsmen and artisans of every kind ready to go to work. Both leaders and people are ready. Just say the word (vv. 20-21).

Next, David addressed the nation and announced he was giving his personal fortune of gold and silver for the project. In 1 Chronicles 29, we read his challenge to the people: "And now, how about you? Who among you is ready and willing to join in the giving?" (v. 7).

The leaders and the people then gave extravagantly! According to verses 6 through 8, campaign contributions totaled 188 tons of gold, 377 tons of silver, 679 tons of bronze and 3,775 tons of iron, plus precious jewels! (Note for the file: God is not short on money.) The Scriptures record the people's response in verse 9: "And the people were full of a sense of celebration—all that giving! And all given willingly, freely! King David was exuberant."

Did they high-five each other? Engrave top donor names on the temple doors or pews? Praise the Platinum Club Members at an invitation-only wine and cheese reception? No. David gave God the glory. Let me repeat that. *David gave God the glory.* Rodin's book names "stealing the glory" from God as the seventh deadly sin.[5] (You *must* read his book!)

Here is David's humble, eloquent burst of praise:

But me—who am I, and who are these my people, that we should presume to be giving something to you? Everything comes from you; all we're doing is giving back what we've been given from your generous hand. As far as you're concerned, we're homeless, shiftless wanderers like our ancestors, our lives mere shadows, hardly anything to us. God, our God, all these materials—these piles of stuff for building a house of worship for you, honoring your Holy Name—it all came from you! It was all yours in the first place! I know, dear God, that you care nothing for the surface—you want us, our true selves—and so I have given from the heart, honestly and happily. And now see all these people doing the same, giving freely, willingly—what a joy! O God, God of our fathers Abraham, Isaac, and Israel, keep this generous spirit alive forever in these people always, keep their hearts set firmly in you. And give my son Solomon an uncluttered and focused heart so that he can obey what you command, live by your directions and counsel, and carry through with building The Temple for which I have provided (1 Chron. 29:14-19).

I believe deep in my soul that God has a better way—a biblical way—for churches and ministries to fund God's work. It must start with a radical revisiting of our methodologies and assumptions about the giver.

> When you spend your days in fundraising, you raise money. But when you invest your life in growing God-honoring stewards, He raises up extravagantly generous givers.

I know many God-honoring fundraising consultants and colleagues who have the right heart. There are thousands of ministry leaders and church leaders who operate with God-honoring motives. But when we survey the Christian giving landscape, the view is bleak. Extravagant generosity is the exception. Sacrificial giving is non-existent. We desperately need pastors and leaders of conviction who have the courage to speak God's truth.

So can a golf-a-thon honor God? Probably—because God looks on the hearts of the organizers and the golfers. Are all auctions and donor dinners inappropriate? No. But do these fundraisers help move people toward becoming fully devoted followers of Christ? Do we use these methodologies because they work, or because they align with God's funding plan?

The trinkets, books and other donor premiums that many ministries offer by mail each month will never change a self-serving heart into a transformed heart. *God changes hearts.* But as long as we continue to use clever carrots to attract donors, we will exacerbate the "What's in it for me?" syndrome. Before God, we are responsible for raising the giving bar and helping Christ-followers transition to a lifestyle of extravagant generosity.

Ball #2:

CREATE a God-honoring Development Plan

Craft your unique stewardship principles and practices
based on prayerful study and research.

Fundraising often looks easy to outsiders. Ask any development professional, however, and you'll quickly understand the challenges. It ain't easy.
You must know what you don't know and then create an action plan that
is in sync with biblical and philosophical principles. You must have a plan
to inspire people to give.

Olan Hendrix writes, "Where there is no vision, the people perish. Where
there is no plan, the vision perishes. Where there is no money, the plan perishes."[6] If your Cause is not supported generously by the donors in your
Community, you will not have a sustainable business or ministry model.

This book is not a fundraising manual, but instead an overview to help
you integrate the 20 management buckets and the most critical balls in
each bucket. Ball #2 is all about conducting thoughtful research and diligent prayer to create a God-honoring development plan. Here are some
selected resources to help you on your stewardship journey.

Organizations

Christian Management Association (www.cmaonline.org) includes stewardship resources and training as part of their comprehensive membership services and benefits to leaders and managers
of Christian organizations and growing churches. Frank Lofaro is
the president.

Christian Stewardship Association (www.stewardship.org) serves
CEOs, senior pastors and development staff with stewardship
training and resources. R. Scott Rodin is the president.

Evangelical Council for Financial Accountability (www.ecfa.org) is
an accreditation agency that helps Christian ministries earn the
public's trust through adherence to seven Standards of Responsible Stewardship. Ken Behr is the president.

Evangelical Development Ministry, Inc. (www.edmi.org) serves evangelical organizations in the critical area of resource management and development so that the cause of Christ and His kingdom is advanced through wise stewardship and increased ministry fruitfulness. Andy Read is the president.

Generous Giving® (www.generousgiving.com) encourages givers of all income levels to experience the joy of giving and embrace a lifestyle of generosity, according to God's Word and Christ's example. Darrell Heald is the president.

Good $ense Stewardship Movement (www.goodsenseministry.com) seeks to empower church leaders to implement a biblically based stewardship ministry within the local church. Dick Towner is the executive director.

Maximum Generosity (www.maximumgenerosity.org) provides a wide array of stewardship resources for churches, ministries and givers. Be sure to read Brian Kluth's booklet, *40 Day Spiritual Journey to a More Generous Life.*

The Gathering (www.thegathering.com) is a small "gathering" of friends in 1985 that has now become an international network of individuals, families and foundations who share a common interest in Christian stewardship. Fred Smith is the president.

Books and Resources

Randy Alcorn, *The Treasure Principle: Discovering the Secret of Joyful Giving* (Sisters, OR: Multnomah Publishers, Inc., 2001).

BoardWise: The Concise Resource for Stewardship and Leadership (Seattle, WA: BoardWise). Subscriptions to this newsletter for board members may be ordered at www.boardwise.net.

John R. Frank, *The Ministry of Development: An Introduction to the Strategies for Success in Christian Ministries* (Dallas, TX: Evangelical Development Ministry Press, 1996).

Olan Hendrix, *Three Dimensions of Leadership: Practical Insight on Management, Finance and Boards for Churches and Christian Organizations* (St. Charles, IL: ChurchSmart Resources, 2000).

Brian Kluth, *40 Day Spiritual Journey to a More Generous Life* (Colorado Springs, CO: Maximum Generosity, 2006).

Patrick G. McLaughlin, *Major Donor Game Plan: Rounding Third and Heading Home* (Grand Rapids, MI: The Timothy Group, 2006).

Henri J. M. Nouwen, *The Spirituality of Fund-Raising* (Richmond Hill, Ontario, CAN: Henri Nouwen Society, 2004).

Bethany and Scott Palmer, *Cents & Sensibility: How Couples Can Agree About Money* (Colorado Springs, CO: Cook Communications Ministries, 2005).

R. Scott Rodin, *The Seven Deadly Sins of Christian Fundraising* (Spokane, WA: Kingdom Life Publishing, 2007).

Andy Stanley, *Fields of Gold: A Place Beyond Your Deepest Fears, A Prize Beyond Your Wildest Imaginations* (Carol Stream, IL: Tyndale House Publishers, Inc., 2004).

Roger Steer, *George Muller: Delighted in God!* (Wheaton, IL: Harold Shaw Publishers, 1981).

Leo Tolstoy, *How Much Land Does a Man Need?* This classic short story is available online at http://www.online-literature.com/tolstoy/2738/.

Wesley K. Willmer with Martyn Smith, *God & Your Stuff: The Vital Link Between Your Possessions and Your Soul* (Colorado Springs, CO: NavPress, 2002).

Wesley K. Willmer, general editor, *Revolution in Generosity: Transforming Stewards to Be Rich Toward God* (Chicago, IL: Moody Press, 2008).

The Donor Bucket To-Do List

❑ *Make a list of your current fundraising programs* and highlight each one that helps move a Christ-follower closer to becoming an extravagantly generous giver.

❑ *Consider becoming involved* with one or more of the listed organizations, knowing that rubbing shoulders with others committed to honoring God in the Donor Bucket will have an undeniable impact on your success.

❑ *Choose two of the resources above* and commit to reading them within the next six months.

TO DO OR TO DELEGATE?				
Priority A, B, C	Point Person	Task	Deadline Date	Done Date

THE VOLUNTEER BUCKET

We reject the notion of a two-tiered Kingdom workforce. Instead, we seek to treat our paid volunteers (staff) and our unpaid volunteers with equal passion and intentionality. We will never have enough paid staff to accomplish our Kingdom assignments, so we continually hone our skills in volunteer cultivation, recruitment, orientation and engagement.

Strategic Balls in the Volunteer Bucket

1. BLESS the socks off your volunteers (and walk a mile in their shoes).
2. ESTABLISH S.M.A.R.T. goals for your volunteer program.
3. VALUE your volunteers with full organizational support.
4. CALCULATE the real costs of volunteerism.

Peter Drucker said, "Accept the fact that we have to treat almost anybody as a volunteer."[1] Whether you lead a for-profit company or a nonprofit organization or church, you have two kinds of volunteers, according to Drucker: paid and unpaid.

Your paid volunteers make decisions everyday about coming to work, engaging in your organization's mission and focusing on results. Unpaid volunteers do the same. From a Kingdom perspective, the presence or absence of a paycheck should make no difference at all.

The Volunteer Bucket is all about people and our biblical view of work and relationships. To get us thinking in this direction, consider two scenarios.

Scenario 1: Skipper the Intern

The junior high ministry is growing in a church of 1,000 adult weekly attenders. The junior high pastor, Butch (all junior high leaders have nicknames), requests funding for one part-time internship position for $1,000 per month. The position is approved.

Butch hires Skipper, a senior theology major from the local Christian college. Skipper has no youth ministry experience, but he does have excellent references and a heart for God.

Skipper's first assignment: Create a training program for junior high parents. He launches it and makes lots of mistakes, but the church survives and Skipper gets paid to learn some valuable lessons.

Scenario 2: Joan of Arkansas

Joan Woodsworth, an executive of a startup software company from Arkansas, recently moved to your city. She has attended your church for three months, completed the orientation class, and is a regular and generous giver.

Joan attends a briefing on the evangelism program, "Coffee with Jesus," and volunteers to serve as a key division leader—but is rejected.

"She's too new," drones the been-at-his-job-too-long associate pastor. "She hasn't worked her way up. What would other volunteers think if we gave her a top spot? Nope. Let her prove herself. Start as an usher, or in the kitchen. She seems too eager to serve. That's not normal."

Undaunted, Joan exits and finds a serving role at the church down the street.

At Friendship Community Church, the volunteer recruitment team interviews Joan and learns her story. It's standard procedure there to interview all members and guide them through C. Peter Wagner's book *Discover Your Spiritual Gifts* and the spiritual gifts assessment process.[2]

Once a person discovers her spiritual gifts and her social style (see the People Bucket), she is then uniquely matched with a volunteer role. The church leadership builds on these spiritual principles and prohibits unpaid *and* paid volunteers from serving where they are not spiritually gifted to serve.

Their approach is pretty radical. It's also biblical.

Guess what? Joan launched campus ministries at three universities (as a student), was a Bible Study Fellowship teaching leader for five years, spent seven summers at a refugee camp ministry overseas, and has written several study guides for apologetic books.

The church leaders realize that she had already been through God's boot camp. In fact, they recognize that her gifts—perfectly fitted to the church's needs—save the church a part-time salary.

Joan is a staff member, with every perk and privilege—except payroll. She's an unpaid, part-time staff member. (But others would call her a volunteer!)

What's wrong with this picture? (Forgive me while I vent for several paragraphs!)

Why do we consistently hire the Skippers of the world when a Joan is patiently waiting in the pew—or in the nursery?

Why do we impulsively hire paid staff and give inexperienced staff highly responsible assignments but require committed volunteers to work their way up (as if "up" is a biblical concept)?

Why do we overwork our paid staff, but underwork and underchallenge our unpaid staff?

Why are the reserved parking places and the anniversary pins allocated to paid staff?

Why do some churches title their paid staff "pastors" or "directors" while none of their unpaid staff have comparable titles? (Where is that in my Bible?)

What does payroll have to do with building the kingdom of God?

Okay, I'm done. Thanks for indulging me.

Ball #1:

BLESS the Socks Off Your Volunteers (and Walk a Mile in Their Shoes)

Eliminate anything that smacks of second-class status for your unpaid staff.

The new COO of a New Orleans ministry was blessed to discover the serving spirit of the one-day-a-week volunteer accountant. This never-miss-a-week servant had a faithfulness record of 14 years. The ministry had treated him like staff—almost.

When the newly arrived COO noticed that his volunteer zealot didn't have a regular desk assignment, he bought a new desk, chair and computer and blessed the socks off his appreciative volunteer. This unpaid staff member now has a regular, permanent place to call home. And guess what? He is so grateful that he now frequently comes in more than once a week!

Visualize life from your volunteer's side of the desk, of the counter, of the bus driver's seat, of the mop, of the carnival booth or of the microphone. Walk a mile in your volunteer's shoes and you'll have a new perspective.

One of my camp director heroes was Enoch Olson at Spring Hills Camp. One school year, he slept in a different camper cabin one night a week, whenever a cabin was vacant. He made notes of improvements needed, maintenance items undone and other changes that would enhance the ministry of his volunteer counselors and their customers—the campers.

If you lead a church or nonprofit ministry, you must ruthlessly eliminate any hint of an idiotic corporate culture that smacks of second-class status for your unpaid staff. "It's good enough for the volunteers" is an unacceptable volunteer management philosophy.

Work at understanding and affirming your volunteers. Start by challenging every person on your paid team to call a key volunteer and ask what your organization can do in the next seven days to create a better working environment for that person. Think of your own volunteer roles over the years, perhaps at your church or another organization. What did they do to bless your socks off?

Ball #2:
ESTABLISH S.M.A.R.T. Goals for Your Volunteer Program
Elevate volunteerism with corporate goals that are Specific, Measurable, Achievable, Realistic and Time-related.

In his movement-making book *Halftime: Changing Your Game Plan from Success to Significance*, Bob Buford writes, "I truly believe that God uses people in their areas of strength and is unlikely to send us into areas in which we are likely to be amateurs and incompetents."[3]

Recently my wife, Joanne, and I were shocked—dumbfounded—to read a megachurch's blurb about their senior adult ministry. The church's four-color brochure and their sophisticated website both had the same message: "We encourage seniors to share their time and expertise by helping others. You can help provide a birthday celebration for foster kids, assemble bulletins for the weekend worship services, or provide a listening ear to others in times of illness, sorrow or need."

Assembling bulletins? That's supposed to be significant volunteer work for retired executives, accountants and sales people in the second half of their lives? Someone, quick! Ship a case of *Halftime* to that megachurch! Buford's book deserves a high spot on my Top-100 Books List (see the Book Bucket). Published in 1994, the message is even more important today because so many

> "When I ask long-term volunteers when they became 'lifers'—people who decide to serve in God's mission for as long as he gives them breath—they almost always point back to a specific serving moment that sealed their commitment. 'In that moment,' they say, 'I felt the God of heaven and earth use me, and I discovered that there's nothing in the world like that. It beats anything else I've ever experienced.'"
>
> Bill Hybels, *The Volunteer Revolution: Unleashing the Power of Everybody*[4]

younger pastors and parachurch leaders don't get it. Buford redefined the "second half of life" for Builders and Boomers.

Bob Buford suggests that people in "halftime" ask the following questions: *What am I really good at? What do I want to do? What is most important to me? What do I want to be remembered for? If my life were absolutely perfect, what would it look like?*

Now Buford's Halftime movement has charged up an entire generation of volunteer zealots. Where do they go? What do they do? Assemble bulletins?

Any venture worth leading must have goals. Is deploying the spiritual gifts of your volunteers at the heart of your ministry, or are you filling slots with warm bodies? Is your volunteer pool used as an inexpensive farm team for the real action: the paid staff? What is your ministry philosophy about volunteers? What are your key goals, and are you measuring results? (See Ball #3 in the Results Bucket to refresh your memory regarding S.M.A.R.T. goals.)

You may need a weekly strategy meeting or an all-day offsite meeting or a two-day retreat. But if you've never been intentional about creating a powerful volunteer program, add this to your To-Do List right now.

Start with a G.N.O.M.E. Chart (see Ball #4 in the Strategy Bucket) to articulate your goals and objectives before you discuss methodology.

Ball #3:
VALUE Your Volunteers with Full Organizational Support
Enhance volunteer satisfaction and mission results.

When you place value on your volunteers, you marshal the full resources of your staff, the board, the budget and all the other management buckets to ensure volunteerism success. If it's worth doing, it's worth doing well.

"It is easy to get lost in the micro-purpose of the ministry and forget the macro-vision of the organization,"[5] write Tony Morgan and Tim

GOALS	NEEDS	OBJECTIVES	METHODS	EVALUATION
THE G.N.O.M.E. CHART: ANNUAL VOLUNTEER GOALS (SEE THE STRATEGY BUCKET)				
Goal #1 for volunteer CULTIVATION is:				
Goal #2 for volunteer RECRUITMENT is:				
Goal #3 for volunteer ORIENTATION is:				
Goal #4 for volunteer ENGAGEMENT is:				

Figure 12.1

Stevens in their incredibly practical book (99 quick volunteer ideas) *Simply Strategic Volunteers: Empowering People for Ministry.* (I know, I know. You can't possible read all of the books I'm recommending. So here's a reminder: See the To-Do List for the Book Bucket and *delegate your reading.* Authors Morgan and Stevens are in-the-trenches gurus at Granger Community Church and at Wired Churches[6] and this is the perfect book for your D.O.V.E.—that is, your Director of Volunteer Efforts. You do have one, don't you?)

Review the Volunteer Program Annual Check-up (Fig. 12.2) to determine if your volunteer program is in alignment with your organization's mission. Do you have a run-away program (led by volunteers, perhaps) that is no longer aligned with the macro-view of your organization? Do your programs flow out of your mission statement and your Big Holy Audacious Goal? When they do, blast off with every gun blazing. Remember, your unpaid volunteers and paid volunteers are on the same team! (That would be Jesus' team.)

THE VOLUNTEER PROGRAM ANNUAL CHECK-UP

The Seven Strategic Standards of an Effective Volunteer Program	Situational Analysis Today	Where We Want to Be in 12 Months	Next Steps & Ideas
1) We have a written volunteerism philosophy and an annual plan with S.M.A.R.T. goals.			
2) We have a volunteer coordinator who receives continuing training in volunteer management.			
3) We enhance the role of volunteers and ruthlessly eliminate anything in our corporate culture that smacks of second class status for unpaid staff.			
4) We have one or more volunteer Senior Advisors who we honor publicly with "Dollar-a-Year" recognition (see the Delegation Bucket).			
5) We validate how much we value volunteers by providing superior organizational support in these key areas: ❑ Volunteer budget ❑ Volunteer position descriptions ❑ Volunteer annual calendar of events ❑ Monthly tracking of volunteer hours, achievements and results ❑ Intentional volunteer celebrations, appreciation and *Hoopla!* ❑ Two-way evaluations: (1) annual evaluations of every volunteer and (2) volunteer evaluations/feedback on the program and the organization ❑ Newsletters, emails, and/or websites, etc., specifically for volunteers			
6) We constantly evaluate the impact and results of our volunteer programs versus employing people to do the same work.			
7) Our board members have clarity on the three hats they wear: the Board Member Hat, the Volunteer Hat, and the Participant Hat.			

Figure 12.2

Ball #4:
CALCULATE the Real Costs of Volunteerism
Establish criteria to determine which jobs should be done by paid volunteers.

What is the real cost of the coffee and doughnuts? Smart leaders and managers keep a calculator close when evaluating their volunteer programs. Take church bulletin assembly work or your annual volunteer spring cleaning day. The staff person who supervises volunteers has multiple functions: volunteer recruiting, training, supervising, thanking, rewarding, celebrating, record-keeping and volunteer gap-filling. Add in the coffee and doughnuts, the occasional lunch to thank volunteers, phone and email time . . . and what is that volunteer team really costing you? Sometimes, it's smarter and more cost-effective to hire a minimum wage person to get the job done.

Other times, the benefits outweigh the costs: Volunteer tasks build community, relationships and even outreach opportunities, and you have expertise well beyond the experience of your paid volunteers.

Effective leaders know that the Volunteer Bucket often has holes in it. Evaluate this bucket at least twice a year based on your written goals and objectives and a thoughtful feedback process. Establish criteria to determine which positions are best done by qualified unpaid volunteers and which roles should be owned by qualified paid volunteers (staff).

> "Sustaining motivation is better understood as a by-product as opposed to a goal of itself. It is my experience that if you pursue discipleship with volunteers, motivation will follow. If volunteers see the fulfillment of their role as 'obeying and serving God' rather than serving you or your organization, it will cause motivation to swell."[7]
>
> Al Newell, High Impact Volunteer Ministry Development

Are the Right Volunteers on the Bus?

Jim Collins uses an important analogy in his bestselling book *Good to Great: Why Some Companies Make the Leap . . . and Others Don't*. He writes:

> The executives who ignited the transformations from good to great did not first figure out where to drive the bus and then get people to take it there. No, they *first* got the right people on the bus (and the wrong people off the bus) and *then* figured out where to drive it. They said, in essence, "Look, I don't really know where we should take this bus. But I know this much: If we get the right people on the bus, the right people in the right seats, and the wrong people off the bus, then we'll figure out how to take it someplace great."[8]

Do you have the right volunteers on the bus, in the right seats, doing the right things? If so, then your volunteer program will likely enhance your mission. But if you are timid about getting the wrong volunteers off the bus (in an appropriate and timely fashion), then your volunteer program may not be saving you money—it may be costing you dearly. The wrong volunteers damage morale, raise havoc with otherwise healthy programs and scare off other qualified volunteers. Get them off the bus! (Read chapter 89 in Morgan and Stevens's *Simply Strategic Volunteers*, called "Sometimes You Have to Fire Volunteers.")

Collins, by the way, understands the challenges of the cultivation, recruitment, orientation and engagement phases in nonprofit volunteer programs. He expanded on his good-to-great thinking with a 35-page monograph titled *Good to Great and the Social Sectors: Why Business Thinking Is Not the Answer.* He writes:

> In the social sectors, where getting the wrong people off the bus can be more difficult than in a business, early assessment mechanisms turn out to be more important than hiring mechanisms. There is no perfect interviewing technique, no ideal hiring method; even the best executives make hiring mistakes. You can only know for certain about a person by working with that person.[9]

Equipping the Saints vs. Paying the Saints

The whole point of God's story is that sinful people (all of us) are reconciled to a holy God through faith in His Son, Jesus Christ. As I discuss in the Crisis Bucket, we then learn to walk by faith and become apprentices to the Master, the God of Miracles.

Our goal is to become increasingly like Christ, not to become employed by a church or a Christian organization. So here's the big announcement: *God's plan is for most of His daughters and sons to be life-long volunteers.* Some will volunteer inside the four walls of the church, while others are privileged to serve outside. Where should you serve? Henry Blackaby suggests we find out where God is working and then join Him!

Paul reminds us in Ephesians 4:11-13, "He handed out gifts above and below, filled heaven with his gifts, filled earth with his gifts. He handed out gifts of apostle, prophet, evangelist, and pastor-teacher to train Christ's followers in skilled servant work, working within Christ's body, the church, until we're all moving rhythmically and easily with each other, efficient and graceful in response to God's Son, fully mature adults, fully developed within and without, fully alive like Christ."

If you are a paid volunteer, be a cost-effective one. If you are an unpaid volunteer, serve with diligence and joy.

The Volunteer Bucket To-Do List

❏ Read *The Volunteer Revolution: Unleashing the Power of Everybody* by Bill Hybels to understand the spiritual foundation for cultivating and recruiting volunteers.

❏ *Devote as much time, resources and care in volunteer cultivation, recruitment, orientation and engagement* as you do when recruiting "paid volunteers." Effective volunteers can make the critical Kingdom difference in churches and organizations.

❏ *Check out the Willow Creek Association's "Network" curriculum,* which "can help you get the right people in the right places for the right reasons."[10] It's based on Bruce L. Bugbee's *What You Do Best in the Body of Christ: Discover Your Spiritual Gifts, Personal Style, and God-Given Passion* (Grand Rapids, MI: Zondervan, 2005).

TO DO OR TO DELEGATE?					
Priority A, B, C	Point Person	Task		Deadline Date	Done Date

THE CRISIS BUCKET

We are prepared for most crises. We have plans in place and a crisis facilitator trained, and we drill our team members frequently and spontaneously. Yet we trust in God, who is our Protector, Comforter and Sustainer.

Strategic Balls in the Crisis Bucket

 PLAN now for your next crisis.

DON'T TRUST your instincts in the middle of a crisis.

DRILL, drill and drill again.

It didn't happen on United in first class, but on a bus. And she wasn't a CEO, but a secretary. And it wasn't about her . . . it was about Him.

After years and years of sterling secretarial faithfulness in numerous churches and at her denominational office, she had retired. She'd cheerfully completed thousands and thousands of projects on time, with no awards, no plaques. She had survived demanding deadlines without email, fax machines or FedEx. For her, "WordPerfect" meant retyping it again—often on a mimeograph stencil.

She had selected a Christian retirement center named after a well-known Baptist pastor. Finally it was time to retire, rest, relax. Time to let others serve her.

Not quite! That community of seniors was a ministry magnet for her spiritual gifts of administration, helps and hospitality. Down every hallway was a to-do list for a seasoned servant. There were projects to organize, people to encourage, the lonely to listen to. One Thanksgiving she invited 12 residents to her tiny one-room apartment where they overwhelmed her three folding tables. Turkey and all the trimmings turned a routine, lonely holiday into a memorable party.

So when the miracle happened, it really came as no surprise to her friends. It was typical of her heavenly Father—quiet miracles in quiet ways. This time it happened on a bus, traveling just 75 miles for a brief overnight visit with friends.

A good planner, even in retirement, she was thinking and praying through the week ahead as the bus bounced along. Once back home, her first priority would be to bake bread—not for herself, but for other residents who needed encouragement. The Lord had already given her the names for this week's deliveries.

The ingredients for a favorite recipe had been purchased. The plan: small loaves of tasty apricot bread. On the bus, she imagined the warm aroma of freshly baked bread and the happy, surprised smiles of the coming week's recipients.

Then abruptly, like screeching brakes, her spirits sagged. The recipe called for a special ingredient—orange zest! She'd forgotten to buy an orange. The loaves would not be the same without that special orange-peel flavoring. How disappointing!—for her and for her unsuspecting friends.

She would be back home the next night, but there would be no time on Baking Day for the inconvenient round-trip bus ride to the grocery store. So her little love loaves would have to go without orange zest.

Not giving in to easy despair, she watched the miles go by, trying to think about other things. It didn't help—she needed that orange!

Then the God of Miracles boarded her bus.

From nowhere, a round object bumped her foot. As she searched the dark floor for whatever had briefly interrupted her sadness, she saw the miracle: An orange! The most beautiful, round, gorgeous orange she had seen in years!

She retrieved the golden treasure for a moment and held it wistfully. But she knew, deep down, that it must be returned to its owner. And so she turned around, smiling as broadly as she could.

But there was no one behind her. No passengers behind her at all.

It was truly a miracle. An orange from heaven. An orange just for her![1]

She wasn't a CEO. She didn't write management books. She didn't lecture on fundraising, marketing or strategic planning. She simply prayed and planned her week. And she saw God provide.

When she told me this miracle story just hours after it happened, it made my heart beat fast. Since then, I've thought many times about that orange. I'll never forget the story and, hopefully, will never forget the lesson.

With lots of management years chalked up, I find it very easy to switch on the autopilot. *Do it this way. Adjust that. Fix this. Monitor eight leading indicators. Re-engineer key programs. Keep it simple. Ask . . . thank . . . ask again. Launch trial balloons. Keep the main thing the main thing.* When I need God's help, I usually ask for it. But the requests are most often for my agenda, not His: "Lord, I've thought up these great ideas for You. Now I need You to provide the funds."

That miracle orange reminds me again that our Father is the God of Miracles. If I'm not experiencing those miracles from time to time in my daily life, I wonder if I'm really about my Father's business?

In his book *A Long Obedience in the Same Direction*, Eugene H. Peterson describes disciples as "people who spend our lives apprenticed to our master, Jesus Christ."[2] Sadly, it's been a long time since I've thought of myself in the apprentice role. I can't say I've seen "Apprentice" listed on any business cards lately. Maybe we should all order new cards. (Of course, the recent reality television series with Donald Trump did not define the kind of apprentice—or boss—that Jesus had in mind.)

We know that being an apprentice to the Master is exactly what Kingdom work is all about. So why do we often miss it? Why are our strategies and priorities so bountiful, yet our miracle stories so few?

Why does God orchestrate an orange festival on a bus for a retired church secretary? Wouldn't His time be better spent at 30,000 feet, helping ministry executives en route to their "Project 2020" meetings? My guess is that church secretaries and thousands of other faithful ministry and marketplace workers often understand more clearly what it means to be "apprenticed to the Master." They have much to teach the rest of us who are skilled at doing ministry, but inexperienced at experiencing God.

I'd like a taste of that orange.

Ball #1:
PLAN Now for Your Next Crisis
It's not if you'll have a crisis, but when.

Peter Drucker said, "Fortunately or unfortunately, the one predictable thing in any organization is the crisis. That always comes. That's when you *do* depend on the leader." He said that the job of the leader is to build an organization that is "battle-ready, that has high morale, that knows how to behave, that trusts itself, and where people trust one another."[3]

- When Dan Bolin (see the Budget Bucket) was general manager of several radio stations in Tyler, Texas, his main radio tower fell over.

- When Alan Bergstedt, one of the founders of Christian Management Association, was the 26-year-old CFO for a national advertising agency, he had to fire his first employee. He sought advice and terminated her on a Friday at 4:45 P.M. After giving her the bad news, he heard the employee leave the office. "But then the door to our department opened again," Alan related, "and I heard this funny sound before the door closed again." When he investigated, he found his dapper summer straw hat—no longer on the coat rack, but now on the floor—had been thoroughly stomped on!

- Hurricane Katrina hit the Gulf States in 2005. Professors, pundits and politicians will write forests of words on this for years to come. What went wrong? Why were we so unprepared?

- When the media swarmed New Life Church in Colorado Springs, Colorado, who was really ready to handle the revelations about Ted Haggard?

- Last year, Norman Maleng, the county's prosecuting attorney in Seattle, Washington, for 29 years, died unexpectedly just one week before the board meetings and commencement exercises of Bakke Graduate University of Ministry. Maleng was the board chair.

Whether your company or ministry experiences ugly terminations (are there any other kind?), moral failure of key people, unfavorable media reports, financial improprieties or just erroneous gossip, it will likely not be the first time or the last.

Effective leaders and managers plan for their next crises because they are inevitable. You can mitigate some of the disasters, but others (such as 9/11) will shock you, upset you and call upon all of your strengths—and potentially put you out of business.

Jesus warned us in Luke 21:10-19 to get ready for a crisis:

He went on, "Nation will fight nation and ruler fight ruler, over and over. Huge earthquakes will occur in various places. There will be famines. You'll think at times that the very sky is falling. But before any of this happens, they'll arrest you, hunt you down, and drag you to court and jail. It will go from bad to worse, dog-eat-dog, everyone at your throat because you carry my name. You'll end up on the witness stand, called to testify. Make up your mind right now not to worry about it.

"I'll give you the words and wisdom that will reduce all your accusers to stammers and stutters. You'll even be turned in by parents, brothers, relatives, and friends. Some of you will be killed. There's no telling who will hate you because of me. Even so, every detail of your body and soul—even the hairs of your head!—is in my care; nothing of you will be lost. Staying with it—that's what is required. Stay with it to the end. You won't be sorry; you'll be saved."

Jesus says, "Make up your mind right now not to worry about it." That's great management counsel. Preparation reduces consternation. Make a plan.

Simple, Step-by-Step Instructions

The Crisis Bucket is rarely addressed in nonprofits and in churches. Marketplace companies do a much better job of it. There are natural disasters—hurricanes, tornados, earthquakes, floods, snowstorms, and much more. And then there's another kind of crisis or disaster that hits below the belt in most organizations—moral failures, terminations, embezzlement, lawsuits, media focus on inappropriate activity, deaths, tragic accidents and financial crises, just for starters. The potential list is immense. Sooner or later, a crisis will knock you flat, so it's prudent to address the Crisis Bucket up front. Be prepared. There are procedures and protections common to all crises.

When the televangelist scandals of the 1970s caught the attention of Congress, Christian leaders leveraged the crisis to avert more federal government control of nonprofit organizations and churches. They got buy-in from most major ministry leaders, who agreed to raise the bar on accountability and transparency in fundraising, board governance and financial management. The Evangelical Council for Financial Accountability (www.ecfa.org) was founded in 1979. Without a crisis, ECFA would likely not exist today. Good can come from a crisis.

World Vision (WorldVision.org) has an Emergency Response and Disaster Mitigation (ERDM) team. Randy Strash, strategy director of the team, was interviewed on the subject for an article titled "We've Got an Emergency: Essential Lessons Every Manager Needs to Learn Before a Crisis Hits."[4] It's the inside story of how World Vision responded to the Southeast Asia tsunami disaster of December 26, 2004.

Strash reported that ERDM team members carry a wallet-size, laminated card with instructions on what to do when disaster strikes. The card has five points (including additional details not listed here):

Five Essential Steps During the First 24 Hours Following a Disaster:

1. Activate the National Rapid Response Team.
2. Send Initial Alert Communication.

3. Mobilize the Initial Evaluation Process.
4. Activate contacts with donors and partners.
5. Mobilize immediate response to affected
World Vision project zone.

Your organization or church may have different needs, but every ministry needs a step-by-step plan. A laminated card, carried 24-7 by the pre-selected disaster team, is an excellent management best practice.

YoungLife (YoungLife.org) distributes a wallet-size "Accident/ Incident/Emergency 24-hour Response Procedure" card to all of their staff and key volunteers across the U.S. The card lists this message:

In the event of an accident, incident or emergency in which medical or law enforcement assistance is required to prevent the loss of life or to resolve an unstable or threatening condition in which persons or property appear to be at great risk of injury or damage: (1) Call 9-1-1, and (2) Call the 800 number below.

The card indicates that "this second call will alert a member of YoungLife's crisis response team to the situation you are facing." The instructions also list names to call about insurance and "faith and conduct" issues.

If you don't have an emergency plan in place, delegate this assignment to a trusted team member and urge them to consult with your legal counsel, your insurance representative, selected board members and other wise leaders.

Ball #2:
DON'T TRUST Your Instincts in the Middle of a Crisis
Involve a trusted adviser immediately.

Blogs and cable news networks have changed the rules for crisis management. If your organization, or one of your people, makes headline news for the wrong reason, how will you respond and how soon? (What you don't want: "No one from the organization responded to our calls or emails.")

As we discussed under Ball #1, thoughtful leaders plan for crises in advance. And when they prepare their response before the media comes a-knocking, they can articulate their message in one sound bite. (They also have at least one well-trained spokesperson available 24-7 to the media.) When you're in crisis mode, it's too late for wordsmithing.

Example: An opinion piece in the *Wall Street Journal* ("The Charity Gap," April 4, 2007) suggested that donors should focus on the poor and redirect giving away from education, health and the arts. If you're the vice president of advancement and alumni relations at Wheaton College, Wheaton, Illinois, how do you respond?

R. Mark Dillon, the Wheaton vice president, already had a well-reasoned case statement prepared in advance. He was ready. His brilliant letter to the editor of the *Wall Street Journal* got top billing in the letters section nine days later.

> When the hurricane comes through or the waters rise or the morality plummets, will your God protect you? Invite the God of Miracles (the One who boarded the bus to start an orange festival) to protect and bless the leaders, managers and faithful people in your company or organization. Make prayer a priority. Proverb 16:9 reads, "In his heart a man plans his course, but the Lord determines his steps" (*NIV*).

Emotions run high in a crisis. If you don't have your act together when the phone rings, don't trust your instincts. Pull out the emergency plan, which should include consulting with a trusted adviser who will not be emotionally involved in your crisis. Trust that person's instincts and counsel.

God will honor your preparation and your thoughtful in-the-heat-of-the-battle diligence. Does your emergency preparedness plan include a team of prayer warriors? Have you prayed about and then selected a team of wise counselors who will be ready when a crisis hits?

Ball #3:

DRILL, Drill and Drill Again

Appoint a crisis facilitator and a back-up person.

Who can speak to the media? Who is in charge in our CEO's absence? Who should be notified in case of death or danger? Under what conditions should we vacate or lock down the building?

Study and prepare! Google "crisis management" and "risk management" and order resources that your attorney and others recommend.[5]

Drill your team with the diligence that would impress soldiers and athletes. Drill again and drill again. Make crisis-prevention prayer part of your drill. Be prepared and practice these scenarios without advance warning. Make up your own scenarios for your unique situation.

Scenario 1: "Joe! CNN just called our receptionist and asked him for a comment on a negative story about us that will air in 30 minutes. What are his CEO-approved instructions?"

Scenario 2: "Sandy! Here's a microphone. Give this reporter a 15-second sound bite on how our organization helps society."

Scenario 3: "Attention All Employees! This is a practice drill for an earthquake. Please vacate the building in 60 seconds." (Is that your planned procedure for an earthquake? What did your employees do?)

Scenario 4: "Cindy, you're VP of HR. Our CEO just had a moral failure, but you can't say anything public yet. Rumors are flying. What should we say at the staff meeting that starts in 10 minutes?"

The Crisis Bucket To-Do List

❏ *Appoint a crisis facilitator today,* even if it's a temporary assignment. That appointment will put the fear of God in that person and he or she will focus on helping your organization become crisis-ready.

❏ *Hold a risk-management planning session* in the next seven days and delegate assignments and scenarios to several teams.

❏ *Seek outside counsel immediately.* Don't depend on your own instincts in a crisis. Your thinking will be fuzzy and your emotions frayed. Ask God to give you an advance team of trusted, wise counselors who will drop everything to serve you and your organization in a time of crisis. Be accountable to them, both in the crisis preparation phase and during the crisis, then debrief with them after the crisis to make changes in your crisis management plan.

❏ *Be prepared!* The Boy Scouts have it right. The amount of time invested in risk management and crisis preparedness will pay dividends of from 100 to 1,000 times (or more!) when a real crisis hits.

TO DO OR TO DELEGATE?				
Priority A, B, C	Point Person	Task	Deadline Date	Done Date

THE CORPORATION

THE CAUSE

Bucket 1: The Results Bucket
Bucket 2: The Customer Bucket
Bucket 3: The Strategy Bucket
Bucket 4: The Drucker Bucket
Bucket 5: The Book Bucket
Bucket 6: The Program Bucket

THE COMMUNITY

Bucket 7: The People Bucket
Bucket 8: The Culture Bucket
Bucket 9: The Team Bucket
Bucket 10: The *Hoopla!* Bucket
Bucket 11: The Donor Bucket
Bucket 12: The Volunteer Bucket
Bucket 13: The Crisis Bucket

THE CORPORATION

Bucket 14: The Board Bucket
Bucket 15: The Budget Bucket
Bucket 16: The Delegation Bucket
Bucket 17: The Operations Bucket
Bucket 18: The Systems Bucket
Bucket 19: The Printing Bucket
Bucket 20: The Meetings Bucket

 # THE CORPORATION

When a leader or manager wears the Corporation hat, we focus on operations, systems, marketing and public relations, boards and meetings. Here, we give our attention to our fiduciary responsibilities, hiring and firing employees, delegation, organizational charts and budgets. Corporation is not the stuff of the touchy-feely Community arena nor the compelling vision of the Cause—but it's no less important. It takes a delicate balance of the three arenas and their buckets and balls to build a sustainable company or organization.

THE BOARD BUCKET

We believe that board members must sense God's call to serve on the board of directors. We invest time in cultivating, recruiting, orienting and engaging board members in their strategic role as stewards of our organization. The first step in organizational sustainability is to inspire board members to be highly committed and generous partners in ministry.

Strategic Balls in the Board Bucket

1. RECRUIT for passion, not position.
2. PRAY before prospecting.
3. DATE before proposing.
4. INSPIRE your prospect to give generously.
5. PROPOSE marriage.
6. CONTINUE dating!
7. LEAVE a legacy.

One day while Jesus was mentoring His disciples, He smiled and said, "Show Me the money!"

Actually, He said, "Show Me your heart."

Well . . . in reality, He said "For where your treasure is, there your heart will be also" (Matt. 6:21, *NIV*). As we discussed in the Donor Bucket, this is one of the most profound stewardship principles in Scripture, yet it is rarely practiced where it matters most—with board members of churches and nonprofit Christian organizations.

The heart issue is the foundational building block for the four stages of building a board: cultivation, recruitment, orientation and engagement. There are six key best practices for recruiting exceptional board members in Christian organizations and churches. Together, they are the first step toward effectiveness—and if you ignore or short-cut any of them, you'll pay for it sooner or later.

First things first. Let's get the right board members on the bus.

Ball #1:
RECRUIT for Passion, Not Position
Invite the already convinced zealots!

Recruit board members for their passion, not their position. Don't swallow the board myth that says you need a CPA, an attorney, a pastor and a fundraiser on your board. People in those positions might make great volunteers, but less-than-loyal, uncommitted board members are the last thing your organization needs.

Instead, recruit highly committed people with board governance skills who are zealots for your ministry—and have already demonstrated multiple times their high passion for your mission.

If you need a volunteer, recruit a volunteer. If you need a board member, recruit a board member.

Ball #2:
PRAY Before Prospecting
Why settle for second best?

Right now—before you finish this chapter—begin your *Top-50 Prospects Prayer List*. Effective CEOs, senior pastors and development officers know that it takes up to 36 months to bring exceptional board prospects into the board circle.

Jim Brown, author of *The Imperfect Board Member*, writes, "The problem is, most board cultures are developed by default, not by design."[1] Change that! The Lord wants you to have an extraordinary board. Imagine the potential when you energize exceptional board members who give spiritual oversight and excellent governance to your God-given mission.

Why settle for second best? Why recruit untested, uncommitted good candidates when—with prayer and hard work—the Lord could bless you with a sterling board team?

Ball #3:
DATE Before Proposing
Bring board prospects inside the circle of involvement.

Thoughtful adults don't propose marriage on the first date. Effective CEOs don't propose board service to untried, B-list prospects. Think of this as a 36-month dating experience, and don't mention marriage (board service) up front. As you pray through the process, slowly bring the prospect inside the circles of involvement (see Fig. 14.1). He or she may be unfamiliar with your ministry today, so add them to your mailing list and invite them to an event. Test their interest with a volunteer role. Just like in dating, continue to evaluate over many months if your prospect demonstrates growing interest, and ultimately passion, for your important mission.

If Cliff turns out to be a lousy volunteer, drop him! You've saved yourself from marrying a lousy board member. If, in contrast, Susan gives 110 percent and recruits friends and families beyond expectation, you've got a live one—keep "dating"!

Ball #4:
INSPIRE Your Prospect to Give Generously
Model and teach The Treasure Principle.

When you're sharing these principles with other team members and board members, take out Ball #1 in the Donor Bucket and review the principles of generous giving (that is, *Your heart follows your money*). Talk about the biblical values in Randy Alcorn's book *The Treasure Principle*. The idea of extravagant generosity is not just for board recruitment. It is not a fundraising gimmick. It is a core value for the fully devoted

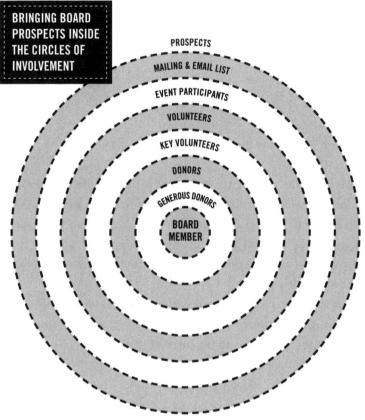

BRINGING BOARD
PROSPECTS INSIDE
THE CIRCLES OF
INVOLVEMENT

PROSPECTS
MAILING & EMAIL LIST
EVENT PARTICIPANTS
VOLUNTEERS
KEY VOLUNTEERS
DONORS
GENEROUS DONORS
BOARD
MEMBER

Figure 14.1

follower of Christ. Don't settle for second best when you're "dating" a board prospect.

Recruit intentionally, with generosity in mind, and you'll breathe new life into your ministry. As you "date" board prospects, spiritually challenge them to become generous givers to your mission. Explain why you need a team of highly committed donors who demonstrate through their giving where their hearts are.

Without waving the carrot of board service—you haven't proposed yet—inspire your prospect (and their spouse, if the person is married) with the opportunity to make your ministry one of their top-three annual giving priorities. That's the definition of a generous giver for your ministry.

If a prospect says no, that's okay. He or she may already be highly committed, even a generous giver, to two or three other ministries, and you've discovered where his or her heart is . . . *before* the wedding. That's the good news: You took the temperature on their passion before you popped the question.

Here's the bad news: There are thousands of nonprofit CEOs that have "married" board members way too soon—and the commitment, the passion, the giving and the heart never followed. Save yourself the agony and do it right by starting your prospect prayer list today.

⑤ | **Ball #5:**
PROPOSE Marriage *generous donor*
Once your prospects have moved into the generous giving circle, it's time to invite them onto the board.

You'll know when it's time to propose marriage (board service). The prospect will have already demonstrated a high level of commitment, all the time moving toward the center of the involvement circle. They will meet all of the previously established board criteria. Plus, the Lord will confirm it to you and your nominating committee.

But again, here's a reminder: Never, never, never invite anyone to serve on your board who is not already a generous giver to your ministry. (In my consulting work, I've found that I can never say this too many times.) The board candidate does not need to be wealthy— just generous. Generally that means that during this person's term of service on the board, he or she will make your ministry their first, second or third highest annual giving priority. No exceptions. Remember,

> Do you have people on your board today who are not generous givers? Your CEO and/or board chair should plan a one-on-one appointment with each board member. Invite each person to lunch or dinner and mentor the member on what Jesus taught about giving and why a totally committed board member is so critical. Then ask your board members for their gifts and their hearts.

Jesus said, "For where your treasure is, there your heart will be also."

Where this core value is practiced, a remarkable culture change happens on the board. Passionate, highly committed board members who follow their money with their heart become incredible zealots for your mission. Wow!

When you have prospects that are highly committed to your church or ministry and meet all the board criteria, pop the question and invite them to serve on your board. Give them a full ministry briefing in advance of asking for their decision. Many organizations provide prospects with a Board Nominee Orientation Binder, filled with helpful background information (staff salaries, board minutes, financials—soup to nuts) so that the nominee can make an informed and prayerful decision about board service.

Ball #6:
CONTINUE Dating!
Help your board members hone their board governance competencies.

The wedding (board member installation) is only the beginning. Ensure that each board member hones their board competencies regularly. Most will bring a diversity of expectations into your board room. They'll also bring the delightful dysfunctional baggage they've picked up from other board experiences.

Use your board meetings, conference calls, mailings and at least one board retreat each year to help members become life-long learners on board best practices. Introduce them to board governance workshops, books, articles, websites and CDs. Invite resource people—consultants, other CEOs, professors, for example—to train, motivate and inspire your board team. Bless your board members and they'll be a blessing to your ministry!

(Memo to CEOs: If your nonprofit board of directors meets monthly, your *board* meeting may feel more like a *staff* meeting. Jim Brown says that "the best boards keep their noses in the business and their fingers out!"[2] Frequent board meetings exacerbate the temptation for board members to become too hands-on. While every board culture is unique, many of the most effective nonprofit boards meet quarterly for 8 to 12 hours. Some board meetings include an overnight stay with spouses invited for the evening meal. Telephone conference calls are scheduled in between quarterly meetings if needed.)

Bonus Ball #7:
LEAVE a Legacy
Grow a great board!

At this point in your management buckets journey, you may be on overload or slightly overwhelmed with the buckets in the Cause, Community and Corporation arenas. You may have a growing list of "I know what I don't know." Don't despair. When you perfect the core competencies in the Corporation buckets, you have the infrastructure for sustainability. Don't neglect the Board Bucket.

When you are effective in the Board Bucket, it creates a remarkable ripple effect in the Donor Bucket, the Results Bucket and the Volunteer Bucket (to name a few). However, when you have low commitment and low passion among board members—and lackluster giving versus extravagant generosity—you will never fully recover and gain organizational momentum until you fix the problems in the Board Bucket.

A Chinese proverb says that if you want one year of prosperity, grow grain. If you want 10 years of prosperity, grow trees. If you want 100 years of prosperity, grow people.

My friend and consulting colleague Bob Andringa says that one of the greatest legacies a CEO can leave to an organization is a great board. He should know: As managing partner of The Andringa Group[3] and President Emeritus of the Council for Christian Colleges and Universities, Bob has consulted with more than 200 boards over the years. When he speaks or writes books on board governance, nonprofit leaders listen!

Another Chinese proverb says, "The best time to plant a tree was 20 years ago. The second best time is today." Start growing a great board today. Here are some resources for the journey:

Books and Resources

BoardSource, *The Nonprofit Board Answer Book: A Practical Guide for Board Members and Chief Executives* (Second Edition) (San Francisco, CA: Jossey-Bass, 2006). The second edition is based on the first edition, co-authored by Robert C. Andringa and Ted Engstrom.

BoardWise, "the concise resource for stewardship and leadership," is published bi-monthly for board members of Christian nonprofit organizations. John Savage is the managing editor and John Frank, president of The Frank Group, is the publisher. Bulk subscriptions are available at www.boardwise.net.

Jim Brown, *The Imperfect Board Member: Discovering the Seven Disciplines of Governing Excellence* (San Francisco, CA: Jossey-Bass, 2006). Brown's book speaks to both corporate and nonprofit boards. The story format has an unusual hero: a senior pastor. Read more at www.strive.com.

John Carver, *Boards That Make a Difference: A New Design for Leadership in Nonprofit and Public Organizations* (Third Edition) (San Francisco, CA: Jossey-Bass, 2006). Every board member today must understand "policy governance." Carver is the policy governance guru.

Fredric L. Laughlin and Robert C. Andringa, *Good Governance for Nonprofits: Developing Principles and Policies for an Effective Board* (New York: AMACOM, American Management Association, 2007). Andringa and Laughlin, partners in The Andringa Group have given a gift to nonprofit leaders with their "add water and stir" template for creating a board policy manual.

Organizations

BoardSource (www.boardsource.org), known previously as the National Center for Nonprofit Boards, is the premier organization for nonprofit board governance resources and training.

John Pearson Associates, Inc. (www.johnpearsonassociates. com) provides board governance training, self-assessment tools and strategic planning facilitation for boards and senior leadership teams.

Policy Governance® (www.policygovernance.com) was created by John Carver and is "the world's most complete theoretical foundation for the board's governance role in business, non-profit (NGO), and government organizations." Jossey-Bass publishes 12 booklets in *The CarverGuide Series of Effective Board Governance.*

The Andringa Group (www.theandringagroup.com) is a group of consultants, led by managing partner Bob Andringa, that provides consulting and other services to both for-profit and nonprofit organizations.

The Board Bucket To-Do List[4]

❑ *Orient your board members!* Board expert Jim Brown jokes that "a greeter at Wal-Mart gets more orientation than most board members ever do." Here's the formula for board success: Multiply the actual meeting hours invested in an annual board retreat times the percentage of board members who qualify as "generous givers." If the number is under 1,000, sustainable success will be doubtful.

❑ *Pray about your prospects.* What is God's vision for your board recruitment strategy?

TO DO OR TO DELEGATE?

Priority A, B, C	Point Person	Task	Deadline Date	Done Date

THE BUDGET BUCKET

We operate with integrity and are accountable for best practices in our financial management. We mentor our team members so that they understand the financial implications of our programs. We monitor our progress monthly.

Strategic Balls in the Budget Bucket

1. BUDGET for an annual surplus and a growing reserve.
2. UNDERSTAND AND COMMUNICATE your cash flow plan.
3. MONITOR monthly reports.
4. IMPLEMENT financial best practices.

Dan Bolin was the young executive director of Pine Cove Christian Camps in Tyler, Texas, when he received some savvy financial counsel from Bob Buford, then a member of the camp and conference center's board of directors. (Bob is the author of the bestselling *Halftime: Changing Your Game Plan from Success to Significance*.) Now with an MBA to his name, Bolin serves as the international director of Christian Camping International.[1] Dan told me that Buford's advice still ranks high on his list of top-10 management insights.

In Dan's first few months as the camp's CEO, Bob had a defining conversation with him. "Dan, let me give you some advice. It may be one of the most important principles I can share with you about ministry leadership," Buford said.

Dan's energy perked up. He was all ears because he knew that Bob Buford was a successful business leader with a heart for God. Whatever leadership lesson Bob was about to share would be memorable.

Bob looked deep into Dan's eyes and whispered, "Don't run out of money!"

This Is Not the Finance and Accounting Bucket

Co-authors George S. Babbes and Michael Zigarelli correctly note the differences between budgeting and finance/accounting in their excellent book *The Minister's MBA: Essential Business Tools for Maximum Ministry Success*. They write, "Mention the words *accounting* and *finance* to a ministry leader and the first thing that comes to his or her mind is budgeting. But mention the words *accounting* and *finance* to MBAs and what instantly come to mind are tools. Power tools. Tools that, as we'll see, help an organization spend in a way that maximizes mission-consistent outcomes, whether that's profitability in a for-profit enterprise or social impact in a nonprofit."[2]

If you're in the marketplace at a for-profit company, you'll recognize that this chapter on Budgeting 101 is slanted toward nonprofit financial issues—but it will still be valuable for you. Your business expertise is needed and appreciated on the church and nonprofit ministry side. If you serve as a board member or key volunteer at a nonprofit, you already realize that finance and accounting are often not the strong points of ministries. You can help change that!

Ball #1:
BUDGET for an Annual Surplus and a Growing Reserve
"Nonprofit" is a tax designation, not a management philosophy.

It may seem obvious, but "nonprofit," a United States tax designation from the Internal Revenue Service, should not be construed as a management philosophy. Many organizations apply for 501(c) (3) status from the IRS. When approved, an organization is designated "nonprofit" and is then exempt from paying federal taxes and is permitted to issue tax-deductible receipts to U.S. citizens who donate to the organization.

So think about this: In 2006 alone, the U.S. Senate passed 635 measures and enacted 248 public laws.[3] Thousands of regulations are written and revised every year. (In the Budget Bucket, you will often be operating at Level 1: "I don't know what I don't know.") That's why every nonprofit organization and church must have either internal or external expertise readily available. You need qualified help from chief financial officers, certified public accountants and legal counsel.

Effective nonprofit organizations always budget for a profit—a surplus—each year. Operating reserves are necessary to maintain programs year-round. The federal government appreciates the work of nonprofit organizations and wants them to be successful. Our government does not frown on healthy annual surpluses or reserves. Neither should you!

Your chief financial officer (CFO) and your board treasurer should consult with similar organizations to determine an appropriate target for your year-end surplus. When you're asking your board to approve the annual budget, remember the One-Cookie-or-Two-Cookie Rule from the Program Bucket. Give several "yes" options:

ANNUAL BUDGET

	OPTION A	OPTION B	OPTION C
Annual Revenue	$500,000	$500,000	$500,000
Annual Expense	$475,000	$450,000	$440,000
NET (surplus)	$25,000	$50,000	$60,000
NET = ___% of Annual Revenue	5%	10%	12%

Figure 15.1

Evangelical Council for Financial Accountability recommends that the board of directors set financial reserve goals for the organization. Dan Busby, vice president of ECFA, writes:

What are the ministry's financial sustainability goals? Yes, ministries are nonprofit but this doesn't mean ministries should not have adequate financial reserves for sustainability. If revenues always equal expenses, appropriate reserves cannot be accumulated.

Ironically, most nonprofit rating organizations actually consider financial reserves a negative factor—the more reserves a ministry has, the more the ministry is penalized in the rating! Can a ministry have too much financial reserves? It's rare, but it can happen. This is why financial sustainability goals are so vital to monitor, including whether the ministry has done better than or fallen short of the goals.

How does a board begin to look at financial sustainability goals? Decide whether reserve goals will be expressed in ratios or absolute dollars. For a large ministry, the focus may be on setting goals for permanently restricted net assets. For others, it may be analyzing unrestricted net assets, after excluding property and equipment-related data, and setting goals based on ministry revenue growth.[4]

In the early years of a ministry, or the re-building years, the financial needs are often overwhelming. The staff and board give each other high-fives if they even come close to a break-even budget. "We'll build reserves later, when we have more margin." That's a mistake.

You'll never have enough cash to do what you want, so you must discipline yourself to create an annual surplus. Year after year, as you faithfully create annual surpluses, those funds will grow into a significant cash reserve.

As we discussed in the Results Bucket, the CEO should submit 5 to 10 standards of performance (SOPs) for board approval each year. Certainly at least one SOP should focus on the budget. For example:

Standard of Performance
To generate a net surplus of $_____ by the end of the fiscal year.

Or:

Standard of Performance
To generate a net surplus of $_____ by the end of the fiscal year toward our goal of growing our cash reserves to $_____ within five years.

Ball #2:
UNDERSTAND AND COMMUNICATE
Your Cash Flow Plan
Pumpkin farmers pray, but they also monitor cash flow forecasts.

Many businesses, nonprofits and even churches have seasonal cash flow challenges. Pumpkin farmers understand cash flow. By faith, they invest time and funds all year to grow pumpkins. Many pumpkin farmers borrow money every spring—again by faith—for equipment, seed and overhead. Their hope is that when the farmers sell their pumpkins every October, their revenue is sufficient to pay down their loans. In a good year, there is a surplus to sustain the farmer until the next season.

A pumpkin farmer has a very simple cash flow forecast: 11 months of expenses with 1 month of revenue. Other seasonal businesses are the same. Some churches experience a major drop in tithes and offerings during the summer months. Colleges

> You'll sleep better at night when your organization has cash reserves equal to three to six months of your annual budget.

and universities experience revenue spikes when tuition is due three or four times a year. Rescue missions often receive more donations during the Thanksgiving and Christmas seasons than at other times.

Astute leaders and managers understand cash flow and recommend a cash flow forecast to the board. Without a detailed plan, board members and staff members who are not financially savvy may interpret a negative cash flow month as a spiritual problem. "Yikes! We have 30 days of unpaid bills. God has withdrawn His blessing from our ministry!" That's usually not the case.

You have two options with cash flow: fret or fix. You can wring your hands, sing another verse of "Woe Is Me" and schedule all-day prayer meetings—or you can be prudent and God-honoring.

To fix the cash flow dilemma, create a 12-month cash flow forecast at the beginning of your fiscal year, with your best-guess estimate of how much money you will receive each month. Break it down by your major revenue sources (fees, donations, sales, and so on).

Then do the same for your expenses, month by month, within your budget categories. Your month-by-month spreadsheet will indicate whether you will have a surplus or a loss each month. If you're a pumpkin farmer, you need a plan to cover the months when you have more expense than revenue. Some organizations dip into their cash reserves and borrow from themselves, while others establish a line of credit at a financial institution and borrow funds as needed during lean months.

Report on Actual Versus Forecast

Here comes the fork in the road for many nonprofit organizations and churches. Some do the forecasting but still get anxious during lean months because they don't like to borrow money internally or externally. If that's your temperament as an individual or as an organization, sell the pumpkin farm. You may not be cut out for ministry work that involves severe cash flow dips.

If, on the other hand, you believe that cash flow is a fact of life (like gravity), be prudent and thoughtful. At monthly staff meetings and quarterly board meetings, focus on your year-to-date forecast numbers and compare them to your year-to-date actual numbers. Hopefully, you'll be able to report something like this:

> "Good news! Our original cash flow forecast predicted we would be $40,000 in the red for the first four months of our fiscal year. However, our actual numbers show we are only $32,000 in the red, which means we are ahead of our forecast by $8,000. Thanks, team, for the excellent work on increasing revenue and watching our expenses carefully! As you know, our largest revenue months are just coming up, so we are on target to hit our year-end budget goals."

Budgeting is part art and part science. Every team member must master the core competencies in the Bucket Budget, yet every team member need not be a financial whiz. Leave the number crunching to the trained professionals, but learn how to communicate cash flow issues and reports with clarity and consistency.

Happy Halloween!

CASH FLOW FORECAST

	4-Month Forecast	4-Month Actual	Difference
Revenue	$135,000	$140,000	$5,000
Expense	$175,000	$172,000	$3,000
NET	$ (40,000)	$ (32,000)	$8,000

Figure 15.2

Ball #3:
MONITOR Monthly Reports
*When you change board treasurers,
don't change your reporting!*

Pardon the pun, but you can take this one to the bank. This scene writes itself all across North America: Your nonprofit board elects a new board treasurer. He's from the hardware industry and he's a smart guy. He tweaks the monthly financial reports based on his experience and his accounting knowledge. Your last treasurer was from the hotel industry, and three years ago, she changed the report formats to align with her financial preferences. The previous treasurer asked Cousin Eddie to install financial software from his dry cleaning business. One problem—your nonprofit doesn't do dry cleaning!

Time out, everyone! This makes absolutely no sense and no thoughtful business person would ever permit this craziness in his or her own business. Resist the temptation to allow elected board treasurers and board finance committees to change the reporting systems at will.

Establish a standard reporting format and stick with it. Dan Busby says there is one basic rule in preparing financial reports: "Prepare different reports for different audiences. For example, a church board would normally receive a more detailed financial report than the church membership. Department heads in a nonprofit organization might receive reports that only relate to their department."[5]

Standard Financial Reports

For most nonprofit organizations, I recommend this level of detail:

Level 1: Monthly Overview
1. One-page Summary
2. Statement of Activity (Statement of Revenue and Expenses)
3. Statement of Financial Position (Balance Sheet)
4. Statement of Cash Flows

Level 2: Standards of Performance Update
5. Leading Indicators (sometimes called "Dashboard Reporting"—progress on key financial goals for the year, including SOPs related to the budget)
6. Cash Flow Graph (12-month cash flow forecast and year-to-date actual)

Level 3: Financial Detail
7. Memo to the Board and Management Team (monthly narrative and notes on highlights, variances and explanations)
8. Appendix (detailed budgets, forecast vs. YTD)

Whether you are reporting in person or in writing, remember that you have a diverse audience with diverse needs. In addition, as we learned in the People Bucket, you are communicating to four social styles: Drivers, Analyticals, Amiables and Expressives. Each style has preferences, and you need to speak their language if your reports are to be meaningful.

Ball #4:
IMPLEMENT Financial Best Practices
Operate with integrity by becoming a member of ECFA.

The Evangelical Council for Financial Accountability (ECFA) has established pass-fail standards of accountability for evangelical Christian organizations and churches. The seven standards also detail best practices that include such topics as the board of directors and audit committee, audited financial statements, use of resources, financial disclosure, conflicts of interest, and fundraising.

The organization publishes the "ECFA Standards and Best Practices," which is an excellent tool for helping your board and staff members move from "I don't know what I don't know" to "I know what I don't know." For example, under the fundraising standards, ECFA members must comply in 11 areas, including truthfulness in communication (donor expectations and intent), incentives and premiums, conflict of interest on royalties, acknowledgement of gifts-in-kind, and acting in the interest of the donor.

Is financial accountability important? In 2 Corinthians 8:19-21, the apostle Paul writes, "[We're] taking every precaution against scandal. We don't want anyone suspecting us of taking one penny of this money for ourselves. We're being as careful in our reputation with the public as in our reputation with God." When you lead and manage your ministry with integrity—and that integrity is affirmed by an independent organization such as the ECFA—you demonstrate a heart for accountability that honors God, safeguards your staff and board, and provides comfort and confidence to your donors. Don't be a spiritual Lone Ranger.

Here are some resources that are especially helpful for non-financial managers and board members:

Resources

George S. Babbes and Michael Zigarelli, *The Minister's MBA: Essential Business Tools for Maximum Ministry Success* (Nashville, TN: B&H Publishing Group, 2006).

Dan Busby, CPA, *2007 Church and Nonprofit Tax & Financial Guide* (Grand Rapids, MI: Zondervan, 2006).

ECFA, *Accounting and Financial Reporting Guide for Christian Ministries*. This is self-published by the Evangelical Joint Accounting Committee and is available at www.ecfa.org. ECFA also publishes a newsletter, *Focus on Accountability*.

J. David Epstein, *Clergy Tax 2007* (Ventura, CA: Regal Books, 2007). An updated edition releases each fall.

Robert P. Fry, Jr., *Minding the Money: An Investment Guide for Nonprofit Board Members* (Washington, D.C.: BoardSource, 2004).

Nonprofit Issues is the newsletter published by Capin Crouse, LLP (www.capincrouse.com), certified public accountants whose passion and mission is to serve the not-for-profit community. The firm's free newsletter provides a wealth of information for nonprofit leaders. My friend, C. E. Crouse, the firm's managing partner, has served many terms on the board of Christian Management Association. He gave me some excellent advice one year, quoting Will Rogers: "If you find yourself in a hole, the first thing is to stop diggin'."

BoardSource (www.boardsource.org).

The Budget Bucket To-Do List

❏ *Don't let non-financial people off the hook.* The core competencies of the Budget Bucket must be learned and applied by every team member. At your monthly meeting to monitor the monthly financial reports, create a Q & A culture that affirms that "There are no dumb questions."

❏ *Review reports early and often.* Monthly financial reports must be reviewed by every team member by the fifteenth of each month—so there's still time that month to make course corrections, if needed.

TO DO OR TO DELEGATE?

Priority A, B, C	Point Person	Task	Deadline Date	Done Date

THE DELEGATION BUCKET

We are experts at appropriate delegation. We invite team members to accept assignments based on their strengths. We value organized delegation and believe in the Point Person Principle. We track our to-do lists and we add to our don't-do lists.

Strategic Balls in the Delegation Bucket

1. MENTOR your team on the "monkey" method of delegation.
2. MAXIMIZE the point person assignment sheet.
3. DELEGATE your delegation.
4. RETHINK your delegation assumptions.
5. DELETE dumb delegation.
6. BEGIN a Don't-Do list.

Peter Drucker wrote, "No institution can possibly survive if it needs geniuses or supermen to manage it. It must be organized in such a way as to be able to get along under a leadership composed of average human beings."[1]

Superman is not a good delegator. (Imagine how dull the movies would be if he enlisted the ordinary citizens of Metropolis to handle each crisis!) Despite the fact that Superman is, in fact, superhuman, while the vast majority of us are not, the Superman Syndrome is alive and well in North America. Many CEOs, pastors, senior leaders, managers and volunteers often tackle their daily work as if they were Superman. As they fly across the screen, rooting out evil, they look back at the applauding crowd. *When the affirmation feels so good, why delegate?*

Think about these symptoms of the "dysfunctional delegation disease." Do you have any? Do the people on your team have the disease?

Dysfunctional Delegation Disease (check all that apply):
- ❑ *If the job is going to get done right, it's faster to do it myself.*
- ❑ *I'm the only one who knows how to do this job—that's why they hired me.*
- ❑ *If I delegate too much, maybe I won't be needed.*
- ❑ *Okay, I admit it . . . I'm a perfectionist. This project is too important to leave to novices.*
- ❑ *I inherited my team—and, frankly, they're ineffective—so it's up to me.*
- ❑ *I get more affirmation at work than I do at home. I love work!*
- ❑ *My boss (or board) says I don't delegate enough. Ha! If they only knew how hard I'm working. I'll show 'em.*

Add your favorites here:

❑ _____

❑ _____

❑ _____

Bottom line: The delegation disease is rooted in sinful behavior. Look at the list above and identify the sin each symptom points to—pride, arrogance, lack of trust, lack of patience. The list goes on.

In my 40s, a caring counselor helped my wife and me understand what had fueled my workaholism for years. When I finally got a grip on that (not a quick fix), it gave me new insight into the delegation disease. I am still a recovering workaholic, and I teach and write about delegation much better than I can practice it.

You may only need Delegation 101 or you may have deeper issues to address. But fundamentally, whether you battle Superman Syndrome or another delegation disease, take some time to reflect on the spiritual issues at the root of effective and ineffective delegation. What you discover may surprise you. If needed, ask a trusted friend, a wise mentor or a pastor to help you become a gracious delegator.

Ball #1:

MENTOR Your Team on the "Monkey" Method of Delegation
Get the monkey off your back!

Why delegate a task to an inexperienced team member when you can nail the project faster, better and with less hassle yourself? If you thrive on being the Problem Solving Guru on your team, stop right now and order this book online. (I'd suggest you delegate the book ordering to someone else, but if you want it done right, you'd better do it yourself!)

The One Minute Manager Meets the Monkey[2] was written by Ken Blanchard, William Oncken, Jr. and Hal Burrows. This humorous classic on delegation is required reading for every leader and manager—and their

> Procrastination is the greatest enemy of delegation. When you fail to plan far enough in advance, you'll delegate less because you're unprepared—or you'll delegate haphazardly due to the tyranny of a deadline. Neither approach will bless your team members.

direct reports. You'll learn how to get the "monkey" (someone else's assignment) off your back and how to avoid accepting monkeys in the first place.

If you've been "delegating" for years, but have never read this book, there's still hope. You'll learn about the three impositions on your time, the four rules for caring for and feeding monkeys (every monkey needs an owner), and the two monkey insurance policies that will lead to your success.

When your entire team understands and uses this powerful "monkey" analogy and language, it will dramatically change your office culture. Think about it. Do any of these statements sound familiar?

- "Suzy, before you finish that project, let me take a look at it. I'll check my library at home and get back to you with that resource." (*Suzy's monkey just leaped onto your back.*)

- "Dick, you've done a great job on this report. Brilliant! I have lunch with Joe today—and he's a great proofreader—so I'll ask him to review it before you send it out." *(Dick's monkey will be busy going from shoulder to shoulder, but the monkey should have stayed on Dick's back.)*

• "Jim, when you delegated the San Diego project to me last month, you promised to do the background memo. I can't move ahead until I have that history." *(The monkey's still on Jim's back, along with a few other monkeys he won't give up!)*

Some managers believe that there is a dangerous downside in delegating: Less experienced people might mess up, miss deadlines or fail miserably. Taking Peter Drucker's wisdom to heart is the antidote to the Superman Syndrome. While it appeared in the Drucker Bucket, here it is again (just in case you missed it):

People who don't take risks generally make about two big mistakes a year. People who do take risks generally make about two big mistakes a year.[3]

Ball #2:
MAXIMIZE the Point Person Assignment Sheet
This simple tool will revolutionize every meeting.

This tool is not rocket science, but it's extremely cost effective. Before we take a look at it, get out your calculator so that you'll have some hard-numbers motivation to hone your team's delegation skills.

Pick a meeting—any meeting—you've attended in the last 30 days and calculate the payroll cost of the meeting. (Suggestion: Do this exercise on a separate sheet of paper so that team members' salaries are not inked permanently into this book!)

Now that I have your attention, how much money would you save per year if your meetings were 20 percent shorter and 20 percent more effective? Christians are stewards of time. Psalm 90:12 says, "So teach us to number our days, that we may apply our hearts unto wisdom"

MEETING COST CALCULATOR		
MEETING NAME:		
MEETING DATE:		
MEETING PARTICIPANTS	**ANNUAL SALARY AND BENEFITS**	**HOURLY RATE (DIVIDE ANNUAL SALARY AND BENEFITS BY 2,080 HOURS.)**
1)		$ per hour
2)		$ per hour
3)		$ per hour
4)		$ per hour
5)		$ per hour
	Cost of this meeting per hour	$
	Multiply length of meeting	X hours
	Total cost of this meeting	$

Figure 16.1

(*KJV*). We do not honor God—or others—if our stewardship of time and delegation is sloppy.

Picture this all-too-familiar scene as fundraising volunteers gather for their monthly planning and accountability meeting:

- "Harry won't be here. I thought Jennifer was inviting him."
- "Was the deadline yesterday? My notes have it down for next Wednesday."
- "The mailing? I thought Susan, Troy and Arch owned that."
- "Oops. Anders brought dinner last night. I just assumed he was bringing it again."
- "Well . . . this was not our best work tonight—but let's close in prayer and ask God to bless our work anyway."

Here's the primo rule of delegation: *Write it down.* Track your assignments on the Point Person Assignment Sheet and update the sheet weekly or prior to every meeting. It's a simple tool that pays spectacular dividends. Everyone is—literally—on the same page and communication is clear. There's no downside. (If you're not the list-making type, delegate it to someone who lives by the list.)

Here's a sample:

Project: Vision 2010 Campaign Project Champion: Julio		POINT PERSON ASSIGNMENT SHEET		
Priority A, B, C	Point Person	TASK/ASSIGNMENT Updated on: July 15 by Julio	Deadline Date	Done Date
A	Julio	Create campaign master timeline	8/1	
A	Cameron	Recommend Standards of Performance for new position	8/15	
B	Chandler	Submit Draft 1 of the key volunteers list	8/15	
A	Tyler	Showcase 4 concepts for logo and website	8/31	
B	Dick	Propose front-end and back-end research activity	8/31	
C	Olga	Review last campaign and submit Draft 1 budget	9/15	
C	Digger	Recommend draft *Hoopla!* ideas for campaign celebration	12/15	

Figure 16.2

Our stewardship of time requires that we understand that time is a gift from God and make effective use of our team's time. Effective delegation is all about managing our time. Heed Ephesians 5:15-16: "Therefore be careful how you walk, not as unwise men but as wise, making the most of your time, because the days are evil" (*NASB*).

> When you know the strengths and social styles of your team members (see the Team Bucket), your competencies in the Delegation Bucket will skyrocket.

Coach John Wooden was a master at mentoring his teams during his 40-year coaching career. From 1948 to 1975, his UCLA basketball teams won 10 NCAA national championships, including seven in a row! ESPN named him the Greatest Coach of the Twentieth Century. Here's Coach Wooden on time:

Time lost is time lost. It's gone forever. Some people tell themselves that they will work twice as hard tomorrow to make up for what they did not do today. People should always do their best. If they can work twice as hard tomorrow, then they should have also worked twice as hard today. That would have been their best. Catching up leaves no room for them to do their best tomorrow. People with the philosophy of putting off and then working twice as hard cheat themselves.[4]

Ball #3:
DELEGATE Your Delegation
Small teams require creative delegation.

I hear the whining already! "I have no one to delegate to. My board of directors identifies a marketing problem and I'm the marketing guy. A volunteer asks for some statistical background information and I'm the statistics guy. A consultant wants fundraising numbers and I'm the numbers guy. I just delegate to the guy in the mirror."

I hear you. I've served on small teams most of my career. Even in large companies, the work is usually done by individuals and small teams. If you focus on why you can't delegate, you never will. H. V. Adolt said, "We are all manufacturers. Making good, making trouble, or making excuses."

Many leaders and managers, in the marketplace and in churches and nonprofits, have attacked this delegation dilemma with creativity, not excuses. Here are some of their best practices.

Idea #1: *Dollar-a-Year Senior Advisers.* Recruit highly committed volunteers and upgrade their status to "Dollar-a-Year Senior Advisers." Create a memo of understanding (MOU) for each person with a customized position description. Set the bar high—you won't be disappointed. (See the Volunteer Bucket.) You'll find top prospects among early retired men and women who, frankly, are bored with golf and the reality of retirement.

Idea #2: *Director of Volunteer Efforts.* Inspire a team member (or a new recruit) to become your D.O.V.E. Many organizations and churches have successful centralized systems for cultivating, recruiting, orienting and engaging volunteers. Be delegation-intentional and think of this person as your Director of Delegation.

Idea #3: *Outsource to contractors.* Not every position needs a full-time team member. Before you've reached your capacity, delegate to an outside contractor. Some churches upgrade volunteers to contractor status. Example: You can compensate a coordinator of 10 small groups (not a full-time position) on a contract basis for a fraction of what it would cost to bring a person onto the full-time staff. The small-group coordinator is more engaged and his or her family is appreciative because the additional compensation helps the family. It's a creative win-win.

Idea #4: *I'll trade you a spreadsheet for a PowerPoint.* You're good at spreadsheets, but PowerPoint presentations give you a headache. Delegate your time-consuming projects by trading tasks with others who have the competence you need.

Idea #5: *Document the potential of future results.* You say, "Boss, I need more people." Your boss hears, "Yada, yada, yada." Next time, explain how the investment in another person (full-time, part-time or contract) will generate more revenue, more results or help your organization achieve its mission. Don't whine . . . design.

Idea #6: *Doughnuts and Delegation.* Invite your team to join you for coffee and doughnuts and brainstorm your delegation dilemma. To document how serious you are about being a more effective delegator, have someone else set up and facilitate the brainstorming meeting. They will be affirmed by your trust in them!

Ball #4:
RETHINK Your Delegation Assumptions
Have more fun by trusting people to make their own decisions.

Dennis Bakke is a champion for a radical workplace. His approach, as described in *Joy at Work: A Revolutionary Approach to Fun on the Job*[5] is thoroughly biblical, as we discussed in the *Hoopla!* Bucket. The fun part of work, according to Bakke, is being trusted to make decisions. It's not a hard concept to sell to team members. The hard part is encouraging bosses and managers to give up decision-making so that their people can experience joy.

The *Joy at Work* approach to management (and delegation) is revolutionary. Decision-making is *not* by consensus. ("We must all agree before we move ahead.") It's *not* by majority-vote. It's *not* dialogue and feedback. The *Joy at Work* plan is designed to intentionally push decision-making down to the lowest practical level.

But with this responsibility, Bakke makes one thing crystal clear:

Everyone must get advice before making a decision. If you don't seek advice, "You're fired."[6]

What's the big deal about seeking advice? Bakke lists five benefits of the advice-seeking process:

1. It draws people in: "They become knowledgeable critics or cheerleaders" and "each person whose advice is sought feels honored and needed."
2. The decision-maker learns humility by asking for advice.
3. It's on-the-job education. "No other form of education or training can match this real-time experience."
4. The decision-maker is far closer to the issue than senior management. He or she will have to live with the decision.
5. And finally, "The process is just plain fun for the decision-maker because it mirrors the joy found in playing sports."[7]

Read the book to understand the "firing" part.

Joy at Work has become a catchphrase for a unique approach to leadership and management, and it's fundamental to the Delegation Bucket. If you're ready to move to the next level, add this to your To-Do or To-Delegate List. (Suggestion: Inspire someone on your team to order and read the book first. It's also legal to delegate your reading!)

 # Ball #5:
DELETE Dumb Delegation
Do you still need that monthly report?

Jim Martin had just completed his degree at Wheaton College Graduate School and was a valued team member at Christian Camping International/USA. One day he gave me an MBA-level course in delegation. He poked his head into my office and asked, "John, do you still need that monthly report?"

"What report was that, Jim?" I asked him.

"You don't remember?" he responded. Upon hearing that I couldn't even recall asking for it—much less remembering why it was so important—Jim made a hasty exit from my office with a mischievous smile and a simple, "Okay." Jim never mentioned the report again. I never received another, and to this day, I still don't remember why it was so important!

Here's the obvious point: Don't delegate useless stuff on a morning's whim or a hurried comment at a staff meeting. Encourage your team members to challenge your every inclination toward dumb delegation. Maybe give an award each month to celebrate the dumbest task someone graciously declined last month.

But what about those never-ending reports and bulging file cabinets? Create a master list of your daily, weekly, monthly, quarterly and annual reports. Add columns to show the point person who creates the report, the time it takes that person to generate the report and the person who needs the report and why. The goal: to eliminate reports that are extraneous, burdensome and rarely read. (*Yikes!* I just encouraged you to create a report to report on the reports!)

Effective leaders and managers must battle the bureaucrats and the paper-pushers every day or the work will overwhelm you and your team. If you need a visual reminder of this ball, grab a magic marker and make a sign for your office: Delete Dumb Delegation. (If you prefer to make the sign less obvious, print out a big "3-D" in 72-point font.)

You must attack dumb delegation because it quickly degenerates into dumber delegation. There's a ball in the Operations Bucket that will help you with this, labeled "Specify 'Good,' 'Better' or 'Best.'"

Ball #6:
BEGIN a Don't-Do List
If a To-Do List is a $10,000 idea, a Don't-Do List is worth $50,000!

The first president of the United States Steel Corporation was Charles Schwab (not the stock guy). He asked a consultant, Ivy Lee, for help on becoming a more effective executive. "Show me a way to get more things done. If it works, I'll pay anything within reason."

Lee introduced Schwab to the To-Do List and suggested that Schwab limit each day's list to no more than six tasks. He should start with the most important task and don't go to the second priority until the first one is done.

This remarkably simple—almost obvious—management tool revolutionized Schwab's work. So he sent Lee a check for $10,000.

I think the Don't-Do List will prove to be just as revolutionary. It's very simple: For 90 days, keep a list on your desk or computer of what you will STOP doing. (My friend Tony Danhelka calls this "selective neglect.") You must rigorously prune your To-Do List every day, every week and every month. You can't keep up—the conveyor belt is hurling work at you faster than the famous chocolate factory scene on *I Love Lucy*.

Get started with this:

MY DON'T-DO LIST							⊗
ITEM NO.	STOP DOING	EFFECTIVE DATE	DELEGATE ☑	IGNORE ☑	OTHER ☑	DELEGATED TO	

Figure 16.3

Send me a check for what this idea was worth to you!

The Delegation Bucket To-Do List

❏ *Start your Don't-Do List in the next five minutes.*

❏ *Ask your team members to point out dumb delegation* and get rid of it. No one—least of all you—will miss it.

❏ Identify other staff, volunteers or board members who are effective at delegation. *Ask for short-term coaching or long-term mentoring* so that you become a master at delegation.

TO DO OR TO DELEGATE?				
Priority A, B, C	Point Person	Task	Deadline Date	Done Date

THE OPERATIONS BUCKET

We affirm the high and noble calling of management and the spiritual gift of administration. We reject the fallacy that leaders lead and managers manage. We relentlessly pursue both effective and efficient operational solutions to organizational challenges. We are experts at ruthlessly eliminating costly bureaucracy that impedes results. We are yes men and women![1]

Strategic Balls in the Operations Bucket

1. AFFIRM the high and noble calling of management and administration.
2. SPECIFY "good," "better" or "best."
3. SHAPE a permission-giving environment.
4. CLARIFY responsibilities and task ownership.
5. BLESS Bob with a binder!

Operations often get a bad rap, yet a well-functioning organization must have gifted people who delight in executing the core competencies in the Operations Bucket. The Corporation arena, while perhaps not as sexy as that of the Cause and the Community, actually has a quiet but life-breathing role to play in the long-term success and effectiveness of your organization. In case you've forgotten:

- Your operations people keep payroll accurate and on time.
- Out of photocopy paper? No problem. There's more in the supply room.
- Software or hardware problem? Call the IT people.
- Is that idea likely to land you in court? The COO is already talking to legal.

If I went on, the list would fill this book and the operational balls would fill buckets of buckets. Here are six balls just to get you started on the core competencies in the Operations Bucket.

Ball #1:
AFFIRM the High and Noble Calling of Management and Administration
Leaders must manage and managers must lead.

Romans 12:6-9, one of the classic texts on spiritual gifts, says in part, "God has given each of us the ability to do certain things well. So if God has given you . . . administrative ability and put you in charge of the work of others, take the responsibility seriously" (*TLB*). The Bible says that teachers should teach, leaders should lead and administrators should administer. It's all about spiritual gift alignment. Yet somehow, the spotlight focuses on leaders and "internationally known speakers" and rarely (if ever) on managers and the gifted team members in operations.

> Results in the Operations Bucket are often less visible than in other buckets, so be more proactive in celebrating successes (see the *Hoopla!* Bucket).

Leadership and management—in truth—are inseparable. Olan Hendrix (see my introduction) writes that "Leaders must learn to manage, and managers must learn to lead."[2] Unfortunately, we often use simplistic definitions and differentiations between the two that minimize the God-honoring work of management. One of the worst statements I've ever heard is "Managers do things right, while leaders do the right thing." What CEO would stand in front of her staff and attempt to inspire team members with that management put-down?

In their book *Execution: The Discipline of Getting Things Done*, Larry Bossidy, a Fortune 500 company chairman, and Ram Charan, author and consultant, write:

Lots of business leaders like to think that the top dog is exempt from the details of actually running things. It's a pleasant way to view leadership: you stand on the mountaintop, thinking strategically and attempting to inspire your people with visions, while managers do the grunt work. This idea creates a lot of aspirations for leadership, naturally. Who wouldn't want to have all the fun and glory while keeping their hands clean? Conversely, who wants to tell people at a cocktail party, "My goal is to be a manager," in an era when the term has become pejorative? This way of thinking is a fallacy, one that creates immense damage.[3]

Bossidy and Charan say you get things done with three core processes: (1) selecting other leaders, (2) setting the strategic direction, and (3) conducting operations. They add, "Many people regard execution as detail work that's beneath the dignity of a business leader. That's wrong. To the contrary, it's a leader's most important job."[4]

When Rolla P. Huff was named president and CEO of EarthLink in 2007, the *Wall Street Journal* highlighted his priorities, which underline the importance of the Operations Bucket. Huff said, "It's all about execution. At the end of the day, I won't be judged on my plan as much as my execution."[5]

Do you want exceptional execution in your organization? Then affirm the high and noble calling of management and administration—and set the bar high. Encourage and mentor people who are called by God to deploy the spiritual gift of administration.

Ball #2:
SPECIFY "Good," "Better" or "Best"
Save huge hunks of time with these three clarifying words.

Some years back, a cracker-jack department head submitted a routine project to me well in advance of the deadline. My heart sank as I read the report. In my (feeble) mind, the project should have taken 15 to 30 minutes, yet my colleague had easily invested two to three hours on the assignment. It was spectacular, it was gorgeous, it was perfect (no typos)—but it was unnecessary.

At the next weekly staff meeting, I announced a new vocabulary for all future projects: "Good," "Better" or "Best."

If the assignment was for an internal document, the standard should be "Good." (Even rough calculations on the back of an envelope might be "good enough" for an internal project.)

"Better" would require more work because a committee might review it. But at the same time, a "better" job might save us time in the long run.

"Best," I announced, would be reserved for times when it must be perfect: website copy, donor letters, corporate annual reports, grant applications, and so on. Our team appreciated the new vocabulary because it saved them time. If I failed to delineate the scope of a future project, I was always asked, "Should this be Good, Better or Best?"

Try it, you'll like it—but don't confuse this operational tool with a commitment to excellence. Notice that the three choices are Good, Better and Best—not Poor, Mediocre and Good-Enough-for-Church Work. Elton Trueblood (1900-1994), the inspirational Quaker author, educator, philosopher and theologian, wrote, "Pious shoddy is still shoddy."

 # Ball #3:
SHAPE a Permission-giving Environment
Ruthlessly eliminate bureaucracy every Friday!

To master core competencies in the Operations Bucket, you must build and shape a permission-giving environment. I had a boss who once posted a sign on his door, "What part of NO do you not understand?" In his case, it was a prudent message for his season of life and the challenges he faced leading the organization.

In contrast, as often as you can, say *yes*. The best way to create a *yes* environment is to push decision-making down to your people in the trenches. Trust your people with budget decisions, days-off decisions and all the decision-making you can possibly give up. But, per Dennis Bakke's bestselling book *Joy at Work*, hold high the principle that people rigorously seek advice before decisions are made (see the Delegation Bucket).

Finally, here's a wild idea: Every Friday morning with coffee, host a *Bagels & Bureaucracy* stand-up meeting. Award Starbucks gift cards to the best ideas for ruthlessly eliminating bureaucracy.

> **Time Management Tip:** What is your most productive time of day—morning or afternoon? Block off time in that slot every day for your A-priority projects. Answer your email only twice a day and turn it off the rest of the time. (When you ultimately leave the company or retire, no one will begin a speech with "Good ol' Ed always stayed on top of his email. Way to go, buddy!")

Ball #4:
CLARIFY Responsibilities and Task Ownership
Eliminate all fuzzy roles—and identify a point person (or champion) for every task.

The Prime Responsibility Chart (Fig. 17.1) has been a critical best practice in my operations tool kit for over 30 years. Bill Benke introduced it to me when he served on my board at Camp Sambica. Benke used a version of this chart when he was a strategic business analysis executive with Boeing.

The chart is simple and straightforward and can be changed at any time. The most important principle: Only one person has "Prime Responsibility" (P) for a task or responsibility.

Ball #5:
BLESS Bob with a Binder!
A three-ring binder will usher in world peace. Almost.

My long-suffering colleagues and board members, over the last generation, would be deeply disappointed if I didn't hold high the perpetual power of a well-organized three-ring binder. It's a core competency you can't live without.

PRIME RESPONSIBILITY CHART P = Prime Responsibility A = Assistant Responsibility AP = Approval Required						PRC
TASKS AND RESPONSIBILITIES	BOARD	EXECUTIVE COMMITTEE	CEO	COO	CFO	PROGRAM DIRECTOR
PERSONNEL						
1) Hire and fire the CEO	AP	P				
2) Hire and fire other senior leaders			P			
3) Staff handbook annual review			AP	P	A	
FINANCE & ACCOUNTING						
1) Annual budget	AP		A	A	P	A
2) Quarterly financial reports	AP				P	
3) Annual audit	AP	P			A	
4) Non-budgeted expenditures under $5K					AP	
STRATEGIC PLAN						
1) Three-year strategic plan update	AP	AP	P	A	A	A
2) Mission, BHAG, core values	AP		P			
3) CEO annual standards of performance	AP	A	P			
Add additional categories below:						

Figure 17.1

Let's say Bob joins your team today and is clueless about your culture, your endless acronyms (CT, NAE, ECFA, CCCA, WCA, CMA, CSA, ETC.), the organizational chart, the code of accounts and your mileage reimbursement policy. *Good news!* It's in the Operations Binder!

Bob's predecessor, Susan, left Bob a complete A-to-Z Binder, including: FAQs, position description, standards of performance, vendor directory, annual calendar, printing schedules, staff birthdays and a one-page snapshot of her boss (strengths, social styles and other helpful info). That binder alone was worth gold.

Bob begins work on the Vision 2020 event and wonders what happened at the Vision 2000 event. *Good news!* It's in the Event Archives Binder!

Bob's wife calls and asks about the health insurance coverage. *More good news!* He'll bring home the Employee Benefits Binder tonight.

You get the point. Binders are a simple way to organize, file and retrieve important documents. If they gave a Ph.D. in Binder Management, I'd sign up. I love binders.

The Operations Bucket To-Do List

❏ *Ask your operations team to identify other core competencies and action steps* (balls) in the Operations Bucket. Then schedule training segments and mentor the entire organization in the best practices that will create a lean, mean operating machine. Ask the HR team, the IT department, legal and other teams to leverage the God-given gifts of administration throughout the organization so that your mission is achieved.

❏ *Paint a picture for your people* of a workplace that honors and doesn't denigrate the administratively gifted people on your team. Eliminate pejorative labels like "number-crunchers," "geeks" and "paper-pushers." Call your people "people" and use business card titles that enhance them and your organization. What would Jesus do?

❏ *Invest one hour once a month with your operations team* to plot and then course-correct your department's activity across Stephen Covey's Time Management Matrix. For every hour you invest in this self-assessment, you'll gain dozens of hours per month in increased productivity and job satisfaction.[6]

TO DO OR TO DELEGATE?				
Priority A, B, C	Point Person	Task	Deadline Date	Done Date

THE SYSTEMS BUCKET

We are passionate about systems thinking and process management.
We encourage systems people to use their gifts and mentor others for
the benefit of our Cause and our Community arenas. We are careful not to
tinker or over-tweak, yet we are tenacious about tickler systems. We have
a heart to create systems that serve people, not the bureaucracy!

Strategic Balls in the Systems Bucket

1. ADD process management to your résumé.
2. SEARCH out best practices.
3. ELIMINATE Tenth-Hole Trash-Can Syndrome.
4. READY! Fire! Aim!
5. TRAIN your team in tickler tracking.

I have good news and bad news about the Systems Bucket at FedEx
Kinko's^SM. First the good news: After sending a written concern to the
company's customer relations department, I received three phone calls—
one each from the store manager, the district manager and the regional
manager. My request for a refund was courteously granted that day, in
an amount exceeding my request. Very impressive!

Now the bad news: In my attempt to send a FedEx to FedEx Kinko's,
the nicer-than-nice customer relations person was not able to give me the
company's street address—only the post office box address in Provo, Utah.

"That's our policy," she smiled. (It was a phone call, but I could sense
her smile.)

Well, as every manager knows (because we've all tried it once, but
only once), FedEx will not deliver to a P.O. box.

"You mean I cannot send a FedEx to FedEx?" I inquired nicely. "Does not the irony of this policy seem, well, ironic?" I asked her (nicely).

Miss Nice agreed, we both laughed and I sent my FedEx instead to the corporate office in Dallas. I attached a note to the president of FedEx Kinko's, asking him to please *mail* my letter to Customer Relations in Provo! (I got the three phone calls the next day.)

There may be a good *internal* reason why you can send a FedEx to the corporate office in Dallas but not to the customer relations office in Provo, but there's not a good *customer service* reason. Maybe we need the Bureaucracy Bucket so that we can use it for pistol practice on our *hoopla!* days! Internal bureaucracy is a morale killer and a business killer.

Inventory is the second highest killer of morale. Last year I went to my local copy and print center at Staples® to use one of their five self-service photocopy machines. Those incredible workhorses were out of staples. Honest! Staples was out of staples!

You must expose your team to the time- and money-saving Systems Bucket. Then help each team member assess their competencies in process management and systems thinking.

 # Ball #1:
ADD Process Management to Your Résumé
Mentor your people to "think systems."

There are genuine experts in your circle who are gifted process managers and systems thinkers. My brother, Paul, is one of those wonderful MBA types: trained as an engineer, but happiest when serving people in a general manager's role. He has brains *and* a heart. He's mentored me often through the years, but I still need the brain transplant.

One year at Christian Management Association's annual leadership and management conference in Nashville, Paul volunteered to lead the three-ring binder assembly team. Paul's team members were all in the local rescue mission's rehabilitation program. On game day, Paul set up the process and the system, assigned the men to the various stations, explained how and why the binders would help managers around the world, and then inspired his men to work as a team.

I would have been happy with that. Not Paul! He's a fully devoted systems guy.

Thirty minutes into the binder marathon, he stopped the assembly line and held a team meeting. Paul began, "Okay . . . now that you see the big picture and your part of the process, what do you recommend we change to make this system run smoother, smarter and simpler?"

The men from rehab—valued people in God's and in Paul's eyes— were at first unprepared for their new consulting roles. But first one and then another made suggestions and, as Paul told me later, they could hardly wait to get back to work to improve the system.

But it didn't stop there. At the end of a fun but physically taxing day, Paul gathered the troops again for his management crème de la crème. After thanking them for their magnificent teamwork, he added this: "When you graduate from your program at the rescue mission, be sure to add this to your résumé. Tell future employers that you have experience in process management and that you worked on a just-in-time production assembly line."

The broad smiles and high-fives in response reverberated across the room. God smiled, too.

Mentor your people to "think systems." You'll see pure genius ooze out routinely. You'll bless your people and they'll bless you.

Ball #2:
SEARCH Out Best Practices
Study the "E-Myth" systems from the franchising world.

Nonprofit ministries and churches often get a bad management rap. A popular assumption is that they are poorly managed and have a high failure rate. *Hello?* Do you read the *Wall Street Journal?* Small businesses fail everyday. Ditto the big ones.

According to Michael E. Gerber, 40 percent of all small businesses fail in their first year. Of those that survive one year, 80 percent fail in the next five years. Only 20 percent that make it past five years are around for 10 years. *Yikes!* Whether you're in a new or established organization, there is much to learn about the power of systems and process management from Gerber's book *The E-Myth Revisited: Why Most Small Businesses Don't Work and What to Do About It.*[1]

Gerber's insights on business development have stood the test of time. Every organization, he says, should study the principles of franchising. Many leaders have built strong organizations by creating great systems (the franchise business model). Franchises use detailed operating manuals, written procedures and consistent sales approaches. Every detail is delineated.

Read why technicians who become business owners (entrepreneurs) often miss the key steps for building a business when stricken with an "entrepreneurial seizure" (the E-Myth). It's likely that your organization has content or program experts who are now managing departments or divisions but still operating as technicians. The systems principles could be a life-saver for them (and you). Ask your team to grade the Systems Bucket in each department.

Ball #3:
ELIMINATE Tenth-Hole Trash-Can Syndrome
Trash distribution is irregular and work never flows evenly in the nine-to-five time slot.

Most golfers are having too much fun (or anguish) to notice this, but my systems radar kicks in on the tenth hole at San Clemente Municipal Golf Course. The trash can on 10 is always overflowing with garbage from golfers' clubhouse stops after the ninth hole. The obvious solution: Place a jumbo-size trash can at the tenth hole. Yet it's not done because a non-systems person ordered identical-sized trash cans for all 18 holes.

Last year, Wal-Mart Stores, Inc. implemented a computerized system that schedules employees' shifts based on customer traffic. Some church offices are now open Sunday mornings and incoming calls go to a live person during the busiest hours of the week. (Why doesn't every church do this?) But more often than not, it's amazing how we still staff and structure our systems as if work, priorities and customer demands flow evenly Monday through Friday from 9 A.M. to 5 P.M.

When you apply systems thinking, you focus on the right steps in the right sequences in the Systems Bucket. Right now, in your mind, wander around your organization and think of several examples of Tenth-Hole Trash-Can Syndrome. Then ask your team: "Do our systems serve our staff or our customers? How will improved systems thinking generate more goodwill among our customers, members, donors, clients, prospects and others?"

Ball #4:
READY! Fire! Aim!
Resist the urge to tinker endlessly to perfect the flawless system. Perfection is not the goal.

It's not always prudent to wait until all your ducks are in a row. Sometimes even systems people must agree that "good is good enough" and now it's time to launch the project. Too much tinkering to get it "right" may create an unintended consequence: *overhead overload.*

Some of your team members are systems zealots and have overused skills. Some may hone the smithereens out of a perfectly adequate system. Others, addicted to perfection, rarely finish a project. You may have a team member—a genius—who is unable to tolerate non-geniuses. "Why don't they get it?"

What can you do?

I encourage my clients to read a unique add-water-and-stir resource that is amazingly simple, yet profound. *FYI: For Your Improvement: A Guide for Development and Coaching* was written by feedback experts Michael M. Lombardo and Robert W. Eichinger.[2] This comprehensive development and coaching guide is organized around 100 topics on competencies, performance dimensions, and career stallers and stoppers. Practical action steps are included for three types of team members: unskilled, skilled and those with overused skills.

Find out how to point each of these types in the right direction and maximize what they have to offer your systems and process management. Above all, get them moving! Systems don't do any good until someone turns the lever to "On."

Ball #5:
TRAIN Your Team in Tickler Tracking
Track your daily, weekly, monthly, quarterly and annual repeating tasks.

Payroll is one of those repeating tasks that must be flawless. The same devotion to details that you require for on-time paychecks can also be routine throughout your organization. Creating a systematic process for repeating tasks is part of systems thinking.

Tracking systems run the gamut from sophisticated software to Post-it Notes on the wall. Start by listing your repeating tasks on a spreadsheet so that you can sort by deadline date, point person, department, task, and so on. Create at least five major sections: "Daily Tasks," "Weekly Tasks" (by day of week), "Monthly Tasks" (by day of month), "Quarterly Tasks" (by date) and "Annual Tasks" (by date).

Your systems thinkers already have binders, tabs and tracking systems, but you might suggest this system for your less organized team members (see Ball #6 in the Operations Bucket):

> The Law of Diminishing Returns fits in many buckets, but it's a frequent sin in the Systems Bucket. Ken Behr, president of ECFA (ecfa.org), cautions leaders and managers to evaluate growth and decline cycles so that they know when it's time to pull the plug on a program, product or service. For example, if you invest $5,000 to increase your customer base by 10 percent, should you invest another $5,000—or will you have diminishing returns? If two staff members are overloaded, does adding a third person make economic and organizational sense? Use systems thinking, Behr preaches, to analyze the Law of Diminishing Returns.

1. Ask each team member to assemble a binder titled "My Operations Binder." (You may want an acronym other than M.O.B., but your graphics guy will love it.)

2. Each person then designates tabs for their personalized "Daily," "Weekly," "Monthly," "Quarterly" and "Annual Tracker," otherwise known as the DWMQAT. (I love easy-to-remember acronyms, don't you?)

3. When repeating assignments are made in staff meetings or one-on-one meetings, they can be immediately listed on the DWMQAT.

Let's say that a team member is hospitalized or a family member dies or is ill. If that person is in charge of payroll, you likely have a Plan B. But what about the zillions of other details that few others know about? When a team member is absent or on vacation, the DWMQAT system kicks in and it's all there in black and white for another person to handle.

Similarly, when a team member is promoted, the DWMQAT is an excellent training tool for their replacement. Train your team in tracking, and cast the vision for both the short-term and long-term benefits.

The Systems Bucket To-Do List

❏ *Encourage team members who have "systems" in their DNA to mentor others* in the fine art of creating and organizing systems that support the Cause and the Community.

❏ *Have fun with systems thinking.* My son, Jason, introduced the Big Red Bowling Ball system to his creative team during his Silicon Valley days. If the Big Red Bowling Ball was on your desk for too many days, everyone knew that you were the bottleneck on the team's primo project. The goal: Finish your part of the project and roll that baby over to the team member who was next in line on the task.

The system worked flawlessly. For their end-of-project *hoopla!* celebration, instead of a clunky bowling trophy, the team's "most valuable player" was awarded the Big Red Bowling Ball! (You too can combine *hoopla!* with systems thinking and add some humor and fun to your routine procedures!)

❑ *Memorize the Six Pointers for Productive Projects.* They are (1) Point person appointed; (2) Prep memo circulated; (3) Project tasks and timeline prepared; (4) Performance standards written; (5) Party planned (for celebrating success); and (6) Post-project evaluation meeting scheduled. It's a system worth remembering!

TO DO OR TO DELEGATE?				
Priority A, B, C	Point Person	Task	Deadline Date	Done Date

THE PRINTING BUCKET

We elevate the power of the written and spoken word and leverage our communication tools to create synergy and alignment between our mission, BHAG, strategic plans and programs. We believe proofreading and style matters!

Strategic Balls in the Printing Bucket

1. LEVERAGE your communication tools to keep programs and projects aligned with your BHAG and strategies.
2. APPOINT and empower a printing coordinator.
3. CREATE a failsafe proofreading system.
4. POST your printing deadline calendar by the coffee maker.
5. SELECT a style and take off!
6. MAXIMIZE new technologies and innovations.

Judy Bryson, president of Pioneer Clubs®, understands the link between the Printing Bucket and the Customer Bucket. At her home church, she asked the office secretary to save all the junk mail she would normally discard. After 30 days, Judy collected the bulging boxes and hosted a meeting with her Pioneer Clubs marketing team.

When she emptied the "junk mail" on the conference table, her colleagues were in shock. Along with the direct mail pieces—easy candidates for the round file—they were amazed to see high-quality, four-color, innovative brochures and product announcements clearly addressed to the youth pastor, the children's department, the music ministry and the information technology team, just to name a few.

On what basis did the church secretary unilaterally determine that a particular brochure or catalog would not find its home in the children's pastor's inbox? Should Pioneer Clubs change their entire marketing strategy to focus on the church secretary—the obvious gate-keeper at this church?

Judy had a second conversation with the secretary and conducted a one-person focus group. The results were startling.

"Well, it's simple," the secretary explained. "We've used Pioneer Clubs materials for our midweek ministry for years—we're not going to switch now. So I just toss the materials from these other companies. Our children's pastor doesn't have time to read half of her junk mail, so I'm just helping her out."

Even if your favorite downtown printer has a Heidelberg Speed-master XL 105, the offset printing monster capable of cranking out 18,000 sheets an hour, you might have missed the most critical balls in the Printing Bucket.

You could call this chapter "the Communication Bucket," but I'm partial to printers—I love the smell of ink in the morning—and (unfor-tunately) I'm old enough to have watched typesetters use lead type while raising a ruckus as the student newspaper editor at Seattle Pacific University.

The Printing Bucket includes all of your communication tools, such as brochures, newsletters, eNewsletters, your website, podcasts, email blasts, signage, magazines, donor appeals, bumper stickers and gospel blimps.[1] There are far more than six balls in this bucket, but I had a dead-line and page limit. Originally, I felt that *Mastering the Management Buckets* was a more significant book than Tolstoy's 1,500-page *War and Peace*. You should be grateful that our friends at Regal know their customers. Some-day I'll write *Buckets and Peace: 20 Critical Strategies* (1,501 pages).

Ball #1:
LEVERAGE Your Communication Tools to Keep Programs and Projects Aligned with Your BHAG and Strategies
Use publication deadlines to fine tune organizational decision-making.

Printers control the world. Every printer's office has the same sign of the *Casper the Friendly Ghost* characters folded over in laughter asking,

"You want it *when*?" I've never seen a project stay on schedule without a few friendly threats from my printer friends.

Your printer calls with this stern warning: "To meet your already ridiculously optimistic schedule, absolutely, without fail, your graphic designer must email me the conference brochure by Friday noon." (Trust me . . . what that really means is "Your designer better work all weekend, because Monday at 9 A.M. is the absolute deadline if you want this printed before the conference!")

There's a big problem, though: Your graphic designer has the concept completed, but those insignificant details like program highlights, conference fees, the names, bios and photos of the speakers, the schedule and (oh, yeah) the brochure copy—none of that is completed yet. The suits on the fourth floor are still haggling over the details. The marketing geniuses on the third floor are still analyzing the customer and what in the world the customer values. The number crunchers (I mean operations all-stars) on the second floor don't even know about this conference yet. (You've successfully kept it under the radar so that it wouldn't be squelched by those budget bullies who care more about bottom lines than changed lives.)

Oops! You just remembered: Is there still time to set up the online registration form?

You've been there and done that. You've screamed, threatened, bribed and prayed for forgiveness—but still, this describes most of your printing projects. There's a better way!

Elevate Execution and the Value of the Printing Bucket

Companies, nonprofits and churches all have the same disease: The senior team focuses on vision and the junior team executes. While this sounds good, it often relegates the incredibly important functions of the Printing Bucket to team members who are burdened with major responsibility and no authority.

The solution, of course, is to *elevate execution*. In the book he co-authored with Ram Charan, Chairman Larry Bossidy writes, "My job at Honeywell International these days is to restore the discipline to a company that had lost it. Many people regard execution as detail work that's beneath the dignity of a business leader. That's wrong. To the contrary, it's a leader's most important job."[2]

At your next senior management team meeting, think differently about the Printing Bucket. Elevate printing by describing how the printing deadlines will help you improve execution. (No jokes please.) Leverage this bucket in new ways so that the printed piece (or your website or a podcast) becomes the eloquent summary of a thoughtful process that integrates all the details of your programs and projects. When you use the printing press as the carrot (the motivator), be it a Heidelberg or FedEx Kinko's, you'll be amazed at how you can align virtually all of the other buckets and balls together: customers, pricing, results, strategy, programs, marketing, volunteers, delegation, budget, and on and on.

When senior people are involved in the Printing Bucket, the top-of-the-line projects like your BHAG (Big Holy Audacious Goal), your key strategies and your passion for ministry results will naturally ooze their way into your communication tools in unique and innovative ways. The results will be breathtaking. The bi-monthly newsletter will no longer be one more task on your To-Do List; it will be an opportunity to inspire and motivate the troops.

Ball #2:
APPOINT and Empower a Printing Coordinator
Your D-Day Dictator will keep your team on schedule and under budget.

Like any key team member, the appointment of the perfect printing coordinator will keep your team on schedule and under budget—*if* you empower this person with both responsibility and authority.

Your printing coordinator needs to have grace and charm, in addition to the organizational authority of a Deadline-Day Dictator! An Analytical (see the People Bucket) is usually superb, but she'll drive you nuts, hounding you with details. A Driver will railroad projects through, but you may have wounded bodies left in the road. An Amiable is often stunning at this role because he or she can leverage warm relationships to meet deadlines. Expressives, however, know how to make the entire process fun and will not be satisfied with boring graphics and same old, same old copy.

Your printing coordinator will be responsible for:

- Maintaining the printing/communication calendar
- Coordinating the team assignments and target dates for every project (customer, concept, cost, color, copy, calendar, quality)
- Monitoring the budget
- Enhancing vendor relationships (printers, designers, and others)
- Ensuring quality (copy, proofreading, correct quantities, and so on)
- Measuring results (with research team help)
- Archiving files, reports and evaluations
- Celebrating team achievements with appropriate *hoopla!*

It's a fun position for the right multi-tasking, versatile team member.

 # Ball #3:
CREATE a Failsafe Proofreading System
Proofreading occurs best after publication!

The buck stopped with me, so it was my mistake. We had outsourced a project to a vendor who would be using their own printer for a quick print run of 10,000 copies. There was one typo in the headline: "Order the audio version of these workshops and encourage your team members to become life-long learner."

We spotted the typo immediately, circled the word "learner" and faxed it back with the instructions to make "learner" plural.

The vendor followed our instructions perfectly. We received 10,000 copies of the order form with this headline: "Order the audio version of these workshops and encourage your team members to become life-long plural."

Yikes! It's funny now. Wasn't then.

The irony is that we had a failsafe system in place for proofreading—but we didn't use it. After all, it was just one typo and we were confident that it would get fixed. Wrong.

One of my favorite Murphy's Laws is: "Proofreading occurs best after publication." The brochure is on the press. The website is live. The order form has been mailed. The CD packaging is on the truck. And, bingo! Someone spots a typographical error.

Many organizations employ a variety of best practices to catch typos before publication (the preferred sequence!).

Printing Purchase Orders

I've always used some version of a Printing Purchase Order (PPO)[3] that details quantity, pricing, paper, ink colors, folds, and so on. The clincher part of the PPO is a section that requires the written sign-off of the project champion and two or three others designated by the project champion.

Some champions use the PPO as an FYI (For Your Information) to be sure that key team members are in the loop. Not every person is a good proofreader. Yet certain team members should still sign off on the project (with a signature) to confirm that they have read the document (or website article or newsletter) in advance.

Frank Hardman at HR Agency Services, Inc.[4] epitomizes the best in the printing world. He served our team at Christian Management Association more like a staff member than a vendor. Truth be told, he bailed us out multiple times. Frank appreciated our PPO and MPI (Mailing Piece Instructions) forms. When I found a system that made his life easier, I used it.

Combating the Fog Factor

Bad, overly complex writing stinks up websites, newsletters, emails, memos, reports, donor letters and signage. There's help!

Bob Kelly, resident wordsmith at Wordcrafters, Inc.,[5] introduced me to the "Gunning Fog Index," a measurement of the number of multi-syllabic words used and the length of sentences. The communication goal: shorter, simpler sentences. Think about your audience. *Reader's Digest* is written at a ninth-grade level while *Atlantic Monthly* is targeted to high school seniors and older.[6]

Your spell check program can give you "Readability Statistics." For example, the Flesch-Kincaid grade level for the paragraphs in this section is 10.7. According to the spell check in Microsoft Word, the Flesch reading ease level for this entire chapter is 47.2 on a scale of 100.

Monitor the reading levels for all of your communication tools in

> **Rewrite this sentence and then measure the "before" and "after" Fog Factor:**
>
> *I'm writing today to inquire about the possibility that you would be open to come and speak to our hard-working employees here at our beautiful international headquarters on the general subject of How to Basically Write Better Memos and Reports When You Haven't Had Any Training, would you?*

the Printing Bucket. You should also write with the four social styles in mind (Analyticals, Drivers, Amiables and Expressives). It's not easy!

Ball #4:
Post Your Printing Deadline Calendar by the Coffee Maker
Out of sight is out of mind.

If you're the printing coordinator, prepare a large visual "Printing Deadline Calendar." Post it by the most frequented location in your office: the coffee maker, the photocopy machine, the water cooler or maybe even the company bulletin board.

Create the master list of printing projects, newsletter deadlines, website phases and changes, and so on for the next 30, 60 or 90 days. The visual reminder will heighten interest in your communication tools and keep projects moving toward the deadlines.

Recommendation: Avoid the temptation to calendarize every project in a software system. You can do it, if that works for you. But remember: Out of sight is out of mind. Most organizations have discovered that the wall works best.

At Association Management Center[7] in Glenview, Illinois, the director of design manages the newsletters and magazines for more than 30 associations. What sophisticated system does he use to track the immense deadline details for these time-sensitive publications? Massive yellow Post-it Notes on his office wall, carefully organized in floor to ceiling columns. *Now you're talking!*

 Ball #5:
Select a Style and Take Off!
Style and spelling matters.

You're seated in the exit row on a Boeing 747-400 at 30,000 feet. You are always anxious about flying, but somehow you have faith that the 147,000 pounds of high-strength aluminum, the 18 tires and the 95,000-pound wings will get you from Los Angeles to London. After all, the 747 fleet has logged more than 35 billion miles—enough to make 74,000 trips to the moon and back. A flight attendant mentions that it took 75,000 engineering drawings to produce the first 747.[8]

While you're appreciating the extra leg room, you review the exit row emergency card and your heart stops. There's not one, not two, but over a dozen typographical errors. Not minor ones—major errors. The airline would be embarrassed with the careless proofreading.

A cold shiver comes next. *Wait a minute. If the proofreading is shoddy— what about the safety precautions? Should I drink the water? Who serviced the engines? Is there enough fuel? Maybe the fuel guy left early for lunch and forgot to fill all the tanks? Who's in charge of pilot training—the same guy that hires the proofreaders?*

Proofreading matters. When your customers, members, donors, volunteers, board members or clients see typos and shoddy materials from the Printing Bucket, it matters.

Here are some suggestions. First, every publication, from the *New York Times* to a one-page bi-monthly eNewsletter, must follow a stylebook and have its own style sheet. A stylebook enables your entire team to follow a consistent set of writing rules. Your style sheet should be a dynamic work in progress and updated regularly. It might include acceptable acronyms, when to use Dr., Rev., Mr., Mrs., Miss and Ms., and the authorized uses of corporate name abbreviations, company slogans and your word-for-word mission statement.

More than two million journalists own the *Associated Press (AP) Stylebook and Briefing on Media Law*, the bible for journalists.[9] This invaluable resource includes more than 5,000 entries on grammar, spelling, punctuation (there is no period in Dr Pepper), capitalization, abbreviations (Calif., not CA), misused words (Canadian geese) and the correct names of countries, organizations, Arabic words and brand names.

Editors at Regal, the publisher of this book, use *The Chicago Manual of Style* as their style guide, which is widely used among academic and trade publishers.

For the punctuation and proofreading zealots on your team, buy them the bestseller *Eats, Shoots & Leaves: The Zero Tolerance Approach to Punctuation,* by Lynne Truss. The author dedicates the book "to the memory of the striking Bolshevik printers of St Petersburg who, in 1905, demanded to be paid the same rate for punctuation marks as for letters, and thereby directly precipitated the first Russian Revolution."[10]

Every publication editor and website writer in your organization should care about consistency—it enhances your brand and blesses the Analyticals!

Ball #6:
MAXIMIZE New Technologies and Innovations
Remember! People are readers or listeners.

Don't get stuck in the routine of the Printing Bucket. At least twice a year, get out of the office, breathe in some fresh air and think deeply about your customers, your mission, your BHAG, your key results and the communication tools you're using to serve your customers. What tools should be dropped, what tools need a makeover and what tools should be added? Research and pray. Pray and research. Ask your customer (see the Customer Bucket).

Peter Drucker said that people are either readers or listeners. Most days I read the *Wall Street Journal* and the *Los Angeles Times*. My son, Jason, prefers customized daily podcasts from the *New York Times*. I'm a reader; he's a listener.

Not every customer, donor, board member, team member or volunteer would select reading as their preferred way to receive your communications. Some prefer verbal messages. Use the telephone. Add video to your website when possible. Meet people personally.

If you're a nonprofit organization reaching out to churches, does your message get past the office secretary? The No. 10 envelope-with-tickler mail piece will not cut it anymore. Innovators with serious budgets have raised the bar.

> When you communicate only from your preferred style, you miscommunicate to 75 percent of your audience! Effective communication is in the eye and the ear of the customer. Analyticals appreciate facts and logic. Drivers want short and sweet messages. Amiables embrace communiqués that are relationship-rich, while Expressives are distracted at the first hint of a boring monologue.

When Metro-Goldwyn-Mayer Studios, Inc. asked Motive Entertainment to promote the 2006 *Rocky Balboa* movie to the faith and family market, Motive understood that a letter, a flyer and a response device might have worked for the first *Rocky* in 1976 but would not have the same punch in this sophisticated decade.

Motive's innovations had helped fuel box office records for *The Passion of the Christ*, *The Chronicles of Narnia* and *Polar Express*, and the team knew that *Rocky Balboa* would need even more creativity. So Paul Lauer, Motive's founder and marketing guru, created a unique resource box for pastors and youth leaders. The colorful box included a boxing glove, a Rocky T-shirt, a cap, a DVD with video clips, posters and an eight-page *Faith-Based Leader's Resource Guide*—with every element pointing to a content-rich website at www.rockyresources.com.

Be assured: The boxing glove made it to the senior pastor's desk. It did not end up in the trash can.

I followed this innovation up close because Motive asked me to write the leader's guide, and my son, Jason, the founder of Pearpod[11] (a marketing and design company), created the resource box and designed the eye-catching materials.

The bell just rang. It's now Round 10, and Motive Entertainment changed the rules for marketing to churches. How will your company, ministry or local church think differently about technology and innovations in the Printing Bucket this year?

The Printing Bucket To-Do List

❏ *Leverage the Printing Bucket for the kingdom of God.* Johannes Gutenberg invented the printing press and gave us the *Gutenberg Bible* in the fifteenth century. The printing press (innovative communication) is even more powerful today in the movement to transform lives for the glory of God.

❏ *Create laser-like messages to move your customers* from ignorance to purchase. Senior pastors understand and leverage the power of the pulpit. Week after week, they zero in on the highest priority task of moving people from no faith to becoming fully devoted followers of Christ. In the same way, effective leaders and managers use their communication tools to move customers in the right direction.

❏ "I learned to write to burn the fuzz off my thinking," commented Fred Smith in his pithy book *Breakfast with Fred.*[12] *Use print deadlines to burn the fuzz off your organization's blue-sky plans* that otherwise would rarely be committed to the printed page (or the website).

TO DO OR TO DELEGATE?				
Priority A, B, C	Point Person	Task	Deadline Date	Done Date

THE MEETINGS BUCKET

We design meetings like an architect designs buildings. We have high expectations that our purpose-driven meetings will enhance team-building, accountability and our commitment to results. We value Holy Spirit-led meetings. We reject boring meetings.

Strategic Balls in the Meetings Bucket

 FOCUS on results with weekly one-on-one meetings.

CREATE a welcoming environment for every meeting.

MAXIMIZE results with four strategic meetings.

Harvard Business School's case studies are legendary. So when Jim Mellado, a 1991 MBA student at Harvard, volunteered to write a case study on Willow Creek Community Church, it attracted wide attention.[1] Mellado had attended a church leadership conference at Willow Creek in South Barrington, Illinois, and was passionate about Jesus and Willow Creek's mission and seven-step strategy.

In 1992, we started the Willow Creek Association, and Bill Hybels, Willow Creek's senior pastor, asked me to be WCA's first president. Later that year, Bill encouraged me to hire Jim Mellado as a vice president. After the association launched, it soon became clear that Jim had the gifts (and the Harvard credentials) to turbo-charge the movement. In 1994, he became the CEO and I focused on U.S. and worldwide conferences.

While enduring my twenty-first winter in Chicago, a headhunter called about a CEO position in Southern California. *Yes!* (Actually, the process was thoughtful and involved the prayer support of the couples in our small group and many close colleagues.)

So picture this: Jim Mellado is encouraged to attend a church leadership conference at Willow Creek. He enters Harvard Business School. He volunteers to write a case study on Willow Creek and then for years, MBA students discuss Willow Creek's mission to help "Unchurched Harry" become a fully devoted follower of Jesus Christ.

Next Mellado joins the new Willow Creek Association team. Now fast forward to 2008: Mellado is in his fifteenth year as president of Willow Creek Association with a membership of more than 12,000 churches in 45 countries and 90 denominations.

Bottom line: Faithful steps produce fruitful results and God is honored.

Okay, now back to the Meetings Bucket. In the Harvard case study on Willow Creek, you'll find a sample of my two-page "Weekly Report" (Exhibit 15). I introduced the report format to Hybels and Don Cousins (having used it for years) and both appreciated staying informed with this weekly update. Mellado saw the value of it, and *presto!*—it ended up in a Harvard case study.

And if it's good enough for Harvard, maybe you'll use it. It's the first ball in the Meetings Bucket.

Ball #1:
Focus on Results with Weekly One-on-One Meetings
Invest time in truth-telling and the Top-3 SOPs.

If you skipped the first chapter on the Results Bucket, you missed Peter Drucker's classic story about meetings and goal alignment. (Take a minute and read it now.) As I indicated, we've all been there. We walk out of staff meetings, strategy meetings and strategic planning retreats and we're absolutely convinced that the assignments and end results are crystal clear. Yet somehow, we have failed to communicate.

Miscommunication happens regularly, often with humorous results. Several years ago, a team member passed the word that Dick Bahruth would miss an important Wednesday meeting because his mother was ill and he was flying to San Antonio to see her. The message didn't make sense to me, because I knew his mother was in Southern California, not San Antonio, Texas. This staff member had always been reliable and she was very careful with details, but she insisted Dick was flying to Texas. Yet it didn't add up.

> "If you have enough meetings over a long enough period of time, the meetings become more important than the problem they were intended to solve."
>
> —Henrickson's Law of Meetings[2]

As I began making alternate Plan B arrangements for the Wednesday meeting, Dick called me. "San Antonio, Texas?" he laughed. "No, no, no. I'm at *Mount* San Antonio Hospital here in the Los Angeles area. Of course I'll be at the meeting on Wednesday!"

Whether you're in a Fortune 500 company, a megachurch or a small nonprofit, the communication challenges are similar. What's the solution?

Weekly one-on-one staff meetings with each of your direct reports can be powerful antidotes to miscommunication. When four eyes are looking at the same schedules, the same calendars, the same concerns and the same targets, excellent communication emerges week after week after week!

CEOs, senior leaders and managers who consistently meet with their direct reports and use a tool such as the "Weekly Update to My Supervisor" form (see Fig. 20.1), affirm that the time and energy invested pays rich dividends. Here are just a few of the powerful things that happen when you meet weekly with your direct reports:

- Team members are affirmed regularly.
- Direct reports more consistently leverage their strengths, their social styles and their spiritual gifts.
- Standards of performance are clear and goals are achieved on time and under budget.
- Staff conflict, gossip and misinformation challenges are dramatically reduced because truth-telling is a practiced core value.
- Bottlenecks and missed deadlines are eliminated.
- Recommendations are more thoughtful and intentional.

- Communication is enhanced as you use your direct report's preferred communication style.
- The pulse (morale, passion and energy) of your team is checked weekly.
- Affirmed and productive team members mean less staff turnover.
- And . . . team members often give you affirmation!

The Weekly Update to My Supervisor tool is not the solution to every management challenge, but it packs a punch when you use it to build the right foundation. In this section, I'll explain how to launch a systematic weekly meeting plan. If you're already meeting weekly with your direct reports but you need a turbo-boost, this process can revolutionize your meetings and your relationships.

First, get buy-in. Some direct reports, frankly, do not want to be held accountable. (A two-page form and a weekly meeting won't fix a deeper problem.) Assemble your team—throw in some *hoopla! (*see the *Hoopla!* Bucket)—and build your case for the value of a weekly one-on-one meeting.

Analyticals will need time to think about this new idea to be sure this isn't yet one more management trend to be tried and then dropped next quarter. An Amiable will appreciate the potential for an enhanced relationship. Tell Drivers that this will save them time—they appreciate structure. Expressives are often irritated by rules and procedures. Give them two "No Written Update Required" coupons and when you meet, just walk through the form verbally.

Second, ask each person to personalize the form. Hand out the Weekly Update to My Supervisor two-page form and email the Word document template to each person. Ask each team member to personalize the update with items that remain the same week after week. While some may prefer to handwrite the update, most will simply create a new document by copying the previous week's form. After a month, each person should be able to complete the form in less than 10 minutes.

Third, set a weekly due date. I asked my direct reports to submit their forms by Tuesday 4:00 P.M. for our Wednesday one-on-one meetings. I scanned the reports before leaving the office on Tuesday to get my brain in sync with the issues, concerns and priorities of my team members. I was then better prepared on Wednesday for the one-on-one meetings. Some emailed me the forms, others hand delivered them or dropped them in the "hot file" inbox by my office door.

Fourth, prepare for the meeting. This is obvious. Your advance preparation communicates that you're interested in them and their work. You care.

Edit this form so that it becomes the tool you need it to be. (You can download the Word document at www.managementbuckets.com.) Bottom line: Inspire your direct reports to think about your meeting in advance and focus on their key result areas.

Some years back, I received the weekly updates from my five direct reports shortly before 4 P.M. on Tuesday. As I scanned each report in preparation for my Wednesday one-on-one meetings, I was shocked to note that all five team members had checked the "Overwhelmed" box on #10. Rather than waiting for more stress to build up overnight, I scheduled a quick management team meeting that afternoon.

I encouraged my direct reports to vent for a while, and then asked them to be prayerful and thoughtful overnight and come back to our Wednesday meetings with recommendations for possible solutions to the Too Much Work, Too Little Time Syndrome.

Remember that you don't have to wait until your weekly meeting to address hot topics.

Ball #2:
CREATE a Welcoming Environment for Every Meeting
The meeting begins when the first person arrives.

Skilled meeting facilitators have a sixth sense about the "WOW Factor." They know that you don't need a knock-your-socks-off extravaganza in every meeting, but you do need to monitor the meeting temperature constantly. The room temperature is important, and the group temperature is critical.

WEEKLY UPDATE TO MY SUPERVISOR[3] (PAGE 1 OF 2)

EMAIL OR HAND DELIVER THIS UPDATE TO YOUR SUPERVISOR EACH WEEK
BY TUESDAY 4 P.M., IN PREPARATION FOR YOUR ONE-ON-ONE MEETING EACH WEDNESDAY.

DATE:	TO:	FROM:

1. MY SNAPSHOT

MY TOP-5 STRENGTHS FROM: *STRENGTHS FINDER 2.0*	1. 2. 3. 4. 5.
MY SOCIAL STYLE FROM: *THE SOCIAL STYLES HANDBOOK*	[ ] ANALYTICAL [ ] DRIVER [ ] AMIABLE [ ] EXPRESSIVE
MY TOP-3 SPIRITUAL GIFTS FROM: *DISCOVER YOUR SPIRITUAL GIFTS*	1. 2. 3.
MY LEARNING PREFERENCE	I AM A: [ ] READER [ ] LISTENER

2. MY SUPERVISOR'S SNAPSHOT

TOP-5 STRENGTHS	1. 2. 3. 4. 5.
SOCIAL STYLE	[ ] ANALYTICAL [ ] DRIVER [ ] AMIABLE [ ] EXPRESSIVE
TOP-3 SPIRITUAL GIFTS	1. 2. 3.
LEARNING PREFERENCE	MY SUPERVISOR IS A: [ ] READER [ ] LISTENER

3. HERE'S THE STATUS OF MY *JOB SUCCESS TOOLS*:

CURRENT	JOB SUCCESS TOOLS	DATE APPROVED
Yes \ No	Position Description	
Yes \ No	Annual Standards of Performance (SOPs)	
Yes \ No	Annual Professional Development Plan (The 3 Cs)	
Yes \ No	To-Do List (A, B and C Priorities)	
Yes \ No	Tickler Tracker (Daily/Weekly/Monthly/Quarterly/Annually Repeating Tasks)	

4. LAST WEEK, I MADE PROGRESS ON THE FOLLOWING:

5. THIS WEEK, I AM FOCUSING ON:

WEEKLY UPDATE TO MY SUPERVISOR (PAGE 2 OF 2)

6. Before I make my decision, I need your advice on:

7. The monkey's on your back! I'm waiting on you for:

8. I am recommending that:

9. FYI! You should be aware of the following:

10. Overall I am:
[ ] OK   [ ] Great!   [ ] Never been better   [ ] Overwhelmed   [ ] Overloaded for the next __ days
[ ] Don't cancel our meeting! We need to talk! [ ] Help! I need more time with you. At least __ hours in the next __ days.
[ ] Other: _____

11. Our next meetings are scheduled for:

Date	Day	Time	Major Agenda Item(s)

12. I continue to affirm our core value on truth-telling. To my knowledge, I have not shared anything inappropriate with others about you (or another staff person) that I have not shared first with you (or the other person). And, to my knowledge, when others have shared something about you (or others) with me that may be "crossing the line," I have stopped them in their tracks—and reminded them about our core values—and urged them to share it with you (or that person) within 48 hours.

This past week, our working relationship has been:
[ ] Excellent   [ ] Great   [ ] OK   [ ] Could Be Better   [ ] Poor
[ ] You blessed me when you _____
[ ] You bugged me when you _____
[ ] I need _____ minutes with you to go into the Tunnel of Chaos.

13. My Top-3 Standards of Performance (SOPs). (These SOPs remain the same all year.)
These are my **3 most strategic SOPs** that were approved by _____ on _____. I understand that the successful accomplishment of these SOPs is our primary focus in our weekly and quarterly meetings. They will account for about _____% of my annual evaluation and future compensation adjustments. (Consequently, this weekly update focuses primarily on these three SOPs and their critical importance to the mission and goals of our organization.)
1.
2.
3.

Internal Bureaucracy Form #98765—Revised January 2008 by GWB   Figure 20.1

The WOW Factor is easy to remember:

Welcoming
Organized
Warm

Routine meetings quickly spiral into boredom and sheer agony. Each of the four social styles (Analyticals, Drivers, Amiables and Expressives) has different expectations for your meetings. If you are not a skilled meeting facilitator and "don't know yet what you don't know," ask two or three people at your next meeting to quietly evaluate the WOW Factor of your meeting with this checklist:

WOW Factor Meeting Evaluation

Evaluation of _____ Meeting

Submitted by _____ Date _____

Rate the WOW Factor for each item below on a scale of 1 to 5.

1 = Utter failure!
2 = Did NOT meet expectations
3 = Met some expectations
4 = Met expectations
5 = Exceeded expectations

WELCOMING
_____ Meeting room was ready 15 minutes before start time.
_____ Meeting facilitator was prepared and relaxed, ready to greet the first person who arrived.
_____ Meeting participants were encouraged to get acquainted and converse with each other.
_____ Guests or new participants were welcomed into the pre-meeting circles of conversation.

ORGANIZED

_____ The agenda, meeting purpose and anticipated outcomes of the meeting were distributed at least 1 to 7 days in advance of the meeting to every participant.

_____ The meeting agenda was distributed or posted on a flipchart, whiteboard or PowerPoint.

_____ The agenda included a time budget for each topic.

_____ The presenters were well-prepared and any materials distributed were helpful.

_____ The assignments and next steps were agreed upon.

_____ The meeting ended 5 minutes early.

WARM

_____ Food and beverage presentation (if provided) was appropriate.

_____ Prayer (if included) was meaningful and not routine.

_____ Room temperature was acceptable.

_____ Facilitator demonstrated warmth and wisdom in leading the meeting.

_____ Participants demonstrated warmth and wisdom and engaged in the meeting.

_____ Meeting room environment enhanced the meeting (tidiness, extra chairs removed, adequate lighting).

Many leaders and managers develop their sixth sense about meetings by reading the body language of the participants. Are they slumped in their chairs or are they engaged? Are they yawning and fidgeting or are they hanging on every word?

Some team members arrive at meetings having just received bad news (family illness, a friend's relational problem, a financial hardship, and so on). Their sad countenance might be misinterpreted as lack of engagement. So, when appropriate, do a quick "around the circle" check-in moment: "Thanks for coming today. Let's take the first six minutes and go around the circle and check-in with each other. Do you have some good news, or even bad news, that you'd like to share with the group today? Take about 30 seconds each and then we'll ask Susan to pray, thanking God for our team and asking for His help today."

Your thoughtful concern will be appreciated by everyone, and you'll be able to get an immediate temperature reading on the group. It's a powerful opportunity to show people that you care. It honors God and it honors them.

Energy Boosters

Eliminate empty chairs before they're empty. If eight people are invited to the meeting and all eight attend, but there are three empty chairs, it feels like three people didn't show. Instead, set up only eight chairs around the table. Put the others on the perimeter or in another room.

If you're expecting 20 people, the chances of all 20 arriving on time are very low. Set up 18 chairs so the room is full when the meeting starts. When the two stragglers arrive, have your assistant prepared to add the extra chairs.

If and when your meeting begins to spiral into boredom anguish, here are some energy boosting ideas to try:

Idea #1: *Stand and Shout.* "Okay! We're almost ready to make a decision. Let's all stand and go around the circle and give your opinion on this. One minute maximum per person."

Idea #2: *Triads.* Use this approach when one or two people are monopolizing the discussion. Break into groups of three and ask the facilitator of each group to report back. Write the conclusions on the flipchart. (Remember: People are either readers or listeners.)

Idea #3: *VideoBreak.* Surprise the group with a humorous one- or two-minute video clip, and bring in some bonus refreshments.

Idea #4: *Best of . . . Awards.* Have an emergency stockpile of Starbucks gift cards, mini-trophies or special candy.

To boost energy, announce that for the next 20 minutes, you'll be giving awards for "Best Idea," "Best Affirmation," "Best Question" and "Best Yawn."

Idea #5: *Kneel and Pray.* When you're prompted by the Holy Spirit, take a time-out and ask everyone to kneel and pray. "Lord, forgive us for making Your work seem so routine and lifeless today. We confess that we need Your energizing power to get over this obstacle we're discussing. We want to move into the Promised Land of Your will. Renew us right now. Amen."

Jim Rayburn, the founder of YoungLife, taught that it's a sin to bore a kid with the gospel. It's also a sin to bore our team members with poorly planned and executed meetings. Remember the WOW Factor!

Ball #3:
MAXIMIZE Results with Four Strategic Meetings
Follow Patrick Lencioni's pattern for four kinds of meetings with your team.

Meetings are boring because there is not enough drama and conflict, suggests Patrick Lencioni, the bestselling author and management consultant.[4] Ask everyone on your team to read his important book *Death by Meeting: A Leadership Fable*. It's all about solving the most painful problem in business: meetings.

Lencioni recommends that every team have four kinds of meetings:

1. Daily check-in meeting (5 minutes)
2. Weekly tactical meeting (45 to 90 minutes)
3. Monthly strategic meeting (2 to 4 hours)
4. Quarterly off-site meeting (1 to 2 days)

According to *Spirit Magazine*, the author "argues that bad meetings lead to poor decision-making, which ultimately creates mediocrity in organizations. In addition, Lencioni says that bad meetings not only exact a toll on the attendees as they suffer through them, but also cause real human anguish in the form of anger, lethargy, and cynicism, and even in the form of lower self-esteem. And that's something those of us who've endured and continue to endure countless lengthy, often pointless meetings can definitely agree with."[5]

The Meetings Bucket To-Do List

❑ *Try the Weekly Update to My Supervisor form for 90 days.* Your To-Do or To-Delegate List is full by now—like after a good Thanksgiving meal, you can't absorb one more good thing. But if you have to select just one strategic ball from the Meetings Bucket, pick Ball #1 and use the Weekly Update to My Supervisor form. That single form and that one hour per week could revolutionize your focus on results, your career and your relationships. Download it, along with other helpful forms and charts, at www.managementbuckets.com.

❑ *Prepare, prepare, prepare.* Every minute the meeting facilitator invests in preparation (advance agendas, task lists, Prime Responsibility Charts, and so on), reduces, on average, the actual meeting time by 25 percent. That's an incredible savings of time and payroll costs that could be invested in the Results Bucket.

❑ *Share the following resources with your team members* as they complete the "My Snapshot" information for the Weekly Update to My Supervisor form:

- C. Peter Wagner, *Discover Your Spiritual Gifts* (Ventura, CA: Regal Books, 2005).

- Bruce L. Bugbee, *What You Do Best in the Body of Christ: Discover Your Spiritual Gifts, Personal Style, and God-Given Passion* (Grand Rapids, MI: Zondervan, 2005).

- Bill Hybels, *Honest to God: Becoming an Authentic Christian* (Grand Rapids, MI: Zondervan, 1992). See chapter 5, "Truth-telling: Pathway to Authentic Relationships."

❏ *Subscribe to Your Weekly Staff Meeting*, the free eNewsletter by John Pearson, which features a book review and a bucket insight each week. Subscribe at www.managementbuckets.com or www.john pearsonassociates.com.

TO DO OR TO DELEGATE?				
Priority A, B, C	Point Person	Task	Deadline Date	Done Date

THE LEAKY, RUSTED-OUT BUCKET

Congratulations! If you've actually read every chapter and carried every bucket, you deserve a medal!

Before you put the book down, pray and reflect on what you've learned and what you still need to learn. Re-read the Introduction and consider how you will integrate the buckets into your life-long learning program. See the learning options for 20 days, 20 weeks, 20 months or 20 years. At your next staff meeting, share the concept of the book and ask your team members to complete the Management Buckets Self-Assessment (available at www.managementbuckets.com) and indicate their level for each bucket:

Level 1: I don't know what I don't know.
Level 2: I know what I don't know.
Level 3: I have an action plan to address what I know I don't know.
Level 4: I am knowledgeable and effective in this core competency and can mentor others.

When I was up to my eyeballs in details and deadlines on this book, my sister-in-law, Marilyn Pearson, often emailed me with the right Bible verse at just the right time. Only Marilyn could have found this verse for me—and for you—from Haggai 1:5-7.

And then a little later, God-of-the-Angel-Armies spoke out again:
"Take a good, hard look at your life.
Think it over.
You have spent a lot of money,

but you haven't much to show for it.
You keep filling your plates,
but you never get filled up.
You keep drinking and drinking and drinking,
but you're always thirsty.
You put on layer after layer of clothes,
but you can't get warm.
And the people who work for you,
what are they getting out of it?
Not much—
a leaky, rusted-out bucket, that's what."
That's why God-of-the-Angel-Armies said:
"Take a good, hard look at your life.
Think it over."

Read the rest of the chapter and you'll be sobered by the high privilege of honoring the Lord our God. As you honor Him, honor your people, your primary customers and your supporting customers by giving them buckets and buckets of blessings. Not leaky, rusted-out buckets, but the buckets in the Cause, Community and Corporation arenas. Remind them that these buckets are on holy ground!

Near the end of the first chapter of Haggai, we read, "And all the people with them listened, really listened, to the voice of their God" (v. 12).

May it ever be so in your workplace!

JOHNPEARSONASSOCIATES

www.johnpearsonassociates.com
www.managementbuckets.com

John Pearson is president of John Pearson Associates, Inc., a management consulting company that helps nonprofit organizations, churches, associations and the companies that serve them. The company's focus is on "Vision Implementation with Detailed Execution."

Management Consulting

- Board governance workshops and retreats
- Strategic planning facilitation
- CEO and senior leader coaching and project implementation
- Fund development strategic direction
- Staff retreat facilitation
- Strategic project development and benchmarking
- Conference and meeting strategic coaching
- Marketing, branding, customer definition and annual communication planning

Management and Board Governance Workshops

- Management Buckets Workshop Experience (two-day sessions)
- Nonprofit Board Governance: Moving the Board from Myth to Mission (one-day session)
- CEO Dialogues (www.ceodialogues.org)

Complimentary eNewsletter

• *Your Weekly Staff Meeting* (a book review and a bucket insight every Monday morning)

For More Information

John Pearson, President
John Pearson Associates, Inc.
P.O. Box 74985
San Clemente, CA 92673
www.johnpearsonassociates.com
www.managementbuckets.com

ENDNOTES

Foreword

1. "Management Guru Peter Drucker," *On Point* with Tom Ashbrook, August 2, 2005. http://www.onpointradio.org/shows/2005/08/20050802_a_main.asp (accessed November 2007).

Introduction: Buckets 101

1. Olan Hendrix at www.olanhendrix.com.

Core Competency 1: The Results Bucket

1. Peter F. Drucker with Joseph A. Maciariello, *The Daily Drucker: 366 Days of Insight and Motivation for Getting the Right Things Done* (New York: HarperBusiness, 2004), p. 346. *Note:* This quotation is from Drucker's book, *Management: Tasks, Responsibilities, Practices.*
2. Peter F. Drucker, *The Drucker Foundation Self-Assessment Tool: Participant Workbook, Revised Edition* (New York: The Drucker Foundation, 1999), p. 5. *Note:* This workbook and a separate process guide is now available from several sources, including Amazon.com, Jossey-Bass Publishers or the Leader to Leader Institute, formerly known as The Peter F. Drucker Foundation for Nonprofit Management.
3. Bobb Biehl, *Stop Setting Goals If You Would Rather Solve Problems* (Nashville, TN: Moorings, 1995).
4. Room to Read at www.roomtoread.org.
5. John Wood, *Leaving Microsoft to Change the World: An Entrepreneur's Odyssey to Educate the World's Children* (New York: HarperCollins, 2006), pp. 137-138.
6. Email from John Wood to Larry Entwistle, March 13, 2007.
7. Leadership Network at www.leadnet.org.
8. Peter F. Drucker, *Managing for Results* (New York: Collins, 2006).
9. Jim Collins, *Good to Great and the Social Sectors* (Boulder, CO: Jim Collins, 2005), p. 7.
10. Ibid., p. 9.
11. Robert A. Watson and Ben Brown. *The Most Effective Organization in the U.S.: Leadership Secrets of The Salvation Army* (New York: Crown Business, 2001).
12. Ibid., book jacket.
13. For subscription information, visit http://cmaonline.org/cmr-magazine/ (accessed November 2007).

Core Competency 2: The Customer Bucket

1. Peter F. Drucker, *The Drucker Foundation Self-Assessment Tool Participant Workbook, Revised Edition* (New York: The Drucker Foundation, 1999). *Note:* This participant workbook, and a separate process guide (see note 5 below), is now available from several sources, including Amazon (amazon.com), Jossey-Bass Publishers (JosseyBass.com) and the Leader to Leader Institute (leadertoleader.org), formerly known as The Peter F. Drucker Foundation for Nonprofit Management.
2. Ibid., p. 5.
3. Ibid., p. 22.
4. "The first JELL-O® advertisement ran in *Ladies' Home Journal* featuring smiling, fashionably coifed women in white aprons proclaiming JELL-O® gelatin 'America's Most Famous Dessert.'" From "The History of the Wiggle: 1845-1924" at Jello.com. http://www.kraftfoods.com/jello/explore/history/ (accessed November 2007).
5. Drucker, *The Drucker Foundation Self-Assessment Tool Participant Workbook, Revised Edition,* p. 5.
6. Gary J. Stern, *The Drucker Foundation Self-Assessment Tool: Process Guide, Revised Edition* (New York: The Drucker Foundation, 1999). See note 1 above.
7. Henry T. Blackaby and Claude V. King, *Experiencing God: Knowing and Doing the Will of God* (Nashville, TN: LifeWay Press, 1990), p. 12.
8. Used by permission of Growing Leaders, Inc., 3550 Corporate Way, Suite C, Duluth, GA 30096, resources@growingleaders.com or visit www.growingleaders.com.

9. Check out Free Wheelchair Mission at freewheelchairmission.org. You can deliver the gift of mobility—a free wheelchair—from the "factory to the field" for just $44.40. As of 2007, more than 285,000 wheelchairs have been donated to people worldwide.

10. Philip Kotler and Kevin Lane Keller, *Marketing Management, 12th Edition* (Upper Saddle River, NJ: Prentice Hall, 2005). Just when you think you've reached "I know what I don't know," go to the library and browse through the 816 pages of this classic test on marketing.

11. James F. Engel and Wilbert Norton, *What's Gone Wrong with the Harvest: A Communication Strategy for the Church and World Evangelism* (Grand Rapids, MI: Zondervan Publishing House, 1975).

12. Ibid., p. 29.

13. Peter F. Drucker, *The Effective Executive* (New York: Harper & Row, 1966), p. 143.

14. Engel and Norton, *What's Gone Wrong with the Harvest*, p. 45.

15. John W. Pearson and Robert D. Hisrich, *Marketing Your Ministry: Ten Critical Principles* (Brentwood, TN: Wolgemuth & Hyatt, Publishers, Inc., 1990), p. 11.

16. Alex Pham and James S. Granelli, "Garry Betty, 49; Shaped EarthLink as a Major Firm," *Los Angeles Times* (January 3, 2007).

17. Marc Gobe, *Citizen Brand: 10 Commandments for Transforming Brands in a Consumer Democracy* (New York: Allworth Press, 2002), p. 216.

18. Pearson and Hisrich, *Marketing Your Ministry: Ten Critical Principles*, p. 42.

19. As of 2007, Best Christian Workplaces Institute had analyzed more than 50,000 employee surveys from over 400 organizations. Visit bcwinstitute.com to learn more about their Employee Engagement Index.

Core Competency 3: The Strategy Bucket

1. "Sputnik and the Dawn of the Space Age," from NASA.com. http://history.nasa.gov/sputnik/ (accessed November 2007).

2. John Naisbitt, *MegaTrends: Ten New Directions Transforming Our Lives* (New York: Warner Books, Inc., 1982), p. 94.

3. Ibid.

4. James C. Collins and Jerry I. Porras, *Built to Last: Successful Habits of Visionary Companies* (New York: HarperBusiness, 1994), p. 94.

5. Jeffrey Abrahams, *101 Mission Statements from Top Companies: Plus Guidelines for Writing Your Own Mission Statement* (Berkeley, CA: Ten Speed Press, 2007).

Core Competency 4: The Drucker Bucket

1. Bob Buford at www.bobbuford.com.

2. Leadership Network at www.leadnet.org.

3. "Peter F. Drucker Quotes" at BrainyQuote.com. http://www.brainyquote.com/quotes/authors/ p/peter_f_drucker.html (accessed November 2007).

4. Ibid.

5. Ibid.

6. Bill Hybels, *Courageous Leadership* (Grand Rapids, MI: Zondervan, 2002).

7. Ken Blanchard and Phil Hodges, *Lead Like Jesus: Lessons from the Greatest Leadership Role Model of All Time* (Nashville, TN: Thomas Nelson, 2007).

8. Marcus Buckingham and Donald O. Clifton, Ph.D., *Now, Discover Your Strengths* (New York: The Free Press, 2001).

9. Tom Rath, *Strengths Finder 2.0* (New York: Gallup Press, 2007).

10. Max Lucado, *Cure for the Common Life: Living in Your Sweet Spot* (Nashville, TN: W Publishing Group, 2006).

11. "Peter F. Drucker Quotes" at BrainyQuote.com.

12. Peter F. Drucker with Joseph A. Maciariello, *The Daily Drucker: 366 Days of Insight and Motivation for Getting the Right Things Done* (New York: Harper Business, 2004).

13. "Peter F. Drucker Quotes" at BrainyQuote.com. http://www.brainyquote.com/quotes/ authors/p/peter_f_drucker.html (accessed November 2007).

14. Peter F. Drucker, *The Effective Executive* (New York: Harper & Row, Publishers, Inc., 1966).
15. Peter F. Drucker, *Managing the Nonprofit Organization: Principles and Practices* (New York: HarperCollins Publishers, 1990).
16. The above list was prepared by the Office of Marketing and Communications at Claremont Graduate University, 165 E. Tenth St., Claremont, CA 91711. http://www.cgu.edu/pages/3899.asp (accessed November 2007). For more information on Peter Drucker, visit www.druckerarchives.net. Other resources are also available at Leader to Leader Institute (www.leadertoleader.org), founded in 1990 as the Peter F. Drucker Foundation for Nonprofit Management.
17. Drucker, *The Effective Executive*, p. 72.

Core Competency 5: The Book Bucket

1. Andy Stanley, *The Best Question Ever: A Revolutionary Approach to Decision Making* (Colorado Springs, CO: Waterbrook Multnomah Publishing Group, 2004), pp. 158-159.
2. Kenneth H. Blanchard and Spencer Johnson, *The One Minute Manager* (New York: HarperCollins Business, Rev. ed., 2001).
3. Online news release, "Bowker Reports U.S. Book Production Rebounded Slightly in 2006," May 31, 2007. http://new.marketwire.com/2.0/release.do?id=738060 (accessed November 2007).
4. J. Grant Howard, *Balancing Life's Demands: A New Perspective on Priorities* (Colorado Springs, CO: Waterbrook Multnomah Publishing Group, 1983), p. 37.
5. Adrian Gostick and Chester Elton, *The Carrot Principle: How the Best Managers Use Recognition to Engage Their People, Retain Talent, and Accelerate Performance* (New York: Free Press, 2007), p. 164.
6. "Put Down the Duckie," words by Norman Stiles, music by Christopher Cerf from *Put Down the Duckie: An All-Star Musical Special* (DVD) (New York: Sesame Workshop, 2003).
7. Leadership Catalyst at www.leadershipcatalyst.org.
8. Bill Thrall, Bruce McNicol and John Lynch: *TrueFaced: Trust God and Others with Who You Really Are* (Colorado Springs, CO: NavPress, 2003), p. 81. All rights reserved. Used by permission.

Core Competency 6: The Program Bucket

1. John W. Pearson and Robert D. Hisrich, *Marketing Your Ministry: Ten Critical Principles* (Brentwood, TN: Wolgemuth & Hyatt, Publishers, Inc., 1990), p. 98.
2. Gateways to Better Education at www.gtbe.org.
3. Pearson and Hisrich, *Marketing Your Ministry*, p. 8.
4. "List of toothpaste brands" at Wikipedia.org. http://en.wikipedia.org/wiki/List_of_toothpaste_brands (accessed November 2007).
5. Colgate Total FAQs: "What makes Colgate Total different from other toothpastes?" at Colgate.com. http://www.colgate.ie/products/oralcare/colgatetotal/whats_different.shtml (accessed November 2007).
6. Crest Products > Liquid Gels: Barbie® BURSTIN' Bubblegum at Crest.com. http://www.crest.com/products/liquidGels.jsp (accessed November 2007).
7. Krista Desens, "Brush Up on New Music with Aquafresh," press release from Net Music Countdown, March 10, 2006. http://netmusiccountdown.com/inc/news_article.php?id=9867 (accessed November 2007).
8. For customizable email surveys, visit www.surveymonkey.com.
9. Pearson and Hisrich, *Marketing Your Ministry*, p. 81.
10. "Peter F. Drucker Quotes" at BrainyQuote.com. http://www.brainyquote.com/quotes/authors/p/peter_f_drucker.html (accessed November 2007).

Core Competency 7: The People Bucket

1. Christian Camp and Conference Association at www.ccca.org.
2. One of the participants in a later institute was Bob Phillips, who at the time was executive director of Hume Lake Christian Camps. A successful author, Phillips created the faith-based version of the four social styles, published by Regal in 1989.

3. This chapter was adapted from Don German, "Who Do You Think You Are?" published in *Christian Camp & Conference Journal*, January/February 2003 (Colorado Springs, CO: Christian Camp and Conference Association) and from John Pearson, "Communication 101: Understanding the Four Social Styles," published in *Christian Management Report*, October 2005 (San Clemente, CA: Christian Management Association). Used by permission of the authors and the organizations.

4. There are several instruments that measure one's social style. The first social style system was developed by David W. Merrill and Roger H. Reid and is described in their book *Personal Styles & Effective Performance* (Boca Raton, FL: CRC Press, 1981). Bob Phillips wrote the faith-based book on social styles, *The Delicate Art of Dancing with Porcupines: Learning to Appreciate the Finer Points of Others* (Ventura, CA: Regal Books, 1989). (*Note:* This book has an excellent "System Comparison" chart on page 67 that lists 16 different "social styles" systems, including Myers-Briggs, Keirsey-Bates, plus Hippocrates' four temperaments (sanguine, choleric, melancholy and phlegmatic), that was later popularized by Tim LaHaye in *Transformed Temperaments*.) Wilson Learning Library has numerous resources and books on this subject, including *The Social Styles Handbook: Find Your Comfort Zone and Make People Feel Comfortable with You* (Herentals, Belgium: Nova Vista Publishing, 2004). (*Note:* Other titles from Wilson Learning Library, based on the social styles system, include *Win-Win Selling: The Original 4-Step Counselor Approach for Building Long-Term Relationships with Buyers* and *Versatile Selling: Adapting Your Style So Your Customers Say "Yes!"*) Florence Littauer and her daughter, Marita Littauer, are popular authors, speakers and trainers. They are the founders of Christian Leaders, Authors and Speaker Seminar (CLASS at www.classervices.com). They have written many books, including *Personality Plus* (Toronto, CAN: Monarch Books, new edition, 2004), *Wired That Way* (Ventura, CA: Regal, 2006), *Personality Puzzle* (Grand Rapids, MI: Revell Books, 2003) and *Communication Plus: How to Speak So People Will Listen* (Ventura, CA: Regal Books, 2006).

5. Phillips, *The Delicate Art of Dancing with Porcupines*, p. 50. *Note:* Phillips adapted this from Merrill and Reid's *Personal Styles & Effective Performance* and Bolton's *Social Style/Management Style*. Phillips also writes extensively on social styles in a more recent book, *How to Deal with Annoying People: What to Do When You Can't Avoid Them*, co-authored by Kimberly Alyn (Eugene, OR: Harvest House Publishers, 2006).

Core Competency 8: The Culture Bucket

1. John Wooden and Jay Carty, *Coach Wooden One-on-One: Inspiring Conversations on Purpose, Passion and the Pursuit of Success* (Ventura, CA: Regal Books, 2003), Day 11.

2. George S. Babbes and Michael Zigarelli, *The Minister's MBA* (Nashville, TN: BH Publishing Group, 2006), pp. 30-31.

3. Bill Hybels, *Honest to God?: Becoming an Authentic Christian* (Grand Rapids, MI: Zondervan, 1992), p. 54.

4. "The Slippery Slope of Conflict," Peacemaker Ministries. http://www.peacemaker.net/site/c.aqKFLTOBIpH/b.958151/k.A519/Slippery_Slope.htm (accessed December 2007).

5. Jack and Suzy Welch, *Winning: The Answers—Confronting 74 of the Toughest Questions in Business Today* (New York: Collins, 2006), pp. 57-61. *Note:* This is just one of 74 quick-reading insights from Jack Welch, named "manager of the century" by *Fortune* magazine in 1999.

6. Bill Thrall, Bruce McNicol and John Lynch, *TrueFaced: Trust God and Others with Who You Really Are* (Colorado Springs, CO: NavPress, 2003), p. 209. Leadership Catalyst, where Thrall, McNicol and Lynch serve, has an excellent "Affirming Each Other" team tool for enhancing an affirming culture. Order at http://www.leadershipcatalyst.org/products.html.

7. Max DePree, *Leadership Is an Art* (East Lansing, MI: Michigan State University Press, 1987), p. 83.

8. Ken Sande, *The Peacemaker: A Biblical Guide to Resolving Personal Conflict* (Grand Rapids, MI: Baker Books, 3 rev. and upd. edition, 2004).

Core Competency 9: The Team Bucket

1. CEO Dialogues at www.ceodialogues.org.

2. Tom Rath, *Strengths Finder 2.0* (New York: Gallup Press, 2007), p. 11.

3. Marcus Buckingham and Donald O. Clifton, *Now, Discover Your Strengths* (New York: Free Press, 2001).
4. Ibid., p. 137.
5. The Master's Program at www.mastersprogram.org.
6. Rath, *Strenths Finder 2.0*, p. iii.

Core Competency 10: The *Hoopla!* Bucket
1. Dennis W. Bakke, *Joy at Work: A Revolutionary Approach to Fun on the Job* (Seattle, WA: PVG, 2005). Bakke wrote *Joy at Work* after he left The AES Corporation (www.aes.com) in 2002. He had served as AES co-founder, president and CEO. According to Bakke, the company affirmed four major shared values: to act with integrity, to be fair, to have fun and to be socially responsible. For more information or to read a short synopsis of the book, visit www.dennisbakke.com.
2. Copyright © 2005, Dennis Bakke. Used by permission. Download PDFs of Bakke's Water Cooler Wisdom posters at http://www.dennisbakke.com/pages/watercoolerwisdom (accessed December 2007).
3. Scott Adams, *The Dilbert Principle: A Cubicle's-Eye View of Bosses, Meetings, Management Fads & Other Workplace Afflictions* (New York: HarperCollins Publishers, Inc., 1996), p. 2.
4. Adrian Gostick and Chester Elton, *The Carrot Principle: How the Best Managers Use Recognition to Engage Their People, Retain Talent and Accelerate Performance* (New York: Free Press, 2007), p. 53.
5. For fast service on business cards and other printing, check out www.missionprint.com. If whimsical business cards are a little over the top for your culture or your budget, consider coffee mugs, T-shirts or bumper stickers with the titles. Several online companies, such as Café Press (www.cafepress.com), feature print-on-demand mugs and lots of other interesting stuff with no minimum purchase. For example, if your receptionist wants her fun title to be "Manager of First Impressions," you can order just one coffee mug with that title.
6. Ball #2 of this chapter was adapted from John Pearson, *"Hoopla!* God Is Honored When We Have Fun," *Christian Management Report*, November/December 1999, p. 46. Used by permission of Christian Management Association.
7. Gostick and Elton, *The Carrot Principle*, p. 9.
8. From my notes while attending A Leadership Summit with Peter Drucker, a four-day invitation-only retreat for 30 pastors and ministry leaders in Estes Park, Colorado, August 19-22, 1986, sponsored by Leadership Network.
9. Les Grossman, *"Time's* Person of the Year: You," *Time* Magazine, December 13, 2006.
10. Gostick and Elton, *The Carrot Principle*, p. 155.
11. Barbara A. Glanz, *C.A.R.E. Packages for the Workplace: Dozens of Little Things You Can Do to Regenerate Spirit at Work* (New York: McGraw-Hill, 1996). Visit www.barbaraglanz.com for information on another helpful book, *The Simple Truths of Appreciation: How Each of Us Can Choose to Make a Difference*.

Core Competency 11: The Donor Bucket
1. Wesley K. Willmer with Martyn Smith, *God & Your Stuff: The Vital Link Between Your Possessions and Your Soul* (Colorado Springs, CO: NavPress, 2002), p. 141.
2. Quoted in Brian Kluth, *40-Day Spiritual Journey to a More Generous Life* (Colorado Springs, CO: Maximum Generosity, 2006), p. 11.
3. Randy Alcorn, *The Treasure Principle: Discovering the Secret of Joyful Giving* (Sisters, OR: Multnomah Publishers, Inc., 2001), p. 23.
4. R. Scott Rodin, *The Seven Deadly Sins of Christian Fundraising* (Spokane, WA: Kingdom Life Publishing, 2007), p. 24.
5. Ibid., p. 52.
6. Olan Hendrix, *Three Dimensions of Leadership: Practical Insight on Management, Finance and Boards for Churches and Christian Organizations* (St. Charles, IL: ChurchSmart Resources, 2000), p. 89.

Core Competency 12: The Volunteer Bucket
1. "Peter F. Drucker Quotes" at BrainyQuote.com. http://www.brainyquote.com/quotes/authors/p/peter_f_drucker.html (accessed November 2007).

2. C. Peter Wagner, *Discover Your Spiritual Gifts* (Ventura, CA: Regal Books, 2005).

3. Bob Buford, *Halftime: Changing Your Game Plan from Success to Significance* (Grand Rapids, MI: Zondervan, 1994), p. 53.

4. Bill Hybels with Lynne Hybels, *The Volunteer Revolution: Unleashing the Power of Everybody* (Grand Rapids, MI: Zondervan, 2004), p. 15.

5. Tony Morgan and Tim Stevens, *Simply Strategic Volunteers: Empowering People for Ministry* (Loveland, CO: Group Publishing, Inc., 2005), p. 136.

6. Wired Churches at www.wiredchurches.com.

7. Al Newell, "Sustaining Volunteer Motivation: One Principle, Five Tips" (Lenoir, NC: Newell & Associates, 2007), available at the High Impact Volunteer Ministry Development website at www.ananet.com.

8. Jim Collins, *Good to Great: Why Some Companies Make the Leap . . . and Others Don't* (New York: HarperCollins Publishers, Inc., 2001), p. 41.

9. Jim Collins, *Good to Great and the Social Sectors: Why Business Thinking Is Not the Answer* (New York: HarperCollins Publishers, Inc., 2005), p. 15.

10. Visit http://www.willowcreek.com/group.asp?action=list&groupid=53 to find out more.

Core Competency 13: The Crisis Bucket

1. The true story of the orange miracle was adapted from an article written by John Pearson, "Miracle on a Bus," *Christian Management Report*, April 1996 (San Clemente, CA: Christian Management Association). Used by permission of Christian Management Association, www.cmaonline.org.

2. Eugene H. Peterson, *A Long Obedience in the Same Direction: Discipleship in an Instant Society* (Downers Grove, IL: InterVarsity Press, 1990), p. 13.

3. Peter F. Drucker with Joseph A. Maciariello, *The Daily Drucker: 366 Days of Insight and Motivation for Getting the Right Things Done* (New York: HarperBusiness, 2004), p. 112.

4. Mark Cutshall, "We've Got an Emergency: Essential Lessons Every Manager Needs to Learn Before a Crisis Hits," *Christian Management Report*, August 2005 (San Clemente, CA: Christian Management Association), pp. 7-10.

5. The risk management resources at www.churchlawtodaystore.com are extensive.

Core Competency 14: The Board Bucket

1. Jim Brown, *The Imperfect Board Member: Discovering the Seven Disciplines of Governance Excellence* (San Francisco: Jossey-Bass, 2006), p. 102.

2. Ibid., p. 88.

3. The Andringa Group at www.theandringagroup.com.

4. A portion of this chapter was adapted from an article by John Pearson, "Six Best Practices for Recruiting Exceptional Board Members," *Stewardship Connections*, Winter 2007 (vol. 2, no. 1). Used by permission of Christian Stewardship Association (www.stewardship.org).

Core Competency 15: The Budget Bucket

1. Christian Camping International at www.cciworldwide.org.

2. George S. Babbes and Michael Zigarelli, *The Minister's MBA: Essential Business Tools for Maximum Ministry Success* (Nashville, TN: B&H Publishing Group, 2006), p. 97.

3. "20-Year Comparison of Senate Legislative Activity" from the U.S. Senate website, www.senate.gov. http://www.senate.gov/reference/resources/pdf/yearlycomparison.pdf (accessed December 2007).

4. Dan Busby, CPA, "The Board's Fiscal Responsibilities," *Focus on Accountability*, First Quarter 2005 (Winchester, VA: Evangelical Council for Financial Accountability, 2005), pp. 1-2.

5. Dan Busby, CPA, *2007 Church and Nonprofit Tax & Financial Guide* (Grand Rapids, MI: Zondervan, 2006), p. 142.

Core Competency 16: The Delegation Bucket

1. Peter F. Drucker quotes at Brainyquote.com. http://www.brainyquote.com/quotes/authors/p/peter_f_drucker.html (accessed December 2007).

2. Ken Blanchard, William Oncken, Jr., and Hal Burrows, *The One Minute Manager Meets the Monkey* (New York: HarperCollins Business, 1991).

3. Peter F. Drucker quotes at Brainyquote.com.

4. John Wooden and Jay Carty, *Coach Wooden One-on-One: Inspiring Conversations on Purpose, Passion and the Pursuit of Success* (Ventura, CA: Regal, 2003), Day 1.

5. Dennis W. Bakke, *Joy at Work: A Revolutionary Approach to Fun on the Job* (Seattle, WA: PVG, 2005).

6. "Water Cooler Wisdom Rule #8," Copyright © 2005, Dennis Bakke. Used by permission. Download PDFs of Bakke's Water Cooler Wisdom posters at http://www.dennisbakke.com/pages/watercoolerwisdom (accessed December 2007).

7. Bakke, *Joy at Work: A Revolutionary Approach to Fun on the Job,* pp. 98-99.

Core Competency 17: The Operations Bucket

1. Selected portions of this chapter were adapted from the article by John Pearson, "Reaffirming the High Calling of Management and Administration," *Christian Management Report*, February 2004 (San Clemente, CA: Christian Management Association, 2004), p. 52.

2. Olan Hendrix, "The Manager Who Leads: Exploring the Unique Qualities of Management and Leadership," *Christian Management Report*, February 2004 (San Clemente, CA: Christian Management Association, 2004), p. 15.

3. Larry Bossidy and Ram Charan, *Execution: The Discipline of Getting Things Done* (New York: Crown Business, 2002), p. 24.

4. Ibid.

5. Associated Press, "EarthLink Hires Huff as CEO," *The Wall Street Journal*, June 26, 2007, p. B8.

6. Stephen Covey, *7 Habits of Highly Effective People* (New York: Free Press, 2004). Where are you investing your best hours of the day, according to Covey's Time Management Matrix? There are four options: Quadrant I: urgent and important (crises); Quadrant II: not urgent and important (planning and preparation); Quadrant III: urgent and not important (interruptions); or Quadrant IV: not urgent and not important (time wasters). The goal is to invest maximum time in Quadrant II.

Core Competency 18: The Systems Bucket

1. Michael E. Gerber, *The E-Myth Revisited: Why Most Small Businesses Don't Work and What to Do About It* (New York: Collins, 1995).

2. Michael M. Lombardo and Robert W. Eichinger, *FYI: For Your Improvement: A Guide for Development and Coaching*, 4th Edition (Minneapolis, MN: Lominger Limited, Inc., 1996).

Core Competency 19: The Printing Bucket

1. Joseph Bayly, *The Gospel Blimp and Other Modern Parables* (Colorado Springs, CO: Chariot Victor Publishers, 1992). This book was originally published in 1960 and is a classic. Buy it!

2. Larry Bossidy and Ram Charan, *Execution: The Discipline of Getting Things Done* (New York: Crown Business, 2002), p. 1.

3. For a sample Printing Purchase Order (PPO) form, along with a Mailing Piece Instructions (MPI) form, go to www.managementbuckets.com.

4. HR Agency Services at www.hragencyservices.com.

5. Wordcrafters, Inc. at www.wordcrafters.info.

6. For more on The Fog Factor, read the Wikipedia.org article on the Gunning Fog Index at http://en.wikipedia.org/wiki/Gunning-Fog_Index (accessed December 2007).

7. Association Management Center at www.connect2amc.com.

8. If you're an Analytical, you'll enjoy reading more information about the Boeing 747 airplane at http://www.boeing.com/commercial/747family/pf/pf_facts.html (accessed December 2007).

9. Norm Goldstein, *Associated Press (AP) Stylebook and Briefing on Media Law* (New York: The Associated Press, 2006).

10. Lynne Truss, *Eats, Shoots & Leaves: The Zero Tolerance Approach to Punctuation* (New York: Gotham Books), p. v.

11. Pearpod at www.pearpod.com.

12. Fred Smith, Sr., and Brenda Smith, *Breakfast with Fred* (Ventura, CA: Regal, 2007).

Core Competency 20: The Meetings Bucket

1. Jim Mellado, MBA, Harvard Business School Case Study #9-691-102 (Rev. 11/20/91), "Willow Creek Community Church" (Boston: Harvard Business School, 1991), pp. 29-30.

2. Winston Fletcher, *Meetings, Meetings* (London: Hodder and Stoughton Paperbacks, 1983), p. 7.

3. A template for the "Weekly Update to My Supervisor" is available as a downloadable Word document at www.managementbuckets.com. Then each week, your direct report simply pulls up the file of the previous week's report and saves the file with the current date. He or she will invest less than 10 minutes to fill in the weekly update for you.

4. Patrick Lencioni, *Death by Meeting: A Leadership Fable . . . About Solving the Most Painful Problem in Business* (San Francisco: Jossey-Bass, 2004).

5. The Table Group, Reviews & Press, Spirit Magazine (published by Southwest Airlines). http://www.tablegroup.com/books/dbm/ (accessed December 2007).

INDEX

More Great Resources from
Regal

Transformation
Change the Marketplace and
You Change the World
Ed Silvoso
ISBN 978.08307.44756

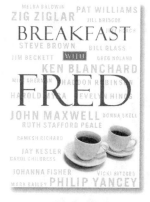

Breakfast with Fred
Fred Smith, Sr.
ISBN 978.08307.44763

The Church in the Workplace
How God's People
Can Transform Society
C. Peter Wagner
ISBN 978.08307.39097

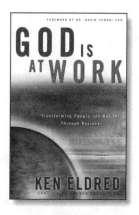

God Is at Work
Transforming People and
Nations Through Business
Ken Eldred
ISBN 978.08307.38069

Available at Bookstores Everywhere!

Visit **www.regalbooks.com** to join **Regal's FREE e-newsletter.** You'll get useful **excerpts from our newsletter** and **special access to online chats with your favorite authors.** Sign up today!

Regal
God's Word for Your World™
www.regalbooks.com